PALM SPRINGS
Legends
creation of a desert oasis

by Greg Niemann

Palm Springs Legends

Sunbelt Publications, Inc.
All rights reserved. First edition 2006. Second printing 2008.
Copyright 2006 by Greg Niemann

Edited by Jennifer Redmond
Book and cover design by Leah Cooper
Project management Jennifer Redmond
Printed in the United States of America
All photographs are from the author's collection, unless noted.

Sunbelt Publications, Inc.
P.O. Box 191126
San Diego, CA 92159-1126
(619) 258-4911, fax: (619) 258-4916
www.sunbeltbooks.com

"Adventures in the Natural History and Cultural Heritage of the Californias"
A series edited by Lowell Lindsay

11 10 09 08   5 4 3 2

Library of Congress Cataloging-in-Publication Data

Niemann, Greg, 1939-
  Palm Springs legends: creation of a desert oasis / by Greg Niemann.— 1st ed.
     p. cm.
  ISBN-13: 978-0-932653-74-1
  ISBN-10: 0-932653-74-X
  1. Palm Springs (Calif.)—History. 2. Palm Springs (Calif.)—Biography. 3. Palm
Springs (Calif.)—Social life and customs. I. Title.

F869.P18N45 2005
979.4'97—dc22
                                                            2005021837

This book is dedicated to Leila,
whose efforts made Palm Springs our virtual paradise.

Palm Springs Legends
TABLE OF CONTENTS

Acknowledgements

This book could not have been completed without the help of others. I sincerely thank all of the authors listed in the bibliography as each book further advanced this project. In most cases it was an idea furnished here or a tidbit offered there. In others it was much more.

Quite helpful was the fine coffee table book by former Mayor Frank M. Bogert, *Palm Springs: The First 100 Years*, both the 1987 and the 2003 editions.

I gleaned information from hundreds of clippings of *The Desert Sun* newspaper through the years and pored over scores of old issues of *Palm Springs Life* and the old *Villager Magazine*. I thank the Palm Springs Public Library and their research assistants who helped me learn much about the Palm Springs of yesteryear. I also spent time in the cozy Welwood Murray Memorial Library.

A special thank you to the Palm Springs Historical Society for the fine photos and helping me link the past with the present. Its long-time president Elizabeth Coffman Kieley, the second Anglo woman born in Palm Springs, took time to review the manuscript. Her daughter Kitty Kieley Hayes, a teacher, spent many hours editing the book. Her insight, knowledge and attention to detail helped render a more accurate and comprehensive final product.

The Palm Springs Historical Society's Director/Curator Sally McManus, whose knowledge of Palm Springs and its history is legendary, pored over the manuscript, suggesting numerous corrections and additions which improved the book's veracity and scope. Steve Nichols, current president of the Palm Springs Historical Society and grandson of two pioneers (P.T. Stevens and Frances Stevens), also reviewed parts of the book.

Special thanks to renowned author Dr. Lowell John Bean, the foremost expert on the Cahuilla Indians of Southern California, for his body of work and personal direction.

Ginger Ridgway, curator of the Agua Caliente Cultural Museum, helped edit the manuscript, primarily checking the complexities of Indian spellings, culture, and lore. A fine editor, she found additional errors in grammar and style throughout the book. I also appreciate Dawn Wellman, curatorial assistant of the Agua Caliente Cultural Museum, for her further editing of the manuscript.

Thanks to owner Diana Lindsay and editor Jennifer Redmond of Sunbelt Publications for their enthusiasm, encouragement, direction, editing— overseeing this project to fruition—and to Leah Cooper for her fine design.

Special tribute should be paid to the pioneers of Palm Springs whose stories are told in this book. A delightful surprise to me was that my research indicated how important women were in the early years. Their contributions are duly noted.

(continued)

This book took off in several directions in the three years it took to research and write it. I wanted to include the Indians but not have it be exclusively an Indian book; I wanted to feature celebrities, but not have it be just a celebrity book; I wanted to recognize the women pioneers, but not exclude the men. I'm happy with the result, an eclectic collection of what it is that makes the city of Palm Springs special, and of all the forces that came into play to make the Palm Springs area the international resort that it is.

—Greg Niemann

SECTION 1

✳

The Land of the Cahuilla

The Cahuilla Indians were the original occupants of Palm Springs, living for hundreds of years in small bands around Mt. San Jacinto, the San Gorgonio Pass, and out across the Colorado Desert.

Today much of the resort city of Palm Springs is still the Reservation of the Agua Caliente Band of Cahuilla Indians. Their heritage, as well as that of neighboring bands and other local tribes, is still very much in evidence today.

Majestic San Jacinto looms over a younger Palm Springs. *Photo courtesy of the City of Palm Springs.*

CHAPTER 1

In the Shadow of the Sacred Mountain
MT. SAN JACINTO

The mountain makes Palm Springs the resort it is. It is from the mountain that Palm Springs and the other valley communities receive protection from coastal dampness, fog, and overcast westerly winds. The mountain provides a natural barrier from one climate to another that is more abrupt than any other place in the United States.

Mt. San Jacinto, at 10,804 feet, is not California's highest peak. Many in the Sierra Nevada range top that. Even Mt. San Gorgonio to the immediate north across the pass, at 11,502, is a bit higher. But that higher peak, nick-named Old Grayback, is not nearly as imposing. Its rounded summit is almost lost among the southern San Bernardino range.

But Mt. San Jacinto, which looms like a jagged tooth straight up from the valley floor, has drawn the attention of visitors for centuries; the Indians considered it sacred, and today's travelers along Interstate 10 have a hard time taking their eyes off the dramatic peak.

There's good reason, too. It is the most swiftly rising peak of any to be found in America, rising vertically from the Palm Springs elevation of 452 feet almost two miles straight up. In close contrast, Mt. Whitney (at 14,491 feet) and other Sierra Nevada peaks over 13,000 feet rise from a valley floor of around 5,000 feet.

J. Smeaton Chase opens his fine 1920 book *Our Araby* with this sentence, "Mount San Jacinto stands isolated and conspicuous, like another Shasta, at the southern end of the great Sierra which forms the backbone of California." He adds, "…this desert face of San Jacinto offers to the view a mountain wall unparalleled for its conjunction of height and verticality—in effect a vast precipice of ten thousand feet."

Mountain sacred to Indians

To the several bands of Cahuilla Indians who inhabited the area in and around Mt. San Jacinto, the mountain was a sacred place, which became home to the evil, powerful demon Tahquitz.

Mukat (Mo-Cot), the legendary creator of the Cahuilla, created Tahquitz (Ta-co-wits), appointed him the first puul (shaman) and bestowed many supernatural powers upon him, expecting that he would use them for good. But Tahquitz violated Mukat's laws, used his powers for evil and was banished to a cave high up on Tahquitz Peak in the San Jacinto Mountains.

There are many Indian legends about the power of Tahquitz. It is said he craved human flesh and beautiful women. People who disappeared on the mountain were reputed to have been carried off by Tahquitz to his lair and eaten. The Tahquitz legends went beyond the Cahuilla tribe and were known by almost every Indian in southern California.

According to Indian Chief Francisco Patencio who published much of his band's oral history in 1943:

> *The man Tahquitz (Ta co wits) was a man of great power. He was one of the first created by Mukat. But he did not do any good. He never tried to cure anybody, or do any good for anyone. So he did not have any friends among his people, and he knew that he did not deserve any.*
>
> *He went on up to one of the Moreno Hills and practised (sic) flying over to the next one. This he did until he became powerful enough to fly. He became a very bad spirit. He lives in the world and makes his home in the Tahquitz (San Jacinto) mountains. He speaks through the lightning and thunder, and is seen everywhere. He kills the people, also the spirits of the people. He kills the animals as well as the people. Causes the wrecks of trains and automobiles, and delights in everything that makes people trouble.*

As the Cahuilla people lived on both sides of the sacred mountain, many of those bands, primarily those on the more easily accessible western slopes, ventured into the mountains for the bountiful deer and other game and acorns and piñon nuts.

The Indians called San Jacinto Mountain *i a kitch*, meaning "smooth cliffs," obviously referring to the rocky cliffs on the peaks. In contrast, they called the rounded dome of San Gorgonio Mountain to the north *queri kitch*, meaning "bald."

Mountain noted by Anza party

The first white men to spot the San Jacinto peak were Captain Juan Bautista de Anza and his party of 34 who crossed the desert in 1774, opening up a route to coastal California. While they missed Palm Springs, skirting the Santa Rosas on the south side at Borrego Valley and Coyote Canyon to the west of the mountains, they could hardly miss the dramatic peak.

The group descended into the present San Jacinto Valley, as Anza wrote in his diary, "keeping on our right a high, snow-covered mountain." Anza himself is reputed to have named the peak 'San Jacinto' after Saint Hyacinth, a Silesian nobleman who later became a Dominican missionary noted for his intelligence and devout picty (1185-1231).

White men had definitely found Mt. San Jacinto by the mid-19th century and lumber was being cut, cattle and sheep were grazing in the meadows, and roads were being created farther and farther up the mountainside. Yielding to pressure, President Grover Cleveland signed a bill creating the San Jacinto Forest Preserve on Feb. 22, 1897.

From the air, Mt. San Jacinto looks like a sharp molar, with the lower peaks of Tahquitz Peak and Apache Peak (weirdly named since there were no Apaches in the area) giving way to verdant valleys, turbulent streams, and bright green meadows, rising past Marion Mountain, through Round Valley to the craggy summit of Mt. San Jacinto.

The view is sublime

The view from the top is sublime. To the south one can see the Santa Rosas turning purple on their long march to the Mexican Border; to the west the view is across the entire San Jacinto Valley to the Santa Ana Mountains of Orange County; and to the north Old Grayback and the entire San Bernardino Mountain range is across the San Gorgonio Pass.

Most impressive is straight down into the San Gorgonio Pass where one can see the town of Cabazon, Interstate 10, the railroad tracks—all dwarfed and looking like toys. One can visualize the dynamics of the narrow pass, where the hot desert air collides with moist, cooler temperatures, creating one of the most effective wind funnels in the world.

To the east, across the vast Colorado Desert with its fertile square sections of land, is the Salton Sea itself, and closer in, Palm Springs and the Coachella Valley communities with squares of greenery amid a light brown desert.

From poolside in Palm Springs, the mountain never ceases to attract. Many times one can see clouds near the mountain's summit, knowing the weather on the "Other Side" is overcast, rainy and about 30 degrees cooler.

Many winter storms stay on the ocean side of the mountains.

The Palm Springs Aerial Tramway's steel cables reflect the sunlight every now and then.

The rocky foothills give way to forests, and pine trees, individually and in small clumps, appear to be marching their way up a crest to the summit.

The mountain is mentioned as "lofty pinnacles above, which seem to pierce the sky" by Helen Hunt Jackson in her popular and ageless 1884 novel *Ramona*. She was not alone in speaking of the mountain with such superlatives. George Wharton James, Charles Francis Saunders, and the aforementioned J. Smeaton Chase were among the many to speak reverently about the mountain.

CHAPTER 2

An Oasis in the Desert
THE PALM SPRINGS SETTING

The vast Coachella Valley, from the foot of Mt. San Jacinto southeast to the Colorado River, is a structural trough formed by the upthrust of mountains during seismic upheavals. The famed San Andreas Fault bisects the valley, running southeast to northwest just north of the present day I-10.

To the south is the Salton Sea, an anomaly in the desert. With the area below sea level, the ancient lake bed was most recently formed in 1905-1907 by a break in the banks of the Colorado River when water flowed into the Salton Sink depression.

While the emergence of the mountain created the arid valley, it also provides sustenance to the desert. Several streams tumble down rocky canyons off the eastern escarpment of Mt. San Jacinto, forming palm-lined pools before disappearing into the sand and gravel. Tahquitz, Andreas, Murray and Palm Canyons provided the verdant heart of Palm Springs to the Cahuilla Indians and to the settlers and visitors who followed.

In addition to the canyons, hot springs welled out of the ground, nurturing broad areas with fan palms, palo verdes, mesquite, willows and smoke trees at several locations on the valley floor. The most notable hot springs became the future site of downtown Palm Springs, right where the Spa Hotel and Casino is today, at the corner of Indian Canyon and Tahquitz Canyon Way.

The "Palm" and the "Springs"

The indigenous and ubiquitous "palm" of Palm Springs is the Washingtonia fan palm (*Washingtonia filifera*), named in honor of George Washington. It received that patriotic and lofty title in 1897 from a German horticulturist named Herman Wendland who saw the palms not in their native canyons but in a Belgian greenhouse where young trees brought from the U.S. were grown from seeds.

Found in California's canyons and in isolated desert oases, the native Washingtonia, with its bright green fan fronds, thrives in the sun with its roots in ground water.

A large, tree-shaded hot mineral springs pool in the center of what would become Palm Springs long ago became home to a band of Cahuilla Indians. The hot springs were called *Sec he* (sometimes spelled *Se khi* or *Sechi*, meaning boiling water) by the Indians, and *Agua Caliente* (hot water) to the Spaniards who later stumbled upon them. The Cahuilla Indians drank from the springs and found sustenance nearby.

The Indians were quite resourceful according to George Wharton James in his 1914 book *California, Romantic and Beautiful*:

> *A brave, hardy, rugged lot of aborigines used the wonderful and scareful spring of hot water at Palm Springs as their health resort, gathering their big-pitted native dates from the palms of Palm Canyon, collecting their acorns from the mountain slopes and making their mush, flour, bread, tortillas, drink and candy from the beans found on the mesquite trees which dotted the desert's face on every side.*

The dryness of the desert area added to the extreme temperature ranges between night and day and between winter and summer. Ice has formed occasionally during the winter months and most summers the daily highs range from 101 degrees to 120 degrees. During 2001, for example, there were 129 days with temperatures over 100 degrees recorded in Palm Springs.

The Indians actually dreaded the winter cold more than the blistering days of summer. For this reason, they considered their hot springs to be important, the place they gathered for social interaction.

The Indian Maiden statue in front of the Spa Hotel is on the site of the original Agua Caliente hot springs.

Explorers "missed" the hot springs

As Captain Juan Bautista de Anza missed visiting the site of Palm Springs in 1774 and 1776, so too did Captain Pedro Fages in his 1772 and 1782 explorations in southern California. It wasn't until the 19th century that the Palm Springs area was visited by white outsiders.

The first recorded event of white man in the Palm Springs area was the 1823-24 expedition of Brevet Captain José Romero who was sent by the Mexican government to find an overland route from Sonora to Alta California.

Romero's diary, written by his diarist and assistant, Commander Lieutenant José Maria Estudillo, noted on the day before they reached the hot springs, December 28, 1823, that there would be no water or pasture for the horses until "Agua Caliente" was reached. While it was the first recorded evidence of the springs and the Spanish name for "hot water," it implies that they somehow had knowledge of the existence of the hot springs beforehand.

In 1826 it was reported that the Spanish padres visited the desert Cahuillas at Agua Caliente.

Over the next 20 years numerous white men crossed the desert but no records exist of any mention of the hot springs. In 1845 there is a record of a B.D. Wilson and his party of 60 men meeting Chief Cabezon at Agua Caliente. Wilson and his men (posse) were sent by Pio Pico, the last Mexican governor of California, into the area to pursue a couple of renegade Indians. Chief Cabezon turned them over to Wilson at the hot springs.

Railroad surveyors arrive

In 1853 young Lt. R. S. Williamson and the Smithsonian Institution geologist William P. Blake led a government survey to find a railroad route to the Pacific and the three-year old state of California. Both wrote about their arrival at the oasis of "Palm Springs."

Lt. Williamson of the U.S. Topographical Engineers wrote,

> *December 15, 1853. The greater part of the valley is entirely dry and sandy and almost as forbidding as the Desert. The monotony is broken by a clump of palm trees on the north of the trail and a green bank from which springs issue known as "Palm Springs."*
>
> *...The water was sulphurous and gave off a slight quantity of sulpherated hydrogen gas. A slight efflorescence quantity of nitro was seen on the surface of the ground around the pools.*
>
> *The water, however, was not so strangely charged with*

these ingredients as to be unpleasant to drink, especially after having used the stagnant and muddy water of the Desert. I found its temperature, under the shade of a palm tree to be 80; air 70....

Blake's description was more social than scientific, "This place was evidently a favorite camping ground for the Indians. When we arrived, many Indian boys and girls were bathing in the warm spring..."

A "therapeutic bliss"

While a few white pioneers began to settle up in the San Gorgonio Pass, the Palm Springs area languished as it had for decades. Occasionally the Indians would throw out the welcome mat to share their oasis with the occasional white man who stumbled upon their land. The canyons and the hot springs provided sustenance and a type of therapeutic bliss rarely seen in native groups.

The therapeutic value of the springs gave rise to the growth of the area after it was first inhabited by white men.

In the 1920 book *Our Araby*, J. Smeaton Chase had this to say about the natural oasis:

> *The Hot Spring is the outstanding natural feature of our village, though not so natural as when one took one's bath in the rickety cabin which antedated the present solid little bathhouse. However, the Spring itself is as natural, no doubt, as any time this five or ten thousand years; and you may get as weird sensation in taking your bath, and as healthful a result afterwards, as bygone generations of Cahuillas have enjoyed. The water, which is just comfortably hot and contains mineral elements which render it remarkably curative, comes up mingled with quantities of very fine sand...and you will come forth with a sense of fitness and fineness all over to which only a patent medicine advertisement writer of high attainments could possible do justice.*

Agua Caliente or the hot springs called *Sec he* were for decades insignificant and isolated, but once the outside world discovered their healthful virtues they would one day provide the central setting of a famous international playground called Palm Springs.

CHAPTER 3

The Cahuilla of "Agua Caliente"
MAN IN PALM SPRINGS

The Cahuilla (pronounced Ka-we-ah), who ranged from present-day Riverside to the Colorado Desert and from the San Bernardino Mountains to the Anza-Borrego area, belong to the Shoshonean division of the Uto-Aztecan linguistic family of Native American Indians.

While its name origin is obscure, Cahuilla is said to mean "the masters" or "powerful ones," and their strength is reputed to be an "inner strength" rather than a physical one. Several sources indicate that the Cahuilla's oral tradition dates back 500 years or more.

Archaeological evidence has proven that Indians occupied the Tahquitz alluvial fan about 350-500 years ago. However, there is evidence, through artifacts and implements, that physical habitation in the area dates back over 2,000 years.

Mountain, Pass, and Desert Cahuilla

The Cahuilla lived in small villages on both sides of Mt. San Jacinto. For identification, W.D. Strong, an Anglo anthropologist, first came up with the idea to divide the Cahuilla into three categories, the Mountain Cahuilla, the Pass Cahuilla and the Desert Cahuilla. He considered the several clans occupying what would later become the Agua Caliente Reservation in Palm Springs as Pass Cahuilla.

Those clans, the *Kauisiktum* of the hot springs, the *Paniktum* of Andreas and Murray Canyons, and other small area clans, would thereafter refer to themselves as the Agua Caliente Band of Cahuilla Indians.

Villages were occupied all year, with periodic departures by some to hunt, trade, visit, or gather plants and food.

Desert shrubs from which the Indians derived food, shelter, clothing and medicine included the hardy creosote, the chuparosa with their bright scarlet blossoms, the small encilia (brittlebush), the mint-smelling desert lavender, the thorny ocotillo, cat's claw (acacia), the very important mesquite and willow trees, and numerous cacti and wildflowers.

The women gathered the food plants (acorns, mesquite beans, seeds, wild fruit, agave, and yucca) and also made the baskets and pottery. The tribe made use of over 200 desert plants.

The men used bows and arrows, nets and throwing sticks to capture small mammals, quail, rabbits, and sometimes deer or bighorn sheep, for food, clothing, and other uses.

Crops in the area were irrigated by water from nearby streams. In a few areas untouched by development, one can even see remnants of the early rock-lined irrigation ditches from the Tahquitz, Andreas, and Chino Creeks.

A Cahuillan woman photographed in 1924 by Edward S. Curtis.

All Cahuilla people belonged to one of two groups: the Wildcat (*Istam*), or the Coyote (*Isil'*). Called moieties, these groups were further divided into clans, of which membership was through the father. A member of one group, *Istam*, was supposed to marry a member of the other, *Isil'*, group. Such intermarriages made for strong social and economic alliances.

The chief is called the "net"

Leadership of the Cahuilla rested upon the shoulders of a person called the *net*, the ceremonial and political leader as well as judge of disputes. His word was final and respected. Additional duties included maintaining the big ceremonial house (kish um na wet) and tribal sacred objects.

His assistant was called the *paxaa* and he was responsible for meting out punishment and leading hunting parties. Both offices passed from father to son.

There were other important people in the tribe including the *shaman*, or medicine man, who enjoyed great powers, and other tribal elders, singers, and dancers who served as oral historians. The close-knit Cahuilla enjoyed their idyllic existence around the hot springs in the desert.

By early in the 19th century it is recorded that Spanish padres from the San Gabriel Mission had made contact with the coastal Indians, the Gabrieleño, the Luiseño, the Diegueño (Kumeyaay), and even a few Mountain Cahuilla. These "Mission Indians" as they would be called, often suffered a harsh life in their adaptation to the "true religion." These gentle and meek Indians were beaten with rawhide whips and often branded if caught trying to escape; later, under Mexican rule, they were often used as slaves.

The situation didn't improve under the Americans. Between 1850 and 1855, the California state legislature passed laws that virtually assured the Indians would be treated as second class citizens, if one can call an indentured servant with virtually no rights a citizen.

The state legislature also opposed U.S. Government treaties with the California Indian tribes that would give them eight million acres of land. They were so vigorous in their objection that even though the treaties were signed, the U.S. Senate did not ratify them.

The Cahuilla still had their independence, their culture, their self-respect, and their pride.

By the mid-1800s other outsiders, like the mounted mail riders and stagecoach drivers, began to visit the land of the Desert and Pass Cahuilla. Making the most impact was the railroad which opened in 1877.

The line was built through the San Gorgonio Pass, and in the early 1870's, the Federal Government granted right-of-way to the Southern Pacific by awarding them alternating sections of land on either side of the tracks for a distance of 10 miles on either side. The odd-numbered sections (a section is a mile-square or 640 acres) went to the Southern Pacific while

Marcus Belardo was a *paxaa* at the Agua Caliente reservation. *Photo taken in 1924 by Edward S. Curtis.*

the even numbered ones were retained by the government.

On May 15, 1876, a total of 880 acres—Section 14 (a mile square area of downtown Palm Springs) and a portion of Section 22 (Tahquitz Canyon)— were set aside as the Agua Caliente Reservation by Executive Order of President U.S. Grant in an attempt to recognize the inhabitants of the area.

The following year President Rutherford Hayes extended the reservation to include those even numbered sections in three townships (48 sections) adding an additional 30,720 acres.

It is reported that some of the Indians were a little confused when some politicians they never met "gave" them something that was already theirs.

In 1885 the U.S. Government restricted the Indians to their reservation. In the process they created the Desert Entry Act of 1885, which opened the non-Indian lands in the valley to homesteading.

Then in 1891, the Mission Indian Relief Act was passed by Congress authorizing various allotments from the reservation acreage to heads of families (up to 20 acres of farm land and 160 to 640 acres of grazing land.) It was a noble gesture but it would take the Indians over 50 years to realize the benefits.

After the early contacts with the white settlers, the Cahuilla continued their existence in a dichotomy, retaining their aboriginal culture, while also working on settlers' ranches and orchards. In the meantime, the Anglos had discovered the springs the Indians called *Sec he*.

CHAPTER 4

Legendary Indian Leaders
TRIBAL CHIEFS AND SHAMANS

Long before and after the Anglos arrived to establish their village, the Cahuilla had trusted their political, cultural, and social leadership to a few strong men. Some of the most notable, powerful, and fascinating Indian leaders were from the Palm Springs area, beginning with the Cahuilla Lion, Chief Juan Antonio.

Chief Juan Antonio

Chief Juan Antonio was a powerful Mountain Cahuilla chief who by 1846 had five Cahuilla clans, from the San Gorgonio Pass to the Colorado River, under his leadership. Called Captain-General by the white man, he was also known as the Lion of the Cahuilla partly because of his stout figure and leonine features.

In some instances he seemed cruel in dispensing justice, allegedly burying a murderer alive, and cropping the ears off two Indian youths caught stealing.

At one time he traded with and hauled timber for mountain man Pauline Weaver, the Anglo who settled in the San Gorgonio Pass. In 1842 with California still under Mexican rule, he and the Cahuilla were invited to an American 4th of July barbecue at the Weaver ranch, witnessing the first raising of the American flag in California.

He and a group of Mountain Cahuilla with traditional bows and arrows later helped guard the large Antonio Maria Lugo ranch and the ranches of his family members and other San Bernardino colonists. They drove off Paiute marauders who were stealing cattle and horses from the ranchers.

When the United States started to take over California, the Indians were caught in the middle of the resulting U.S./Mexican War and didn't know whom to support. Juan Antonio's Cahuilla group joined forces with the Mexican and Spanish settlers and fought one battle against a group of Luiseño Indians who had allied with the U.S., killing many and capturing others. The prisoners in Juan Antonio's custody were later killed as well.

The settler Lugo chastised the Cahuilla chief for the apparent cruelty, but Juan Antonio reminded Lugo that as an Indian, had it been the other way around, every last Cahuilla would have been roasted alive.

Juan Antonio was also called upon by Lugo's relative José Maria Lugo in 1851 to help track down the Cahuilla chieftain Antonio Garra and his men. Garra had organized a revolt protesting unfair taxation by the San Diego tax collector. Together Chief Juan Antonio and Lugo captured Garra at Juan Antonio's stronghold thus thwarting Garra and some of the southern California tribes' plan to attack and destroy Los Angeles. During the capture, Garra's son, also named Antonio Garra, knifed Juan Antonio in the arm and in the side. The elder Garra was turned over to the Americans, found guilty of treason, blindfolded over an open grave, and a San Diego firing squad ended his plans and his life.

In 1852 Juan Antonio and other Indian leaders signed a treaty with the U.S. Commissioner of Indian Affairs which gave them exclusive use of land 40 miles long by 30 miles wide in the San Gorgonio Pass. But it was never ratified and, to the confusion of the Indians, not fulfilled.

For years Chief Juan Antonio helped the Mormon settlers ward off marauders from San Bernardino, yet the Mormons still began settling on Cahuilla land without permission. Not only that, they were zealously trying to make the Indians convert to Mormonism. Juan Antonio, who was named Captain-General by U.S. Army General Stephen W. Kearny, was called to diffuse the situation. By then, 1855, the army had reported that the Cahuilla numbered 3,500 males, of whom 1,500 were fighting men, all under the power of Juan Antonio.

The more confused the situation, the more the Indians and whites alike looked to Juan Antonio for leadership. He was an eloquent spokesman and ruled in a solemn and impressive manner.

In 1862 a smallpox epidemic that ravaged many throughout southern California also afflicted Juan Antonio. Per Indian custom, he tried sweat baths and plunges into icy water and then eventually dragged himself out of his hut and died alone in early 1863. According to the *Los Angeles Star* on February 28, 1863, he and the bodies of four other Indians who died of smallpox were not buried but shamefully left to the animals. It was an inhumane end to a powerful leader.

Before he died, Chief Juan Antonio had turned bitter toward the white man. He had listened to decades of promises and saw Indian lands dwindle and imported diseases ravage his people, including ultimately himself. He regretted capturing Garra and lamented that he should have had his Cahuilla men join forces to aid Garra's battle. He was truly one of the bravest, most loyal, and intelligent Indian leader in California history.

Chief Cabezon

White-haired Chief Cabezon was allegedly so-named because of his big head (*Cabeza* means *head* in Spanish). He ruled his people firmly and had held back the Colorado River tribes from massacres.

Chief Cabezon was given papers by the Mexicans giving him broad control over all the Cahuilla tribes as well as the Serranos, from the San Gorgonio Pass throughout the desert areas.

By 1878 he too had become disillusioned. According to Lowell Bean and Harry Lawton in *The Cahuilla Indians of Southern California*, he summed up his people's plight for new Indian Agent Rev. S.S. Lawson:

> *When white brother come, we make glad, tell him to hunt and ride. He say, "Give me a little for my own," so we move little way, not hunt there. Then more come. They say move more, and we move again. So many times. Now we are small people, we have little place, but they say move to new place, away from white friends, go out from valley.*

He then added with a sigh, "I know not. I know not."

Chief Cabezon (white beard) poses with some of his leaders. Front row (l to r): Captain Habiel, Captain Will Pablo, Chief Cabezon, Captain Manuel and Captain José María. Back Row (l to r): Captain Ramón, Captain Jim and Captain Sastro. *HB Wesner photo courtesy Malki Museum.*

Chief Cabezon died in 1883, allegedly at the advanced age of 120. His son took over the reign until he passed away a few years later. The Cabazon Reservation—spelled differently—was named in his honor and eventually Cabazon also became the name of the town in the San Gorgonio Pass.

Medicine Man Pedro Chino

Pedro Chino was a powerful Cahuilla *shaman*, or medicine man, who also lived to be a reputed 120 years old.

As a shaman, Pedro Chino was a *partlid*, or seer who was noted for his extraordinary powers, and according to Cahuilla belief, capable of predicting future events, making rain, stopping catastrophes, and performing other miracles. Supposedly according to legend, he could change into a crow, mountain lion, coyote, or any other bird or animal.

As a youth, he became a highly skilled cowpuncher, and worked for Pauline Weaver who ran 4,000 head of cattle on his San Gorgonio Pass ranch. He was reportedly still rounding up horses when he was 100 years old.

Pedro Chino. *Photo courtesy Palm Springs Historical Society.*

Pedro Chino's 1880 sale of land—for $150.00—to two white men became Palm Springs' first real estate transaction. He became friends to the white men who followed and even had a young white boy, Jim Maynard, accompany him to help him see as his eyesight had deteriorated with age. Young Jim learned much of the Cahuilla way, and old Pedro Chino learned more about the white man.

Maynard recalled that while Pedro Chino didn't say much, what he said had much meaning. Once in a tribal meeting where a prominent white citizen was trying to explain why the Indians should be satisfied with the rent they were receiving from having their water diverted away from them, the old chief said to Jim Maynard in Cahuillan, "You tell the white man that they didn't give us anything! They took everything else away from us."

When he died in 1939 Indians from all over southern California attended his funeral.

Alejo Patencio

Alejo Patencio was the net, or headman of the *Kauisiktum* clan in 1925. Marcus Belardo was his assistant, or paxaa. During the 1920's Alejo Patencio shared some of the stories of the Cahuilla with outsiders. As the Cahuilla history was not written, but oral, the accounts of Cahuilla life were reported by Alejo Patencio to anthropologist William Duncan Strong.

Strong wrote it down so people who could read English could understand it, and the ensuing story of the Cahuilla creation and beliefs is considered a sacred and literal account.

Alejo's brother Francisco Patencio also became a respected chief, or *net*, of the Cahuilla.

Francisco Patencio

The 1943 book *Stories and Legends of the Palm Springs Indians* by Chief Francisco Patencio (as told to Margaret Boynton and published by the Times Mirror Company of Los Angeles) became the definitive printed work of the many beliefs and lore of the Agua Caliente Band of Cahuilla Indians.

And well it should, as its author Chief Francisco Patencio was an Agua Caliente net, or headman, for years. He was born in the 1850s, the fourth of 13 children, in what is now Chino Canyon (where the tram is), their summer home. His parents were given Spanish

Francisco and Dolores Patencio in 1928. *Photo courtesy Palm Springs Historical Society.*

names and married by the Catholic Padres at Mission San Gabriel.

Francisco Patencio became an excellent farmer and for a time worked in the Craft family orchard in Yucaipa. In 1881 he met and married Dolores San a va, of the Los Coyotes band near Warners Ranch. Dolores became known as one of the most exquisite basket weavers of the Agua Caliente band.

Patencio took on responsibilities that had him travel not only throughout southern California, but even to a convention of the American Indian Society in Minneapolis in 1919 where he admittedly "made speeches."

Totally unschooled, Chief Patencio studied reading and writing. He wrote, "I began to learn and write Spanish. That was not so hard, for I had spoken that all my life. But the English. That was hard. I have never stopped studying English." Before he died at age 90, Chief Patencio reportedly could read and write English, Spanish, French, and speak seven Indian dialects.

But most important was his ability to put the legends and traditions of the Agua Caliente band of Cahuilla Indians on paper.

Fig Tree John

Fig Tree John was a notable character of the desert. He was a Desert Cahuilla Chief of the Agua Dulce clan, but he preferred to live alone and be left alone. He lived at a spring near the Salton Sea where he claimed he was born in the late 1700s. It is hard to separate fact from fancy as that would have made him about 130 or more when he died of the flu in April 1927.

Apparently his given name was Juanita Razon, and he claimed that he was once an Indian guide for Gen. John C. Fremont. He preferred to be called Juanita, with an "a," and not Juanito, with an "o."

Mystery always surrounded Fig Tree John and, because he allegedly spoke Apache, some claimed he was really an Apache renegade. According to Harry C. James in the book *The Cahuilla Indians*, the rumor started when a white friend brought an acquaintance to visit. The guest thought Fig Tree John looked like an Apache, so he spoke a few words in Apache. Old John nodded his head, seeming to understand, which gave birth to the rumor.

Based on that, an Edwin Corle wrote a fictional novel called *Fig Tree John*, about an Apache, modeled after the Cahuilla Chief. He was under the opinion that his main character was an Apache taking sanctuary in California.

Fig Tree John received his name because of the black mission figs he planted around his springs. His original springs near Travertine Point were inundated with the filling of the Salton Sea in 1905-07, so he moved his primitive jacal of arrowweed and mud north to Agua Dulce Spring. He also salvaged railroad ties that were being flooded and sold them for a profit.

A recluse, he put a barbed wire fence around his springs and kept trespassers off with an ancient Winchester rifle, which some said had enough parts missing to render it inoperable. Nevertheless, his menacing attitude compensated for the lack of a proper weapon. He acquired a black stovepipe hat and long military coat with brass buttons which he often wore even while his feet were bare.

Around 1910 he and his wife acquired a buggy to take them to various fiestas and social events, with Fig Tree John, of course, resplendent in his quasi-military attire. His crusty countenance and

Fig Tree John in uniform. *Photo courtesy Field Studio, Riverside.*

dignified appearance in his "uniform" made him a favorite for those wishing to take photos or sketches. The old man agreed, for a fee of course. His son, Johnny Mack, said that his father was given the clothes at "some important Indian meeting in Los Angeles."

Fig Tree John was known as a shrewd trader and had a string of horses. According to one rumor, he reputedly paid for his purchases in Banning with gold dust, setting tongues wagging about the possibility he might have come across a lost gold mine in the Santa Rosas. More stories attest that it was not Banning, but Mecca, where he once paid a storekeeper in gold nuggets. Did he get the gold through his constant trading or did he really have a mine? While most historians doubt the veracity of the mine's existence, it does make a good tale, especially with a character like Fig Tree John.

Even though he liked to appear menacing, stories leaked out about how he rendered aid to those in need who might chance upon him. Many whites in the area spoke favorably of Fig Tree John. Miss Cornelia White of Palm Springs was with him on a long desert trip and not only found him an excellent guide but a trustworthy companion. That kind of destroys the image, doesn't it?

CHAPTER 5

A Woman Possessed

HELEN HUNT JACKSON

"Just five years after President Grant affixed his historic signature to the document granting Section 14 to the Agua Caliente Band of Cahuilla Indians, a wrathful woman aroused America with a crusade in behalf of better treatment for all Indians," noted author Ed Ainsworth in *Golden Checkerboard*. He continued, "Her name was Helen Hunt Jackson."

Jackson was born in 1830 to a literary family in Amherst, Massachusetts. Among her schoolmates and friends were poet Emily Dickinson and Harriet Beecher Stowe, author of *Uncle Tom's Cabin*. Jackson herself was a poet of note and writer of numerous children's stories. By age 35 she had lost her husband and two sons to accident and illness. After being widowed by U.S. Army Captain Edward B. Hunt, she later remarried wealthy banker and railroad executive William S. Jackson.

She got involved in Indian rights after hearing Ponca Indian Chief Standing Bear in 1879 describe to a Boston audience his tribe's forcible removal from their Nebraska reservation. The evangelical fire was lit and the crusade that would consume the rest of her life had begun.

Jackson became, as one writer noted at the time, a "holy terror." Incensed by what she heard, Jackson wrote letters to the *New York Times*, circulated petitions, and raised money on behalf of the Indians.

According to *The Indians of the Southwest* by E.E. Dale,

> *"Mrs. Jackson was a highly emotional woman and, like most reformers, she was far from realistic in her views. She saw only the wrongs committed against the Indians, and their sufferings; and wrote a vivid story about them, and blamed the people of the country."*

In 1881 Jackson's book *A Century of Dishonor: A Sketch of the United States Government's Dealings with Some of the Indian Tribes* was published, and the crusading Jackson sent a copy to every member of Congress admonishing them that their hands were stained with the blood of their relations. She was disappointed that the book had little impact.

The Smiley Commission

U.S. Congress established the Mission Indian Commission (more commonly known as the Smiley Commission) to investigate Indians in southern California being pushed off their lands. Due to her scathing book *A Century of Dishonor*, Jackson became a member. She went to southern California to see the situation first hand.

Her zeal landed her the appointment as an Interior Department agent. In that capacity, with the respected California promoter Mr. Abbott Kinney, she criss-crossed southern California, documenting Mission Indian conditions. They toured the backcountry of Riverside and San Diego Counties in a two horse, double seat carriage. By that time the few remaining Mission Indians (former Gabrieleño, Luiseño and Diegueño/Kumeyaay) were living in slum shacks near white settlements.

Mrs. Jackson wrote of the contrast between those poor dependent wretches and the non-mission Cahuilla who were happily living in industrious, peaceful communities "cultivating ground, keeping stock, carrying on their own simple manufactures of pottery, mats, baskets, etc., and making their living—a very poor living, it is true; but they are independent and self-respecting in it and ask nothing of the United States Government now, except that it will protect them in the ownership of their lands."

Jackson and Kinney did not visit the Palm Springs Cahuilla, but sent a former Indian agent, Captain J.K. Stanley, to represent them. He met with Chief Cabezon and about 100 Cahuilla Indians from eight different village groups. His report indicated that one community of those Cahuilla in a region called The Potrero (The Waterhole) set a fine example of an industrious settlement under cultivation. He added that the Desert Cahuilla were unsullied by the Christian missionaries and were still following their traditional customs and religions.

Not so the Mission Indians, who had not been as fortunate as the Cahuilla in remaining isolated from the Spanish invaders and those who followed.

In 1883 Mrs. Jackson submitted a 56-page report calling for massive government relief, including purchasing more land and establishing more schools for the Mission Indians. To her credit, a lot of her recommendations were put into a bill which passed the U.S. Senate, but died in the House.

A novel to "move people's hearts"

Undeterred, she soon realized that perhaps a novel might better explain the plight of the Indians. She wanted "to move people's hearts" in a manner that succeeded for her friend Harriet Beecher Stowe and her novel *Uncle Tom's Cabin*.

Jackson began writing *Ramona* in a New York City hotel room in December 1883. It was completed in three months and published in November 1884. She later remarked that "every incident in Ramona is true."

While the incidents might have been true, there was apparently a little bit of literary license. For example, the fictional husband of Ramona was Alessandro, a Luiseño, whose father was chief of the San Luis Rey Indians. In real life, the husband of Ramona Lubo was Juan Diego, a Mountain Cahuilla who did odd jobs.

According to Cahuilla Chief Francisco Patencio,

> *I think that Miss Helen Hunt Jackson, who was Special Indian Agent through this Southern California years ago, made the story up from different things that happened at different places. There was a couple living at Juan Diego Flats. Juan Diego was shot by Sam Temple about a horse. He was shot in his own yard just as the book says. His wife's name was Ramona. They are both buried in the Indian Cemetery at the Cahuilla Indian Reservation near the Juan Diego Flats. The spring, the falling rock corrals of the goats, the foundation of part of the house, are still to be seen there. All as Mrs. Jackson told it.*

In *The Cahuilla Indians of Southern California*, authors Lowell Bean and Harry Lawton noted, "Alessandro, the tragic hero of *Ramona*, was a Cahuilla named Juan Diego, shot down by Sam Temple of San Jacinto. The real Ramona was also a Cahuilla, Ramona Lubo. She died on July 21, 1922 and is buried in the old Cahuilla cemetery in the San Jacinto Mountains."

I visited the cemetery on a small hill near the Cahuilla Creek Casino. The Casino employees did not know of the nearby cemetery nor its significance. The grave of Ramona is

The real "Ramona" and "Alessandro" lie buried in the Cahuilla Cemetery, located in the San Jacinto Mountains.

simply marked "Ramona, Died July 21, 1922. It is at the right hand side of one marked "Juan Diego 'Alessandro' Ramona's Martyred Spouse, Died March 24, 1883." At the Ramona Pageant offices in Hemet I saw photos of Sam Temple, a belligerent looking man with mean eyes and a big bushy handlebar mustache.

Ramona Lubo's lineage can be further traced. According to Frank Bogert in *Palm Springs—The First 100 Years*, the legendary Ramona's grandson, Harry Hopkins, was married to Celia Patencio, the sister of the last Cahuilla ceremonial singer Joseph Patencio.

The book *Ramona* was immensely popular, but Jackson would only see a portion of the success. She died of cancer on August 12, 1885, less than a year after *Ramona* was published. The name Ramona lives on, in towns, streets and businesses throughout southern California. Along with several movies and songs, the Ramona Pageant, an outdoor stage adaptation of the novel, opened in 1923 in Hemet and, still running, is the largest and longest-running outdoor play in the country.

On January 12, 1891, Congress passed the Act for the Relief of Mission Indians, which using Smiley Commission recommendations, formally established reservations for southern California Indians.

The voice of one person can make a difference.

The Ramona Pageant is an annual event commemorating the story by Helen Hunt Jackson.

CHAPTER 6

Pursuit of a Renegade Indian
THE LEGEND OF WILLIE BOY

The wild west had been pretty much tamed by the early part of the 20th Century. In the areas around Palm Springs, relationships between the white settlers and the local bands of Indians had, apart from occasional differences of opinion, been at least neutral overall.

But if an Indian committed murder, as did Willie Boy, that was a different matter. After the murder, lawmen were able to relive the days of yore as they formed posses and set out to find Willie Boy. The dramatic manhunt received big press coverage across the country, and convinced some easterners that the west indeed was still living in savage times.

Willie Boy was a Piute-Chemehuevi Indian born in 29 Palms in the high desert. He was raised by two aunts after his parents drowned in one of those desert thunderstorms that can rapidly change sandy washes into raging torrents of water, mud, and sand within minutes.

He fell in love with Chemehuevi Indian Mike Boniface's 16-year-old daughter Mabel (while some accounts indicate her name was Lolita, Carlota, Isoleta, or Neeta, a review of her death certificate or "Record of Funeral" clearly says Mabel) and ran away with her once. Boniface, 60, known as "Old Mike," brought her back at gunpoint, admonishing Willie Boy that because the young couple had a distant blood relationship they were forbidden to marry under Indian law.

In late summer 1909 the Bonifaces went to the Gilman Ranch near Banning to help with the fruit harvest. Willie Boy followed and also got employment there. He was a good worker, even though he had once, four years previous, been jailed in San Bernardino for drunkenness and disorderly conduct.

Willie Boy shot Old Mike

As Riverside County was dry at the time, folks had to go into San Bernardino to drink. Late Saturday night, September 25, 1901, two white boys returned to the Gilman Ranch from San Bernardino with a bottle of whiskey almost three quarters full. Apparently, sometime during the night it rolled down to Willie Boy's bunk who discovered his bonanza in the morning.

Thus on Sunday, September 26, 1909, emboldened by the booze, Willie Boy shot Mike Boniface in the eye, grabbed Mabel, a rifle and some cartridges, and set out across the desert. Accounts of the murder vary, including one version that has him killing Old Mike while he slept and another that reported a struggle over the rifle. But that he committed the murder was never challenged.

Outraged over the murder, a posse led by the Riverside County sheriff quickly gave chase. The posse, and those which would follow, contained several Indian guides including the Yaqui John Hyde and Cahuilla tribesmen Henry Pablo and Segundo Chino, and later Willie Pablo.

Even so, and with a warm trail, the couple slipped away from the pursuers. The posse camped near Whitewater, not sure whether Willie Boy went south into Palm Springs, or north toward his home turf at 29 Palms. In the morning the posse discovered fresh tracks that indicated Willie Boy had circled their camp while they slept.

As the posse later followed the tracks over the Morongo Basin into the Mojave Desert, they found indications that Mabel had been pushed and dragged over the sand. Finally they came across her still-warm body lying in the desert, a gunshot wound in her back. Willie Boy was now on his own. The first posse ended with them bringing Mabel's body back.

A "red-skin lady killer"

It was Mabel's death that ignited the flames of journalists and, trying to outdo each other, reported rumors, untruths, and many inaccuracies, calling him a "red-skin lady killer." His partial bottle of booze in some accounts had grown to "a suitcase full of whiskey." Stories circulated about Willie Boy being responsible for almost every death and crime that occurred anywhere within hundreds of miles of his location.

Other posses were formed, some also led by the San Bernardino County sheriff, and overall leadership appeared to be by ego and politics rather than effectiveness.

Willie Boy circled through the desert, even slipping past posse members to visit his home in 29 Palms. Finding the village abandoned and receiving no help, he went back into the desert, knowing where to find springs and waterholes. He killed rabbits and lizards and raided miner's caches to survive.

On October 7, on Ruby Mountain, Willie Boy doubled behind his pursuers and laid a trap. As an advance party of the posse approached he started shooting. He killed three horses and seriously wounded lawman Charlie Reche. Indian guide John Hyde broke several ribs falling down on his long run back to the main party. They got Reche down to a doctor in Whitewater and decided to regroup for another posse.

What created the drama for most Americans was the fact that in the midst of this manhunt, President William Howard Taft was on a cross-country speaking tour and was a guest at Riverside's Mission Inn on October 12, 1909.

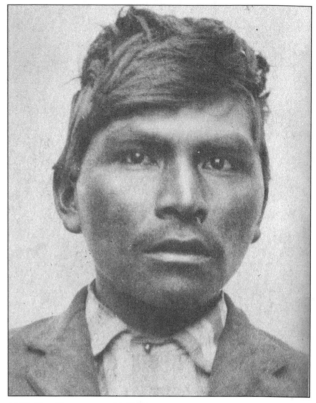

Willie Boy. *Photo courtesy Malki Museum.*

It had been a boring and mismanaged trip for the presidential party and accompanying media. Half the time the president did not identify well with his audience and the press was constantly hurried here and there and had to suffer long speeches by local politicians.

At Riverside, reporter E.A. Fowler of the *New York Sun* picked up on the Willie Boy story and he realized it made far better copy than boring speeches, especially when the pursuit stories left an implied threat that the President of the United States might be scalped by wild Indians. No matter that the lone outlaw was about 60 miles away.

A media frenzy

Rumors ran rampant and there were stories about imminent "Indian uprisings." Scores of media descended upon the scene to feed upon the frenzy.

Sensing a scoop, the *Los Angeles Record* sent a young reporter to join what would be the last posse. Randolph W. Madison, a 22-year-old Virginian; was thus in the right place at the right time.

Madison joined that group led by Riverside County Sheriff Frank Wilson which was scheduled to rendezvous later with the San Bernardino County faction.

They went first to Ruby Mountain, the site of the ambush and the last known place of Willie Boy. Some in the ambushed party had earlier said they heard a shot as they were leaving but they were unsure of its significance.

It turned out to be a suicide shot as Wilson and his group found Willie Boy's decomposing body on Friday, October. 15, 1909, one week after the ambush. He had one shoe off, having used his toes to pull the trigger aimed at his chest and had thrown his meager possessions far into the bush, honoring the Piute custom of ridding oneself of possessions before one dies. After several photographs by Madison, they cremated the body on site, but not before pillaging for souvenirs.

Willie Boy had put fear into many, eluding over 75 pursuers in five organized posses. Some Indians had fled their villages fearing rebuke from the outcast. Most whites had really become incensed only when he shot Reche—Indians fighting other Indians was one thing, but they should never shoot a white man.

While most newspapers reported more fancy than fact, Madison got his scoop and his stories were picked up across the country. He even wrote a story told from Willie Boy's perspective. Citing Indian customs and system of revenge, he noted that Willie Boy knew he was a marked man early on.

According to Indian Agent Clara True at the time,

> It was an Indian feud. It is difficult for white people to understand affairs of this kind. The girl was recovered once, and I believe Mike's family only waited a time of vengeance. This likely made Willie Boy more desperate than white people would understand. He killed Mike in all probability because Willie Boy was marked for death when the band went back to the desert after the fruit picking season.

Madison even presumed that the posse's relentless pursuit made killing Mabel inevitable. Willie Boy shot Mabel rather than leave her to the enemy.

Reporter vilified

Madison's story (trying to understand Willie Boy's motives and background) ran in the eastern press, but was not printed anywhere in southern California. In fact, many westerners vilified and ostracized the reporter for looking at the story from the Indian point of view. Their version of the story is full of misrepresentations and fabrications. After all, Willie Boy was called "a good Indian" by some reports, alluding to the racist saying at the time, "The only good Indian is a dead Indian."

The Indians themselves have their own inaccurate versions of the Willie Boy story, told and retold in different versions depending on band of Indians. Some had him escaping and fleeing to Mexico, or Nevada, or somewhere in California. Take your pick. Years later, some Indians glorified him for what he represented, but were not specific about what that might be.

For whatever reasons, the legend of Willie Boy grew. Years later, a plaque was placed on the site of the suicide, saying in eulogy, "Willie Boy, 1881-1909 The West's Last Famous Manhunt." By 1969 a Hollywood movie, "Tell Them Willie Boy Is Here," featuring Robert Redford and Robert Blake, immortalized the murder and pursuit.

The facts were, he was a young man who shot and killed the father of his affection, then killed her for whatever reason, and fought off a widening search for almost two weeks before taking his own life.

Those were the facts. To a public thirsty for the old wild west he was much more than that. He was the last of the breed—the last wild Indian.

SECTION 2

✿

A Settlement is Born
(Late 1800s)

With the beneficial effects of the dry hot desert climate, all Palm Springs needed was someone with vision who could recognize the potential and share that with others. That some- one was Judge John G. McCallum. Modern-day Palm Springs owes much to his tenacity in bringing in settlers, establishing a community, and bringing in the water to support them.

CHAPTER 7

Palm Springs Discovered
STAGECOACHES AND RAILROADS

The first white men to encounter the Cahuilla Indians was the 1774 Anza expedition, but, as mentioned earlier, that party missed visiting what would become Palm Springs.

Historical records do indicate that by the early 1800s some Cahuilla Indians were among those indigenous people baptized into Catholicism and given Spanish names through Mission San Gabriel. The Cahuilla were also noted to have helped the Franciscan padres with irrigation projects and farming in the Redlands and San Bernardino areas dating from 1819.

But none of those Anglo/Cahuilla encounters was in the Palm Springs area. By the mid-1850s several white men had settled in the San Gorgonio Pass area, but there is no record of any of them living at or around the hot springs occupied by the Agua Caliente. even though it had been visited several times.

Soon, more and more people, stagecoaches, freight lines, and others began passing through the area on their way to and from points east of the Colorado River and southern California.

The mail riders on horseback had stopped at Agua Caliente for water. Many years later stage coaches also stopped at the springs. The first overland stage in California was the San Antonio and San Diego Mail Line, followed by the Butterfield Overland Mail, which ran from 1857 to 1861. Their routes were south of Palm Springs, but they opened the door to other enterprising stage companies.

In 1872, the Grant Stage ran from Prescott, Arizona, to San Bernardino, but the biggest impact upon Palm Springs was the Bradshaw Stage Line which ran from 1863-1877.

Gold was discovered in La Paz, New Mexico Territory (near present-day Erhenberg, Arizona) and people from Los Angeles needed to get there. So, an enterprising southern gentleman named William D. (Big Bill) Bradshaw, scouted the area in 1862, meeting with Cahuillan Chief Cabezon and a Maricopan Indian, who showed him the best route.

Later that year, Bradshaw wrote the *Los Angeles Star* and described sites and stops along the new trail, including: Agua Caliente, Sand Hole (now

Palm Desert), Indian Well, Torro, Martin's House, Lone Palm, Dos Palmas and more.

Bradshaw then went into partnership with a William Warrington and established a ferry across the Colorado River to complete the route. The Bradshaw Trail then went from San Bernardino, through Beaumont, Banning, Cabazon, and Whitewater to Agua Caliente (now Palm Springs), Indian Wells and on past the Colorado River. His route became the most popular road for many decades.

Jack Summers was first settler

The Bradshaw Line not only stopped at Agua Caliente, but had a station built there. Bradshaw hired Jack Summers to operate the Agua Caliente way station; Summers, the first white settler in Palm Springs, lived in an adobe hut from 1865 until 1877.

According to Chief Francisco Patencio in his 1943 book,

> Jack Summers was agent at Palm Springs. He was the first white man to live here. He rented from 10 to 12 acres where The Desert Inn now stands, and hired the Indians to raise barley for his horses. He also rented about the same amount just south of where the new school house is built. He paid the Indians who worked the land for him, a team of horses, a set of harness, a plow, and some money for the year's work....
>
> ...Summers and his wife lived in a Adobe Station. It was made of sticks and brush plastered with adobe mud. This adobe was bought from the Indians. It came from the Spring....This station was where the Post Office now stands.

The hut of mud from the hot springs remained standing until the 1920s.

The Bradshaw Line carried U.S. Mail along with travelers, gold seekers, prospectors, and assorted wanderers. It is said that the stage was ambushed on its first return trip going through the pass and the driver and another man were murdered. The other man lost his life for the $5,000 of gold dust he had on him.

While the stage lines brought travelers, the new railroad nudged them out of business. It was the railroad that brought Palm Springs and the surrounding area to the public's attention. President Franklin Pierce and the U.S. Congress wanted a southern route across the United States and allocated funds for the project and even awarded the railroad alternating sections of land for 10 miles on either side of the tracks.

Railroad arrives in 1877

The Southern Pacific Railroad got busy surveying and laying tracks. In 1875 the railroad hired some of the Agua Caliente Indians, including future Chief Francisco Patencio, to haul timber and logs and lay track. It finally opened in 1877, sounding a death knell upon the stage lines. The stage station closed and the train tracks passed to the north of Agua Caliente at a place called Seven Palms, about six miles away. There would be a train stop there which remains to this day (Interstate 10 and North Indian Canyon Drive).

That same year the competing Santa Fe Railroad reached Los Angeles—forcing the Southern Pacific into a rate war. The low fares created a land boom for areas served by the railroad. And it wouldn't be long before the old hot springs once called Agua Caliente would be one of those areas.

The title of "first land speculators in Palm Springs" certainly must go to W.E. Van Slyke and M. Byrne of San Bernardino. They had already bought 320 acres of prime Palm Springs land from the Southern Pacific Railroad and had their eyes on more. In 1880 Van Slyke and Byrne paid Pedro Chino $150 for his 10-acre ranch between the hot springs and the mountains. Fruit trees irrigated by canyon waters surrounded his one room adobe house.

It was the valley's first real estate transaction and the fact that Pedro Chino didn't even own the land (it belonged to the railroad) didn't deter anyone. He'd lived there for years and figured he had the right; he also guessed that sooner or later the lands would be taken away from the Indians. And then too, the land was bought on "spec," calculating that people would soon be settling in the valley.

The stage was set for John Guthrie McCallum.

CHAPTER 8

The Settlement Begins
JUDGE JOHN GUTHRIE McCALLUM

It was a sick child, a concerned father seeking a healthful, warm, dry climate, and a knowledgeable Indian that led to the development of Palm Springs.

Judge John Guthrie McCallum already had abandoned a successful law practice and moved to San Bernardino seeking a more salubrious climate for his son Johnny, who suffered from tuberculosis. There he was told about an even warmer, dryer climate and the healing properties of the hot springs called Agua Caliente by his Cahuilla Indian friend/interpreter Will Pablo.

Together the two men left the old Mormon town of San Bernardino in a surrey and, upon arriving at the oasis, McCallum knew immediately that this "Palm Valley" as he called it was the place to relocate his family. It was 1884 and the McCallums became the first permanent non-Indian residents of Palm Springs.

That the task of establishing a settlement fell upon the over-achieving Judge McCallum is fortuitous because a lesser individual might not have prevailed. McCallum was a man who did not know failure.

The son of a Scottish farmer, McCallum was born in Indiana in 1826

John Guthrie McCallum. *Photo courtesy Palm Springs Historical Society.*

and by 1854 had a thriving law practice. It was interrupted, however, by a letter from California that mentioned one of his two brothers who went there to seek their fortunes had been stricken in an epidemic. At his mother's pleadings, he closed out his law practice and went around Cape Horn to California to find his brothers. When he arrived in San Francisco he found that both had died and he had the onerous task of writing the news to his mother.

An important politician

California agreed with McCallum and he remained, settling in Placerville where he became a lawyer known for settling mining disputes. He bought the *Georgetown Weekly News*, a prominent voice of the American "Know-Nothing" Party, became a state senator, and eventually president of the American Party. He was appointed by American Party Governor John Neely Johnson to several key committees. After the brief meteoric rise and fall of the Know-Nothings, McCallum returned to private practice.

While he was never a "judge," the title was bestowed upon him by colleagues and friends. He was admitted to practice law before the California State Supreme Court.

McCallum was an advocate of a railroad to the Pacific, a plank on Abraham Lincoln's presidential platform. He switched parties and was elected president of the State Republican Committee and an elector. When he went to Washington D.C. to deliver the vote for Lincoln, he attended the president's second inauguration and was also admitted to practice before the U.S. Supreme Court. He experienced the horrors of the assassination and was one of a delegation to pay final respects over Lincoln's bier.

Back in California, McCallum put his energies to work fighting what many considered the selfish interests of railroad's "Big Four" (Crocker, Huntington, Hopkins, and Stanford), who were so concerned about his vendetta they tried to buy him off.

In San Francisco McCallum met and married Emily Freeman in 1861 and they had four sons and two daughters (one son died in infancy). John Guthrie Jr. was born December 22, 1864, and, as the oldest, was the favored child. Thus it was a difficult blow that while the four older children were stricken during the 1881 typhoid epidemic that Johnny was the only one who did not fully recover. He almost died, then caught pneumonia which so weakened him he lapsed into tuberculosis.

Even though he was at the height of a successful public and private career, Judge McCallum decided to devote his remaining fortune and his future to the restoration of his son's health.

Appointed Indian agent

The popular remedy for tuberculosis up to that time had been high altitudes, cold weather, and strenuous exercise, but a more modern medical theory, understood by McCallum's doctor, prescribed rest and a warm, dry climate. McCallum was able to secure an appointment, signed by President Chester A. Arthur, as Indian agent for the Mission Indians in warmer San Bernardino. It was there he met Will Pablo.

After that first visit to Agua Caliente, he resigned his position as Indian agent and moved his family to the newly renamed Palm City. They took the train as far as Seven Palms (also later called Garnet) and took off across the desert on a buckboard with Johnny on a stretcher. Originally they moved into a rough camp by an old grey-trunked fig tree but soon, with the aid of his friend Will Pablo, built a fine adobe house.

California's Section 14, which contained the hot springs, was set aside by the government for the Agua Caliente Indian Reservation, but two speculators, W.E. Van Slyke and M. Byrne, had purchased the adjoining areas from the railroad. They had also formed the Palm City Water Company. From them, on March 24, 1885, McCallum bought a one-fifth interest in those bordering sections (13, 15, 23 and 25), a total of 320 acres, and a one-fifth interest in the water company.

Then on November 5, 1885 he bought 150 acres from Byrne for $1,800. Over the next eight years he continued to buy land from Van Slyke, Byrne and the railroad until he owned more than 6,000 acres of land.

He dreamed of starting a colony of people to relocate in the desert and hired a surveyor, T.M. Topp, to lay out the town of "Palm City." The original subdivision was called the Colony Tract and consisted of 76 lots of various sizes totaling 199 acres. He began selling right away and by 1886 had deeded 11 of the acre lots and about 35 acres of outside tracts.

First store in Palm Springs

He set up the area's first store using one room of a small building and began laying stock of canned foods and other materials needed by the settlers and other travelers.

McCallum now had a vision and set about to accomplish it. His vision included an influx of people. From their small ranches and home sites, they would develop an agricultural settlement where produce could grow all year.

With this in mind, he went to Los Angeles and set up a law practice. There, with three partners and a capitalization of $100,000, they syndicated under the name Palm Valley Land and Water Company in 1887. Their first order of business was to survey 320 acres (the eastern half of section 15), what would become downtown Palm Springs. They also commenced construction of 19 miles of rock-lined irrigation canals from the nearby canyons.

The partners signed a written agreement with McCallum, assigning him sole responsibility for all the promotional activities and plans for the auction of the lots. McCallum took the baton and ran with it. He wrote the railroad requesting reduced fares for his planned land auction. He blanketed the state with seductive advertising. One ad read: "Perfect climate, wonderful scenery, pure mountain water; the earliest fruit region in the state; absolute cure for all pulmonary and kindred diseases."

The Original Palm Valley Store. *Drawing by Carl Fytel.*

Parcels sold at auction

The people came, and they bought. On auction day, November 1, 1887, some 137 parcels of land were sold for a total of more than $50,000. Palm Springs was about to come into being. Soon the purchased acreage began to blossom with a variety of crops in efforts to determine the most hardy. Alfalfa, figs, apricots, grapes, melons, corn, oranges, grapefruit, and even the now-prolific date palms were grown.

By 1888 land sales were booming. Special trains stopped at Seven Palms and residents picked up prospective settlers in buckboards.

A post office had been established at nearby Palmdale (now Smoke Tree Ranch) for another development. Then McCallum's son Harry, who began doing more and more for his father, established another post office in downtown Palm Springs and officially began using the new name which was also the name of the town's only hotel. In a letter he wrote, "And by the way, I might inform you that after July 1, 1890, 'Palm Springs' is the P.O. address and not Palmdale, which it has been."

No more Palm Valley, nor Palmdale, nor Palm City. The idyllic agricultural settlement at the base of Mt. San Jacinto would henceforth be known as Palm Springs.

A devastating drought

Crops grew, settlers moved in, and optimism prevailed. Then Mother Nature with a one-two punch struck the newly named Palm Springs with a fury. A 21-day record rainfall in 1893 flooded crops and wiped out irrigation ditches; then a devastating 11-year drought (1894-1905) succeeded in driving many of the settlers away.

While the climate improved Johnny's health for some time, he eventually had a relapse and died at the age of 26 on January 17, 1891. Another son Wallace died in 1896 at age 30, of heart disease brought on by alcoholism.

The patriarch himself, Judge John G. McCallum, died at age 70 on February 5, 1897, of heart failure. He died (perhaps thinking his life a failure) shortly after learning of the federal government's decision to cut McCallum and the white settlers off from the water supply from the Tahquitz and Andreas Canyons in favor of the Indians.

Son Harry, who tried to carry on for his father, died at age 30 of pulmonary tuberculosis while visiting Chicago in 1901. Then daughter May McCallum Forline died in 1908 leaving a three-year-old daughter, Marjorie. The only surviving McCallum child, the one who would care for her aging mother Emily until her 1914 death, and the one who would continue the legacy begun by her father, was the determined Miss Pearl McCallum.

Early Palm Springs orchard, part of the McCallum land near the present day Tennis Club. *Photo courtesy Palm Springs Historical Society.*

Years later, the original McCallum adobe house that was built by the side of a large old fig tree in downtown Palm Springs was moved to the Village Green on South Palm Canyon Drive in the early 1950s and is the current home of the Palm Springs Historical Society.

Even though the last decade of the 19th century was tough on not only the McCallum family but all of the settlers of Palm Springs, those who would follow continued to lay the groundwork for a world-class resort.

Welwood Murray, owner of the Palm Springs Hotel, with his wife Elizabeth and their son Erskine. *Photo courtesy Palm Springs Historical Society.*

CHAPTER 9

Scotsman Opens First Hotel
DR. WELWOOD MURRAY

By 1887 Judge John G. McCallum had a lot of people coming out to Palm Valley to look at lots, but no lodgings were available for them. He needed accommodations and prevailed upon his literate Scottish friend who lived near Banning, Dr. Welwood Murray, to establish some type of inn.

Dr. Murray did not graduate from medical school; his title was bestowed upon him for outstanding medical service he rendered to the wounded on a battleship during the Civil War.

So it turns out that a judge who was not a judge got the assistance of a doctor who was not a doctor to run a hotel in a village that was not yet a village.

Welwood Murray was a lanky Scotsman, born September 17, 1832, who came to the United States from Edinburgh when he was 26 years old. He was employed as a copyreader for a publishing firm in New York City before he came to the Banning area in 1876 because of failing health. He became the manager of the San Bernardino Fluming Company, a corporation formed to cut and transport lumber, fuel, and ties for the Southern Pacific Railroad.

He bought 80 acres near Banning, built a two-story house in a canyon, and with his wife began ranching and establishing an orchard. He also became manager of the local orchards of a San Jose company and supervised the growing and canning for them.

Murray and the Indian Agent Judge McCallum enjoyed an intellectual friendship as they were the only two in the area with similar education and literary interests. Even so, they were dissimilar in personality and disposition, and often disagreed on numerous subjects.

When shown the possibilities of the new Palm Valley village by his friend, the normally cautious Scot "went for it" and bought a five-acre plot just across the way from the McCallum adobe. From that date in 1886, he too shared McCallum's vision.

The Palm Springs Hotel

Murray soon became one of the founding fathers of Palm Springs. Hiring local Indians, he constructed and opened the Palm Springs Hotel in time for the great Land Auction of November 1, 1887. He located his hotel across the street and southwest of the hot springs, which he then leased from the Indians for $100 a year. An old bathhouse and dressing room were erected just over the springs and remained standing until 1916 when the Indians replaced it with their own structure. (The Spa Hotel stands on the site of the springs today).

Old bath house on the site of the original Agua Caliente springs. *Photo courtesy Palm Springs Historical Society.*

The Palm Springs Hotel was a rambling, one-floor ranch style structure of Murray's own design, capable of sleeping 26 guests. It occupied the entire block of (what is now) Tahquitz Canyon Way between Main (now Palm Canyon) and Indian Canyon Drive. For the auction, Murray hired the local Indian Willie Marcus, had him dressed in flowing Arabian attire, placed him on a camel, and sent him out to Seven Palms to meet the trains and pass out literature. The Murrays had buckboards pick people up at the train station and also organized forays and picnics into the nearby canyons.

Dr. Murray left most of the hotel managing business to his wife, Elizabeth Erskine Murray, also a native of Scotland. She had been a teacher at the Indian School on the Potrero Reservation before she and her husband relocated to Palm Springs. A stout woman, she became known for entertaining her guests, her great home-cooked meals, her nursing abilities, and the pleasant accommodations she offered.

Welwood Murray was more interested in horticulture and planted 22 varieties of fruit trees and all sorts of plants and shrubs on the adjoining acreage. He quickly became an expert in the field and one of the leading horticulturists in California. In the book *Palm Springs, The Landscape, The History, The Lore*, author Mary Jo Churchwell revealed much about Welwood Murray when she wrote, "Murray was mad about trees. He loved them. He understood them. He cared for them as if they were his—I'm tempted to say *children*."

Notables begin to arrive

Many notables were drawn to the new colony at Palm Valley and they all stayed at Dr. Murray's Palm Springs Hotel. In 1905 the naturalist John Muir arrived with his two daughters, Wanda and Helen, the latter ill and in need of a hot, dry climate. U.S. Vice President Charles Fairbanks came, as did Mrs. Fanny Stevenson, the widow of Robert Louis Stevenson (who had fought a tuberculosis condition most of his life and died before Palm Springs became known for its healing properties).

Welwood Murray became the first trustee of the Desert School District in 1893. Often called the "Patriarch" of Palm Springs, he was considered by some as the village's greatest benefactor. He was well-read, garrulous, opinionated, and passionate. The lanky man with his Scottish tam and accompanying thick brogue could and did expound upon most any theory (from evolution to the Bible to Shakespeare to the politics of foreign countries), sometimes to the boredom and chagrin of his boarders and charges.

He loved to use pompous English and familiarize the Indians with it. As an example, when John Muir paid a surprise visit and Murray was forced to clean up the place mid-summer, according to guest Helen Lukens Gaut, he ordered the Indians to "exterminate the superfluous accumulation of dirt."

When the village was ravaged by flooding in 1893 and then followed by the drought, many of the settlers were forced to flee leaving just a handful of people, including the visionaries McCallum and Murray.

Murray lost so many trees during the devastating 11-year drought that he became disillusioned and tried to sell the Palm Springs Hotel. He had earlier ticked off the Indians when, to save his trees, he desperately diverted the remaining flume water. Saddened, he tried to sell the hotel and it closed forever in 1909; it was finally torn down in 1954.

Welwood Murray was a friend of Indian Chief Francisco Patencio and worked for the betterment of the Agua Caliente Band of Cahuilla Indians. While he was involved in water disputes with them, especially during the drought years, he continued to exhibit an interest in their welfare.

The Welwood Murray Cemetery

When the Murrays' son Erskine (born 1867) died in 1894, rather than take him to Banning, they buried him on a triangular shaped lot at the west end of Chino Drive. (As the Indians used the Patencio cemetery on Section 14, the Murrays allowed a few other burials on Chino Drive). When Mrs. Murray died, she was buried there, and when Dr. Welwood Murray himself died in 1914, he was also buried in the cemetery that would be named after him.

The Murray heirs deeded the cemetery to the public which formed the Palm Springs Cemetery District. Miss Cornelia White and J. Smeaton Chase were among the trustees. Today looking at the names on the tombstones is revisiting the past of Palm Springs as many of the town's early settlers and notable citizens lie in repose there: The White Sisters, J. Smeaton Chase, Alvah Hicks, Nellie Coffman, Ruth Hardy, Zaddie Bunker, Albert Frey and many more.

Murray's hotel, the house he built in 1893 out of railroad ties from the old Palmdale Railroad, and much of the block to the south was bought by Dr. Florilla White and her sister Cornelia White.

Concerned with the lack of reading materials in the village, Murray made several attempts to help people borrow books. He even built a small adobe building at the rear of the hotel for a library. There he loaned out his own books.

So it was fitting that in 1938 his son George Welwood Murray donated land in the heart of Palm Springs to the city to provide for the construction and maintenance of a library. Thus the Welwood Murray Memorial Library (which opened in 1941) now graces the southeast corner of Palm Canyon Drive and Tahquitz Canyon Way. It was the main library of Palm Springs until 1975. In addition to the cemetery and library, Murray Canyon is named in honor of that garrulous Scotsman, Welwood Murray.

The Welwood Murray Cemetery, taken from the mountainside.

CHAPTER 10

Lifeblood of the Valley
WATER TO THE DESERT

The early settlers might have called it "Palm Valley," but regardless of what you called it, it was still a desert. Oh, the warm dry air and benevolent mineral hot springs were the drawing cards, but the price for that was living in a desert. And while the climate was salubrious, in the desert the main desideratum was, and always will be, life-sustaining water.

In the beginning there was only the mineral-laden, sulfur-tasting hot water that bubbled up from the springs. The Indians had been drinking it as it was for years, and many felt they were healthy because of, not in spite of, that. The first white men to the area drank it, but usually from ollas which they'd filled and let sit awhile to let the strong mineral taste dissipate.

With the emergence of the village, many of the settlers claimed therapeutic results from drinking the spring water. For example, J. Smeaton Chase in his 1920 book *Our Araby*, claimed "Good results have been found to follow the use of the water of the hot spring, both for bathing and drinking, in cases of kidney disease."

Additional water came from a small stream at the base of the mountain in Tahquitz Canyon that the Indians had lined with stone, affording an 18-inch flow of water.

Judge John G. McCallum went to the source of the springs in Tahquitz Canyon and, with the help of the Indians, enlarged the flow of water to 75 inches. But it was reported that the Indians shunned drinking it because of the evil spirits of the Tahquitz legend.

Our Araby is a popular book by J. Smeaton Chase.

To start an agricultural community, McCallum knew more water was needed. There was some water in nearby Andreas Canyon but it belonged to the Indians living there and was used by them.

A flume from Whitewater Canyon

Then there was the Whitewater River which tumbled down from the slopes of Mt. San Gorgonio before disappearing into the sand. So with an investment of $60,000 of his own money and the assistance of the Indians, McCallum had a 19-mile flume built bringing water from the Whitewater River. Rounding the point of the desert on big redwood flumes on high trestles, and tunneled through the mountain to an eight-mile long stone canal, it brought the water for citrus trees, grapes, alfalfa, apricots, dates and much more. Water flowed, and the community was off to a start, even though the flume constantly needed repairing from the ravages caused by the winds and sands.

On February 1, 1887, McCallum incorporated his Palm Valley Land and Water Company with 5,000 shares of stock values at $100 each.

The irrigation ditch flowed full, irrigating orange groves, melon patches and vineyards on the 80-acre McCallum Ranch and for all the settlers. Waterwheels were even used to fill water storage barrels.

The Indians eventually got their share. It did, however, take complaints from them for the government to insure that they too would benefit from this water that was diverted across their land. In a sensible ruling, it was declared that the company would have the rights to the water as long as the Indians would be guaranteed free water for their 160 acres of land on section 14 and an additional 160 acres should that area be developed.

No one, however, could have predicted a drought, especially one so prolonged and devastating. The drought caused the Whitewater River to finally become only a trickle and caused most of the new settlers to abandon their lots and their dreams. Only a few remained.

Welwood Murray, who allegedly loved his trees and plants more than any-thing, was especially distraught over the lack of water. He even diverted the last remaining trickle of flume water for his trees. This act infuriated the Indians and they complained to Mr. Collins, then the Indian agent from Riverside, who issued a dictum stating that all the water belonged to the Indians.

Finally one flash flood filled the flume, and the Indians, emboldened by the earlier dictum, opposed the opening of sluices to irrigate the white man's land. Frantic for water, at night the colonists opened them by force, using crowbars and hammers.

While the Indians were the original occupants of the land, even though they had little cultivation or growth, they had still been awarded the first 30 inches of water to develop their 160 acres. That was then increased by the agent to 40 inches once the Indians had some further acreage planted.

It appears the drought, or lack of any water, took a situation that was working and created such an imbalance that hard feelings and drastic measures were bound to result, and did. This apparently was exacerbated by the ruling of the Indian agent from Riverside who apparently didn't understand all the ramifications. The white settlers saw it as an uninformed action of a meddling government.

During the 1890s Judge McCallum was gone a lot from the valley, visiting his sick daughter May in Chicago and left his son Harry in charge. As the drought continued, many ranchers got behind in payments for the land and the assessments to keep the ditch in good repair.

Finally, after McCallum's death, his family was forced to sell the family interest in the Palm Valley Water Company to liquidate a debt and provide necessary funds. They sold the water company to Los Angeles land promoter Ralph Rogers. Rogers got the Indians to help and they made the necessary repairs to the ditch.

The initial water system changed hands several times after that and today the Palm Springs water is supplied by the Desert Water Agency and the Whitewater Mutual Water Company.

An enormous aquifer

The desert-like Coachella Valley sits on an enormous aquifer. As early as 1853, it was predicted by the geologist who accompanied the government railroad survey, Professor William P. Blake, that artesian water should be found. In 1888 the Southern Pacific successfully dug a few wells at Thermal and Walters (now Mecca) in the east valley.

By early in the 20th century, the U.S. Government had begun digging wells in the Coachella Valley. Instantly, although at great depth, fresh, pure water was found. Scores of wells were dug with successful results.

In some places the water lies at a depth of from 50-200 feet, or deeper, and needs to be pumped, where in others, like Thermal and Mecca in the east valley, the water pressure is so strong that many of the wells were gushers rising several feet above the surface.

In his 1914 book *California, Romantic and Beautiful*, author George Wharton James talks about his Coachella experience, "In 1913 I put in a well on land I had purchased from the Southern Pacific Company. We went down in the neighborhood of nine hundred feet, and there came rushing out, with great force over the casing, a flow of between fifty five and sixty inches."

In 1918 the residents of Indio and the east valley voted to establish the Coachella Valley County Water District. They brought in water from the Colorado River to supplement and replenish the great underground flow. It took 30 years, but in March 1948, a 123.5 mile canal, the Coachella Branch of the All-American Canal, began delivering water to continue helping turn the desert green. The terminus reservoir would be called Lake Cahuilla, a 183-acre site in Indio that holds about 1,500-acre feet of water.

The Coachella Valley County Water District became the premier water district in the valley and through the years acquired some of the smaller water companies and districts, including the Tamarisk Water Company, the Rancho Mirage Water Company, and the oldest of them all, the Palm Valley Water Company.

Desert Water Agency

The smaller Desert Water Agency currently serves a 325-square mile area, which includes all of Palm Springs, some adjacent county areas and parts of Cathedral City. Only five percent of its drinking supply is from the mountain streams of Chino Creek, Snow Creek, and Falls Creek. The remaining 95 percent is groundwater captured in four huge natural basins that is pumped from deep wells. Natural groundwater replenishment comes not only from the streams but also from the aforementioned aqueduct.

Unlike many bottled brands that are stripped of mineral content, DWA water is rich in minerals required for healthy growth and development.

According to DWA General Manager Dan M. Ainsworth, "Desert Water is fortunate to have some of the best drinking water available anywhere. The Board and our employees are committed to preserving quality while ensuring a plentiful supply for our growing population."

The agency also encourages recycling water to keep the area's scores of golf courses and parks green.

Most locals will agree with the high quality of DWA water even though it sometimes looks funny. The Palm Springs water, which has been tested at 99.6 pure, sometimes comes out of the tap with a cloudy, milky look, which soon dissipates. Many locals drink it from the tap, unlike some communities where the tap water often has a metallic or dirty taste. It may not be directly from the hot springs anymore, but it apparently is just as beneficial.

CHAPTER 11

The Little Train That Couldn't
PALMDALE/SMOKE TREE

Other settlers moved to the Coachella Valley following the 1885 act that offered non-railroad lands to homesteaders. Down at the east end of the valley, a few pioneers began establishing an agricultural community in the Indio area. In Agua Caliente (Palm Springs) itself, Judge McCallum was the first to subdivide—but there would soon be others.

Several other groups tried to make a go in Palm Valley, one a subdivision called "The Garden of Eden," promoted by B.B. Barney of Riverside. Located near the mouth of Andreas Canyon adjacent to Indian homes (about where the Canyon Country Club is today), it was an unusual circular tract with small plots on streets named after biblical characters radiating outward from a proposed central Grand Hotel Eden.

The only water available to the Garden of Eden was that from the Andreas Canyon, and that belonged to the Indians. The once grandiose plan was deserted and after years of litigation the government bought out the remaining settlers and gave the land to the Indians.

At the end of McCallum's big November 1, 1887, auction, one group of three investors bought unsold land by taking an option on about 2,000 acres and shares of unsold stock in the water company. The men, S.W. Ferguson of Oakland, H.C. Campbell of San Francisco, and L.B. Holt of Riverside, were part of McCallum's Palm Valley Land and Water Company—in fact Ferguson was the auctioneer.

The three had $100,000 invested and set out to develop the new town they called Palmdale, where Smoke Tree Ranch is today. They planned to sell 100 acres at a time in 10 or 20-acre parcels at $150 per acre. The price would escalate after each offering of 100 acres, from $150 to $175, to $200, to $225, with the fifth offering at $250 per acre.

The syndicate went out of their way to bring prospective settlers to Palmdale. By 1876, the Southern Pacific Railroad went to the Seven Palms station, near present day I-10 and North Indian Canyon Drive, and continued on to Indio and points east.

Rather than having buckboards meet the train, the enterprising developers of Palmdale built a 12-mile-long narrow-gauge railroad from a point near the eastern end of Garnet Hill at Seven Palms in an almost straight line south down present-day Farrell Road to the Smoke Tree Ranch just south of Highway 111. In addition to passengers, it was built to haul equipment and supplies, and, hopefully, to haul out produce grown by the settlers.

Seven Palms Railroad Station. *Drawing by Carl Eytel.*

They appointed their land development company manager Herbert W. Bordwell as rail superintendent, got a small wood-burning locomotive named "Cabazon," three flat cars for baggage and freight, two cable cars from San Francisco, and they were in business.

The locomotive had a flaring smokestack and a small attached coal and wood tender at its rear. The cable cars were quite a sight, one flat-sided and the other bulging outward. Their names were still displayed on them indicating their original Baghdad by the Bay destinations: "Market Street" and "Sutter Street."

There was a "Y" at each end of the railroad permitting the engine to turn around and a roundhouse at the Palmdale end.

One of the first shipments on the flat cars was reported to have been orange tree nursery stock from Florida.

On March 9, 1888, a post office was established in a small store at Palmdale, with Thomas M. Sweet installed as the first postmaster, and things looked promising. But while there was a ranch, the development never took off. In fact the ranch employees and railroad track-laying crews lived in tent houses.

The trains on this special one-of-a-kind railroad, so noble in planning, ran just a few trips, from July until September 1888, only two months in operation.

That summer, the water from the 19-mile irrigation ditch from the Whitewater River petered out before it got to Palmdale. Palmdale could get very little water. The few fruit trees that survived the trip from Florida soon died, a vivid signal that perhaps the end of the ambitious project was near. The developers ran out of money and couldn't even pay the ranch laborers. The project was abandoned.

The little train that could, couldn't continue. The locomotive sat out in the desert until 1892 when the last engineer, A.D. Spring, loaded the engine, two flat cars, and most of the rails on a Southern Pacific train and they were taken to Bakersfield.

The two cable cars laid abandoned in the desert for years. J. Smeaton Chase took a photo of them resting forlornly in the desert sun in the early part of the 20th century. Finally they were destroyed by fire, and the wheels, axles, and old frames could be seen until as late as 1916 lying on the desert. That year flooding buried the remnants under many feet of silt and sand.

The railroad ties suffered a slightly better fate. Welwood Murray gathered up many of the old ties to build his home. Cornelia White purchased the house from Murray and today it has been moved to the Village Green on South Palm Canyon Drive as part of the Palm Springs Historical Society.

The two cable cars of the little train to Smoke Tree Ranch abandoned to the desert. *Photo courtesy Palm Springs Historical Society.*

Of the abandoned right-of-way, there is very little evidence. Searchers today looking for some tangible evidence of the poor little railroad might be disappointed. In the lot adjacent to what is now the upscale community of Smoke Tree Ranch there is a slight rise in the ground in a few places and a few rotten old pilings, but it is unsure if they were from the roundhouse or not.

CHAPTER 12

After The Drought
REBUILDING A DREAM

The early settlers of Palm Springs could not have known during those heady days of 1893 that much of their efforts would shrivel and die from the prolonged drought, and that many of them would be leaving the village, forever abandoning their properties.

Before the drought, an 1893-94 *History and Directory of Riverside County* had this to say about the fledgling village, along with the list of residents:

> PALM SPRINGS — *(formerly San Diego County)* A small settlement on the Southern Pacific Railroad twenty-seven miles south of Banning at the eastern base of Mt. San Jacinto, almost enclosed by Mountains. They have a post office, hotel, mineral water and water for irrigating. Some fruit is raised: also a resort for consumptives.
>
>> *Benson, M.J. — farmer*
>> *Bowman, F.H. — laborer*
>> *Broesawaite, C. — laborer*
>> *Campbell, A. — mail carrier*
>> *Chase, M. — assistant postmaster*
>> *Chase, W. — carpenter*
>> *Coombs, R. H. — laborer*
>> *Coombes, W. laborer*
>> *England, U. — laborer*
>> *Gilman, J.H. — farmer*
>> *Hoyman, G. — superintendent irrigation ditch*
>> *Langford, C. — laborer*
>> *Maine, G. — laborer*
>> *McCallum, H. F. — real estate*
>> *McCallum, W. — farmer*
>> *Murray, Welwood — proprietor, Palm Springs Hotel*
>> *Pierce, O. — laborer*
>> *Taylor, H. — laborer*
>> *Wheaton, H. F. — farmer*

That Palm Springs survived and endured those 11 dry years is a tribute to those who stayed. Of interest today is that this older directory does not include the approximate 50 Indian residents who were there before, during, and after the drought.

When the drought was over, from about 1905 through World War I and up to about 1920, a new village emerged, one bolstered with health resorts, hotels, stores and businesses all geared to attract visitors and tourists from all over. That has been the destiny of Palm Springs ever since.

SECTION 3

❊

Women Revive a Village
(1905-1920)

So many women played vital roles in the development of Palm Spring during the early years that it was close to a matriarchal society.

Most notable were Nellie Coffman, Pearl McCallum McManus and the White Sisters. But they were not the only women to leave their mark upon the fledgling city of Palm Springs.

Through the years the impact of women in business, education, politics, and society has been legendary.

The first sanatorium established by Lavinia Crocker in 1893 set the pace for the many scores

(continued)

of women-owned businesses to follow. One prominent example is Zaddie Bunker who owned the first garage and other real estate in downtown Palm Springs.

In 1893 Palm Springs also received its first teacher, a Miss Annie K. Noble, and numerous women educators since, including the illustrious Katherine Finchy, have served the village with distinction.

Palm Springs residents owe much to the pioneers who made the former village what it is today, and a good lot of that history was created by hard-working and strong-willed women.

CHAPTER 13

The Desert Inn
NELLIE COFFMAN

God's Garden of Peace
by Nellie Norton Orr Roberson Coffman

God gave to mankind the beauties of the earth,
Of mountains, and lowlands and sea,
Rivers and lakes, forests and glades,
These wondrous gifts gave He.

But He kept for His own a Garden,
Rugged, forbidding, austere,
Surrounded by peaks uplifted—
Snow-capped through the year.

And He walks in His Garden at twilight,
And all who would have surcease
From life's toil and struggle, many find it
In the Desert, God's Garden of Peace.

The remarkable woman who penned the above created her own Garden of Peace.

There's a plaque at the former site of The Desert Inn in downtown Palm Springs (northwest corner of Palm Canyon Drive and Tahquitz Canyon Way) that reads:

> *On this site in 1909, Nellie N. Coffman (1867-1950), her husband, Harry, and two sons, George Roberson and Earl Coffman, established a small health resort hotel, The Desert Inn. Her ability, determination and charm extended the resort's reputation and people came from all over the world. In 1927 a modern hotel replaced the earlier structures. Nellie's love and charitable works for the community earned her the title of Mother Coffman. The hotel gave way to a shopping complex in 1967.*

While Nellie Coffman wasn't the first settler in Palm Springs, she arrived at a propitious time when only a few settlers (10 whites) remained with about 50 Indians after a long drought. She established The Desert Inn and, through her efforts, she has often been referred to as the "Mother of Palm Springs." Some even called her the "Patron Saint of Palm Springs."

Once she saw the desert shimmering in the distance from horseback on a day trip out of Idyllwild to the mountaintop, she wanted to visit it. She arrived with her family in December 1908 and stayed at Welwood Murray's Palm Springs Hotel.

She had been ill and recognized the healthful properties of the desert air. She was taken by the serenity of the place. Here she and her husband, Harry Lee Coffman, M.D. could establish a hotel and a "sanatorium"—later more commonly called a sanitarium—to treat people suffering from pulmonary ailments.

Entrance to The Desert Inn. *Photo courtesy Palm Springs Historical Society.*

It began with $2,000 down

Harry selflessly gave up his medical practice, and sold his Santa Monica rental properties so he and Nellie could realize their dreams. They bought 1¾ acres across the road from Welwood Murray's hotel for about $2,000 down.

Family members today are pretty sure they paid about $10,000 for the property. There was a comfortable structure on that lot that was originally the vacation home of a wealthy San Francisco widow, Eleanor Martin, who left permanently during the drought. The house was solid and comfortable with thick granite fireplaces. There were also stables to the rear of the land and a fence across the front. The property was owned briefly by a Denver merchant and then sold to the wife of a San Diego businessman, Mrs. McKenzie, from whom Harry and Nellie purchased it in September 1909.

Upon arriving in town with her husband and older son George Ball Roberson on October 16, 1909, Nellie immediately hung a printed sign on the wooden porch post out front, the first advertisement for what would one day be a world renowned resort. The sign said simply, "The Desert Inn."

The Coffmans also bought Lavinia Crocker's Green Gables Health Resort which consisted of a home and some tent houses located to the west of the property. They soon had an additional 35 acres for the expansion of The Desert Inn.

Nellie brought more tent houses of canvas and wood from Los Angeles for $85 apiece to the site and opened The Desert Inn within six weeks. For decades it would remain the village's most important destination, and one of the country's premier desert hotels.

Nellie and Harry's credo was to provide good food, clean and comfortable accommodations, and warm hospitality. The first two clients were reporters from the *Los Angeles Times* who went on to extol the merits of the new desert resort, and the rest is history.

Nellie's father managed hotels

Born in Illinois in 1867 to James and Ruth Orr, Nellie Norton Orr had a younger brother and two sisters. The family moved to Texas when Nellie was 10 years old and her father became manager of a Dallas hotel.

Nellie married George Ball Roberson in 1887, and he tragically died in a fire before their son, George, was born on July 5, 1888. Meanwhile her parents and three younger children had moved to Ranchito (now Pico Rivera), California, where they were neighbors of walnut grower Charles Alan Coffman.

Nellie and her son George followed and there she met Coffman's son Harry Coffman, whom she courted. The Orrs sought better opportunity and moved to Santa Monica where both James and Ruth Orr got into the hotel business. Nellie and Harry Coffman continued their courtship and were married on March 5, 1891, at the St. James Hotel in Santa Monica. Their son, Owen Earl Coffman, was born on March 28, 1892.

Nellie and Harry were not the only Orr-Coffman match up. Nellie's sister Edna would marry Harry's brother Edgar.

At Nellie's encouragement, Harry went to school, eventually obtaining his degree in medicine from a school in Philadelphia in 1901. He established a medical practice in Santa Monica.

With some of her parents' hotelling experience rubbing off on young Nellie and an opportunity to put her husband's medical practice to good use, the move to the desert and acquiring The Desert Inn seemed a sound one.

Although it was originally a sanatorium, their vision went beyond that as they added rooms and permanent guest accommodations making it a true hotel. Harry and Nellie provided excellent care and good meals and the word spread about The Desert Inn.

The Coffmans were friendly with everyone and were highly regarded by the community. They helped the Agua Caliente Indians by employing many of them at the inn.

In 1914, Fanny Stevenson, widow of famed author Robert Louis Stevenson, spent some time at The Desert Inn and wrote a letter about it to an English friend, part of which reads:

> There is, also, a climate of extraordinary purity and dryness, and almost no rain or wind. Wonderful cures of tuberculosis have taken place here; one of the former patients I know very well; he was considered a hopeless case, and is now perfectly well. If I had only known of Palm Springs in my Louis's time! There are very few people except patients, and perhaps an old prospector or two; everything is very simple and plain, but the food is excellent, and the "penthouses" in which the patients live, are as comfortable as one could wish. I came here partly for asthma, and partly to recover from a bad attack of influenza. The influenza is gone, the asthma is nonexistent, but I plan to stay for another month.

While Nellie's husband was instrumental in the development of The Desert Inn as a sanatorium, it was Nellie herself whose foresight turned it into a class resort. According to Marjorie Belle Bright in her 1981 book *Nellie's Boardinghouse*, it was a lot of little things that finally eroded the Coffman's marriage and they legally terminated it in 1917.

Harry was the first practicing physician in Palm Springs. He went on to practice medicine in Calexico and later had a ranch in Cherry Valley. He died in 1935 with his boots on, treating patients in Alpine, San Diego County, California. He was buried in the old Welwood Murray Palm Springs Cemetery.

Both sons served in WW I

Both of Nellie's sons went off to serve in World War I leaving Nellie to manage the hotel, a task for which she showed considerable ability. She was aided by her double niece, "Pat" Helen Ruth Coffman (daughter of Nellie's sister Edna and Harry's brother Edgar), who worked tirelessly helping her aunt run the inn. One of Nellie's great granddaughters, Kitty Kieley Hayes, reports, "Granny (Nellie) never forgot and Pat received the first bequeathment from Granny's estate." When the sons returned from the war, the family set up The Desert Inn in corporate form with Nellie as president, George as vice president, and Earl as secretary-treasurer.

Los Angeles doctors began sending flu patients to The Desert Inn to escape possible contagion during the 1918 influenza epidemic, and not a single case was reported in Palm Springs. Still, by 1920, Nellie had visions to change The Desert Inn and was not encouraging patients for respiratory and pulmonary ailments. By then she had developed a "no invalid" policy. In fact, by 1915 she had been excluding guests with communicable diseases. The tent houses were gradually replaced by comfortable wooden bungalows with screened porches.

Then Nellie borrowed money to expand and change the hotel forever. By 1928 with the help of architect Charles Tanner, it was mostly completed with Mission Revival style guesthouses amid her beautiful 35-acre garden. The new main building featured a large, inviting lobby, an intimate bar, and beautiful expansive porch built in old California Mission style with handcrafted furnishings to match. The first swimming pool in the desert, originally a reservoir used to collect water for Whitewater Mutual Water Company, opened at The Desert Inn in the early 1920's. Later guests were also offered golf privileges with the newly built O'Donnell Golf Course behind the property.

The sons of Nellie Coffman, Owen Earl Coffman (left) and George Ball Roberson Jr. (right) flank fellow pioneer Harold Hicks. *Photo courtesy Palm Springs Historical Society.*

A social director was hired and the guest list reads like a who's who of the times. W.K. Kellogg (cereal), King Gillette, John Ford, and film idol Rudolph Valentino were among the many early guests. Businessmen, the media, and film luminaries began flocking to Palm Springs, virtually all of them at one time or another staying at The Desert Inn.

Other Desert Inn guests included Irving Berlin, J. Edgar Hoover, and child star Shirley Temple. Berlin, famous for his "White Christmas," stayed in Nellie Coffman's house and used her piano to compose several pieces. Hoover was a friend of the family.

Desert Inn developer and owner Nellie Coffman shares a moment with Shirley Temple, the most famous child star of the 1930s and 1940s. *Photo courtesy Palm Springs Historical Society.*

UPS founder Jim Casey and his family were frequent guests. J.C. Penney stayed there as did the Heinz family—Mrs. Heinz passed out pins shaped like small pickles. Leo Carrillo, Gilbert Roland, Dolores Del Rio, and Monty Montana stayed at The Desert Inn. Montana actually rode his horse into the lobby and lassoed some of the guests. The only person allowed to bring his dog was Lee Duncan, and the dog—Rin Tin Tin.

High standards

Nellie had high standards and would not allow just anyone to visit. Once a movie star brought a female companion who was not his wife and the pair was asked to leave. She expected her guests to dress fittingly for dinner in the De Anza Room which featured candles, white linen, and a string trio.

She served as not only the official greeter of The Desert Inn but also of

Palm Springs at large. She was a "one woman city council" according to some and was also the entire Palm Springs Chamber of Commerce. The Palm Springs "season" revolved around the opening of The Desert Inn on October 1, and its closing on May 1 of each year.

Nellie became involved in many community efforts. With the exception of two years, she served on the school board from 1923-1946. In 1939 a school opened that, against her protests, was named in her honor. She was a dynamo in helping those who were unfortunate, making sure that all of the people, regardless of their background or heritage had food and blankets. Many of the local Agua Caliente Indians worked for Nellie or her sons through the years. She founded the Palm Springs Welfare and Friendly Aid, which eventually became the local United Way.

At the hotel, she clung to her few simple tenets that served so well. The cuisine at The Desert Inn became widely known and respected. Nellie was a good cook and liked to wear an apron, a large bonnet and looked rather, well…"motherly" behind those specs.

A "Boardinghouse in the Sky"

Nellie was sought after as a speaker and addressed many southern California groups talking about "Hotel Keeping." Nellie loved running the hotel. In a 1946 address she commented, "When my time on earth comes to a close and I stand at the Pearly Gate, I'm going to ask the gatekeeper if I can start a boardinghouse in the sky."

Through the years she added to the family holdings. She bought a property in Banning called Lazy Acres, then later 1,920 acres (3 sections) up Highway 74 off the Palms to Pines Highway. The two upper sections were called Upper Ramada, and the lower (present site of Big Horn Country Club), the Lower Ramada. Along what is now Tahquitz Canyon Way, the upscale Le Vallauris Restaurant was for years the home of her son George Roberson and his family. The Cape Cod building that was next door was the home of her other son, O. Earl Coffman.

Her sons were also involved in community activities. George was a member of the police and fire protection board and became one of the town's business leaders. Earl was the first chairman of the Mt. San Jacinto Winter Park Authority which runs the Palm Springs Aerial Tramway. He held that position for over 20 years.

For some years Nellie and her sons spent their summers when the Desert Inn was closed up at Lake Arrowhead, where Nellie managed the Lodge at Lake Arrowhead.

In recognition to their "Patron Saint," the City of Palm Springs threw an 80th birthday party for Nellie Coffman on November 1, 1947. A front-page banner announced the Nellie Coffman Day activities in Palm Springs' *The Desert Sun* newspaper on its October 31, 1947 issue. It included a photo with the caption: "Village Mother, Nellie Coffman, founder of The Desert Inn, acclaimed the *mother* of Palm Springs, who will be honored on her 80th birthday tomorrow in the form of an old fashioned picnic. Pictured with her two sons, Earl Coffman, on the right, and George Roberson, who now operate the world-famous hotel."

Nellie died three years later, in 1950, and was buried in the Welwood Murray Cemetery with the marker simply stating, "Mother-Nellie N. Coffman, 1867-1950." Earl, who died in 1967, and George, in 1968, are buried nearby.

Her sons sold The Desert Inn in 1955 to Marion Davies, who was long associated with William Randolph Hearst, for $1.3 million. It later became the Desert Fashion Shopping Plaza occupying the long block on Palm Canyon Drive to the north of Tahquitz Canyon Way.

In 1976 a new Nellie N. Coffman Middle School opened on 35 acres in Cathedral City just east of Palm Springs.

Nellie was gone but her legacy lives on not only in Palm Springs but in resorts everywhere. The legendary World War II correspondent Ernie Pyle wrote a series of columns about Nellie Coffman and her indomitable spirit. He wrote,

> *She started what was to become the whole, vast vogue of desert vacationing. All the great resorts—Tucson and Phoenix and Death Valley—the fancy hotels and the Southwest dude ranches and the thousands in trailers who have discovered the uncanny lure of the desert, it all began with Mother Coffman. The whole thing was built on one woman's spiritual love of the desert!*

CHAPTER 14

Reclaiming a Heritage
PEARL McCALLUM McMANUS/TENNIS CLUB

If there ever was a woman with a birthright on the village of Palm Springs it would be Pearl McCallum McManus, a member of the first permanent settler family. Pearl, the daughter of John G. McCallum and only surviving McCallum, eventually developed much of her father's land in the desert.

While Nellie Coffman was enjoying widespread fame as the "founding matriarch" of Palm Springs, a role that perhaps should have gone to a McCallum, Pearl was in the process of resurrecting the neglected family estate. She would eventually become known for establishing first the Oasis Hotel, and then the still-famous Tennis Club.

Pearl was born in 1879, the second daughter of John and Emily McCallum. At age five she and her older sister, May, and three brothers, Johnny, Wallace and Harry, came to settle Palm Valley with their parents. Aside from her siblings and a little burro she enjoyed, her only playmates were Indian children.

She spent much of her youth, however, living in the family's Los Angeles house on West Adams Street. There she attended Marlborough Finishing School for young ladies. She remained in Los Angeles to help her ailing mother and became a teacher.

Starting over in Palm Springs

By 1909, her father had been dead for 12 years, the drought was over, and Pearl and her by now invalid mother returned to Palm Springs. Along with the lack of water, indifferent hired help had allowed most of their ranch to revert to the desert it had originally been. Only a few grapes, apricots, and a half-acre of oranges were left. The income from that meager yield at first sustained Pearl and her mother. They even had the Indians cut down the dead apricot trees to be sold for firewood. There were times when Pearl and her mother were so broke that Nellie Coffman sent them food.

Over the next few years Pearl found herself in the middle of water disputes between the Palm Springs settlers, water agencies, the Indians, and what many, including Pearl, referred to as meddlesome government agents.

Having already lost her brothers, Pearl would also lose her sister May Forline who died from being weakened by a typhoid attack when she was a girl. May realized she was dying and asked Pearl to take care of her daughter, Marjorie Forline. So "Auntie Pearl" and Marjorie became inseparable for the next thirty plus years.

In 1914, her mother Emily died and Pearl assumed control of all the McCallum holdings. About all that was left was the land, between 5,000 and 6,000 acres that her father had bought from the railroad for $2.50 an acre. One of her first transactions was to sell a parcel of land, part of her father's original 80 acres for $500. Remembering her father's admonitions to hang on to the land at all costs, from then on she only very reluctantly sold land.

Pearl had little but the land in 1914, the year she met and married Austin G. McManus, a former owner of a men's clothing store who was at the time working in real estate in South Pasadena. It took a while for the well-groomed Irish city boy from New Jersey to adapt to the desert, but he and Pearl set up a real estate business, Pioneer Properties, in Palm Springs. Pearl became president and Austin was the secretary. They lived in the old McCallum adobe and spent their summers at the McManus home in Pasadena. Pearl spent much of her life re-acquiring Palm Springs land formerly owned by her father and at one time was the town's largest single property owner.

The Oasis Hotel

In 1924 Pearl and Austin began construction of the village's newest hotel on McCallum property across the road from The Desert Inn. They hired Lloyd Wright, the then estranged son of famed architect Frank Lloyd Wright to design The Oasis Hotel, which opened in 1925.

It was a Modern/Art Deco building of solid concrete using an innovative slipform technique. Its most distinctive feature was a 40-foot tower which provided access to upper floors and a rooftop terrace. Years later actress Loretta Young had the uppermost room named after her as she claimed the view from it was her favorite place in Palm Springs.

Pearl had leased the hotel and turned the management over to W E. Hanner and his brother who were operating the Hotel Cecil in Los Angeles at the time. The Oasis Hotel featured a 90-foot dining room and guest rooms surrounding a fountain. The Oasis Hotel still stands today, (at the corner of Tahquitz Canyon Way and Belardo Road.), the oldest hotel in Palm Springs.

The historic Oasis Hotel on Tahquitz Canyon Way.

Pearl sold the corner lot which housed the family's original home. The new owner was going to level the home to put in a commercial building. Rather than see that happen, Pearl was forced to dismantle the family's original adobe home and relocate it, brick by brick, a few blocks south where it rests today in the Village Green on South Palm Canyon Drive. She also had the old fig tree, under which her family had originally camped, (by then weighing 18½ tons), relocated. It took two days to move it.

After the adobe was moved, Pearl and Austin relocated to a small cottage and then built what became their famous "pink mansion" on the side of the mountain, just north of the Tennis Club.

Austin's business acumen helped Pearl become known as an astute businesswoman herself. While she was often referred to as "Auntie Pearl," her serious demeanor caused many to respect her and many to fear her. She was finishing-school correct, opinionated and proud, and wielded great power. Her demeanor was quite different from the village's other female power, Nellie Coffman, who was a much more earthy individual.

She also methodically set about buying as much land as possible. She performed title searches on land seemingly abandoned by early settlers, contacted them, and bought many original land sale lots that way. She built the Hacienda Apartments, the first apartment house in Palm Springs.

Pearl sold acreage to the fledgling city of Palm Springs for a landing field. During World War II that landing field was appropriated by the federal government for a U.S. Army air transportation center. It is now the Palm Springs International Airport.

She developed the city's first main subdivision, Tahquitz River Estates, and many individual homes, often living in them before offering them for sale. She had designed and built the first Sak's and Robinson's stores, working closely with the architect.

Tennis Club became resort model

Of all her projects, one which made her most proud was the Tennis Club. It started with tennis courts for some of her English visitors. When completed they were considered the finest courts in the world. The Club's famous oval swimming pool, under two graceful palms which formed a "v," became a much photographed model for resorts for decades.

Pearl traveled widely and brought back ideas from Europe in her designs. She recalled a monastery on the Amalfi cliffs in Italy for the terrace and clubhouse of the Tennis Club, and hired well-known designer/architect Paul Williams of Los Angeles to make her ideas become reality. He was the first black member of the American Institute of Architects. The dining room featured one wall of rugged stone replete with waterfall.

The original clubhouse and buildings have been recently renovated in 2001-2002. Today the Tennis Club and Spencer's, the accompanying restaurant, is owned by Harold Matzner. There are currently 11 tennis courts, five spas, and three swimming pools, with one and two bedroom units creating a true resort destination.

Pearl was a sophisticate and a socialite and felt right at home entertaining guests and celebrities from around the world. She was active in much of the social activities of the

The famous oval pool of the Tennis Club.

desert. She made the Tennis Club facilities available free for charitable events. She was a charter member of both the Desert Riders and the Palm Springs Polo Club. To some, to be sure, if "Auntie Pearl" wasn't involved, it was not a significant event.

Austin on First City Council

Austin McManus served on the first city council when Palm Springs was incorporated on April 20, 1938. He died in 1955 and was buried in the Welwood Murray Cemetery.

In 1959, chartered buses brought people in from Los Angeles to The Desert Inn to help celebrate Pearl's 80th birthday party.

While she could be frugal for herself, Pearl became a tireless benefactor, giving back much to the city she helped found. She donated to all sorts of charities, the schools and the arts. She also established scholarships that would put a recipient all the way through college. She gave so much to the Palm Springs Women's Club, including land, that the first meeting in November each year is now known as Pearl McManus Day. She also donated land to the Boy Scouts and the chamber of commerce.

Pearl McCallum McManus died on Jul. 24, 1966, and was buried beside her husband in the Welwood Murray Pioneer Cemetery.

After her death, the McCallum Foundation was responsible for millions of dollars of civic improvements and educational projects. The beautiful airport fountain built with her financial assistance was named in her honor. Probably more through her efforts rather than her father's is the name 'McCallum" so dominant in the Coachella Valley. It is on buildings, parks, theaters, and schools. It was mostly a result of "Auntie Pearl" picking up the pieces, making them work, and giving back to the city she loved.

Mr. and Mrs. Austin McManus. *Photo courtesy Palm Springs Historical Society.*

CHAPTER 15

Women of the Desert
EARLY WOMEN SETTLERS

As noted, some of the early Palm Springs women were astute business-women, but others were also instrumental in the development of the village. Some endured difficult conditions as they accompanied their husbands trying to create and maintain families, homes, and lives in the harsh desert environment.

Imagine being Mrs. Jack Summers, who lived with her husband in a small adobe hut from 1865-1877. Summers was the stage line agent based in Palm Springs, and the couple were the only non-Indians living there at the time. She helped her husband raise barley for horses on the 10 acres they rented from the Indians.

Emily Freeman McCallum

We've met John G. McCallum, but consider his wife, Emily Freeman McCallum, a frail and gentle socialite who was never comfortable in the desert. Her hardships went way beyond living in a simple adobe brick house her husband constructed with the help of Indians. She lost one child in infancy and had four of her five surviving children stricken during a typhoid epidemic and all four precede her in death.

According to her only surviving daughter, Pearl McCallum McManus,

> *Mother never recovered from the heartbreak of Johnny's death, then Wallace died, and this was followed by the sudden death of her husband. She was a beautiful woman, with a lovely singing voice, but she was a little girl woman—not a pioneer. She did the best she could in this strange and, to her, relentless world, and when it was unbearable she cried like a little girl.*

Elizabeth Erskine Murray

Dr. Welwood Murray's wife was one of the first teachers in the land of the Cahuilla, instructing at the Indian School on the Potrero Reservation near Banning.

Once the Palm Springs Hotel was established by her husband, Mrs. Murray became known far and wide as a gracious hostess, preparing comfortable accommodations and cooking abundant and hearty meals. Reportedly, she served as a nurse, advisor, and provided heartfelt motherly care to their many guests. Probably considered more significant, especially by today's standards, was that she remained a devoted and understanding wife to a difficult and, by all accounts, cantankerous and opinionated Dr. Welwood Murray.

A stout woman, considered overweight for that decade, she enjoyed puttering in her garden, and with age suffered increasing deafness, toning down some of her husband's bellowing. Born in Scotland in 1830, she died in 1911.

Ramona Lubo

There really was a Ramona, whose true tragedy inspired the famous 1884 novel by Helen Hunt Jackson. A Cahuilla Indian, she was married to Juan Diego, a man who was known to have suffered erratic spells. It is said that it was during one of those spells that he made the mistake of going out for a ride on a horse that belonged to Sam Temple, a white rancher.

When informed of the incident, Temple shot Juan Diego 22 times in the chest. Ramona was the only witness, but being an Indian she was not allowed to testify. The all-white jury trial concluded that Temple had acted in self-defense and was acquitted.

Widowed and poor, Ramona Lubo lived out her life on the Cahuilla Reservation in Anza, bringing in a little income from selling baskets and allowing visitors to have their pictures taken with the "real Ramona." She died in 1922.

Dolores Patencio

While many of the Cahuilla Indian women could be mentioned here, we'll single out one of the more famous of them. Dolores Patencio was the wife of Francisco Patencio, one of the Patencio brothers who were all leaders of the Agua Caliente Band. Francisco, one of the last ceremonial leaders of the Agua Calientes, became widely known for his story telling and preservation of tribal legends. Dolores, who hailed from the Cupeño Band, was originally from Warners Ranch near Warner Hot Springs.

Cahuilla basket weaving became widely known as some of the finest among North American Indians, and by many accounts the most famous of the Cahuilla basket weavers was Dolores Patencio. She gathered and prepared the traditional plant materials that she painstakingly wove into beautiful baskets, some of which are still displayed at the Palm Springs Desert Museum.

Dolores Patencio, circa 1920. She was known for her fine baskets. *Photo courtesy Malki Museum.*

Clara True – Indian Agent

The 1891 visit of the Albert K. Smiley Commission to the Banning area found a troubled situation with about 100 Cahuilla Indians of the Morongo Band being exploited by about 300 white settlers. Commissioner Smiley could not effect any progress, commenting that strong racial prejudice in the area would virtually prohibit any legal justice for the Indians.

Instead of improving, relations deteriorated badly over the next 20 years. Indian agents were non-existent or ineffectual. Indian/white tensions were extremely poor, with whites considering Indians "good for nothing." Liquor had become a serious problem among the Indians and their lands were unsuitable and lacked the water for farming.

Indian Commissioner Francis Leupp, in recognizing that the situation had to be turned around, reviewed his field staff and concluded, "The very man to do the job was Miss Clara D. True. I gave her a man's work," he said, "and she has done it better than any man who has been in there for 30 years."

Leupp felt she could cope with any problem, but she almost didn't get started. She arrived in desolate Morongo, looked around, and decided to resign on the spot. She reconsidered, and went on to become one of the most productive Indian agents of the era.

Working out of her headquarters on the Morongo Reservation in Banning from 1908 to 1910, she was also placed in charge of the Chemehuevi Reservation in 29 Palms and three other reservations. She was the first Indian Service employee to visit the 29 Palms Reservation and obtained a surveyor to establish proper legal boundaries there, ending disputes over the local water hole.

On all the reservations, the feisty agent fought not only the bootleggers who supplied the Indians but also all alcohol sales, even enlisting the aid of William "Pussyfoot" Johnson, a noted saloon-breaker, to help her drive booze-peddlers from the area. Described by someone who knew her well, Miss True was "A short, dynamic, little old maid." The national issue of the day was the vote for women but Clara True herself said she was no suffragette and wouldn't vote if she could.

Miss True just set out to help and was able to assist Indians in sustaining themselves. She taught them new methods of irrigating their land, and had them create tunnels and ditches. They were so successful, with so many Indians working their own fields, that by late 1908 the white farmers in the area had to bring in Indians from outside reservations to help them harvest. Their success actually created a labor shortage!

Clara True made a huge impact in her two years as Indian agent among the Morongo Cahuilla and other Indians, not only for the Indians but also in Indian/white relationships. She spoke Spanish and conversed with the Indians in that language. Her immediate supervisor once described her as "a woman of 40 years of age, small in stature but strong and wiry, with an indomitable will and courage, thoroughly able to handle the Indians and all questions arising in connection with her work."

One old photo of petite Clara True shows her with a group in a desert camp. Her long sleeved shirt with bandanna, long skirt and boots seemed appropriate for the clime and the decade. But the large, straw, Mexican-style sombrero tends to dwarf the diminutive woman. A close up photo shows what was under that large sombrero, a friendly, proper woman with compassionate eyes and a strong determined jaw. She didn't need the right to vote. She made a difference all by herself.

Lavinia Fryatt Crocker

Lavinia Crocker, born in 1861, came to Palm Springs in 1898 and opened one of the first sanatoriums, the Green Gables Health Resort on Spring Street (Tahquitz Canyon Way), due west from what would become The Desert Inn. She had a home and tent houses for her patients.

Nellie Coffman desperately wanted to buy it, not only to incorporate it into The Desert Inn property, making the house into her home, but also because the meticulous Nellie felt Crocker's lackadaisical refuse disposal (allowing trash to pile up) was an eyesore.

Crocker had her ups and downs with her Green Gables, and according to the *Red Front Store News*, a paper put out by Otto Adler in 1914, "Mrs. Crocker, proprietress of the Green Gables Health Resort, after one of the most prosperous winter seasons Palm Springs has ever experienced, is having her place repaired and repainted and it will be quite inviting to the health seekers the coming season."

Crocker eventually sold it to Dr. Harry and Nellie Coffman who moved into the Crocker home. Lavinia Crocker had to sell because of misfortune, but was astute to sell for enough to take care of her during her twilight years.

According to Mother Nellie Coffman,

> *There was about an acre of ground in all. We had to have it and the woman who owned it [Mrs. Crocker] knew it...The poor thing had a tragic life, and he[Mr. Crocker] did too. He'd lost a leg in a railroad accident, then contracted T.B. [tuberculosis]. They just had no money. Used up their last dollar...so for six months we cooked and carried luncheon and dinner for them....Anyway, after things got straightened around, she began to think about what she could do. "I am going to make them pay me enough interest to take care of me as long as I live." I paid the woman forty thousand dollars for that property....we had to borrow the money....I don't know if I could ever do a thing like that, but she could see far ahead of her time.*

Mr. Walton Nye Crocker of Massachusetts died in 1911. Lavinia survived him by 40 years, eventually passing away in 1951. Both are interred in the Welwood Murray Cemetery.

CHAPTER 16

Sisters of Adventure

DR. FLORILLA, CORNELIA, AND ISABEL WHITE

The White sisters, especially Dr. Florilla Mansfield White and Miss Cornelia Butler White, seemed destined to help settle Palm Springs. A third sister, Isabel, also arrived and remained in the small village, but it was primarily Florilla and Cornelia, both earthy nature lovers whose idea of a good time meant exploring a nearby canyon, who left a lasting imprint upon the budding resort town.

One of 10 children of a New York state farming family, Dr. Florilla White was born in 1871. She first visited Palm Springs during the winter of 1912 and stayed at Welwood Murray's hotel.

Dr. Florilla later joined younger sister Cornelia, born in 1874, in Mexico for a while and then the two of them returned to Palm Springs in 1913 to stay. They ended up purchasing Welwood Murray's Palm Springs Hotel and continued to rent out rooms, sans meals, with much of their business handling overflow from The Desert Inn.

When Murray died in 1914, the sisters also bought the block across Tahquitz Canyon Way, north of the present-day Welwood Murray Memorial Library, for $10,000. It was the entire 100 North Palm Canyon block, extending to Indian Canyon Drive, minus the northeast corner, which Welwood Murray had given to the Community Church.

The White sisters pose in their finery at early ages: (left to right) Florilla, Cornelia, and Isabel. *Photo courtesy Palm Springs Historical Society.*

Miss Cornelia, as she was known, also bought the entire block in which she lived (to the south of the present Tahquitz Canyon Way) for $5,000. The house Cornelia White lived in was the one built by Dr. Welwood Murray in 1893 from railroad ties taken from the erstwhile Palmdale Railroad. It was moved once when Cornelia White sold the property in 1944 to the southeast corner of Indian Canyon Drive and Tahquitz Canyon Way where it became part of the original Palm Springs Desert Museum. Then in 1979 it was moved again to the Village Green on South Palm Canyon Drive. where it sits today.

From the Arctic to Mexico

At age 18, the adventurous Cornelia White left the family farm in Utica, N.Y., and set out on her own. She first spent a year in Europe in 1894-95, then returned to the United States and later joined a mining expedition in the Pacific Northwest.

She also went above the Arctic Circle with a brother. There, the pair met up with the polar explorer Vilhjalmur Stefansson, whom they had known earlier. Stefansson was a Canadian explorer of Icelandic parents who had spent time living among the Inuits (Eskimos).

Miss Cornelia also sailed up the Nile River in Egypt before she settled down at the University of North Dakota. There she became a teacher and taught practical domestic science courses like plumbing and carpentry (highly unusual for a woman circa 1911). A restless adventurer in a static setting, she jumped at the opportunity to head off to Mexico.

It was 1912 and the Mexican Revolution was raging, but a U.S. Senator from North Dakota had subdivided some land in the state of Sinaloa on the west coast. Cornelia White joined the colony of Americans—mostly North Dakotans—who went to settle there. In Mexico, she renewed a friendship with Carl Lykken, an engineering graduate from the University of North Dakota, and a fellow settler. In Sinaloa, Mexico, Miss Cornelia became a farmer, raising bananas and papayas.

While they enjoyed the warmth of Mexico, many colonists were forced to flee in 1913 as the rebels neared their location. Due to the tense situation, U.S. President Wilson had earlier ordered all American citizens home.

According to Mary Jo Churchwell in her book *Palm Springs, The Landscape, The History, The Lore*, a small band of six refugees (Carl Lykken, Cornelia and her sister Florilla, and three others) escaped by securing a hand car and taking turns pumping over rails that had some of the ties already burned away. They took a ship from Mazatlán to San Diego and Lykken went on to Los Angeles.

From Florilla's visit to Palm Springs the previous year, she suggested to her sister that they would much prefer the adventures that might await there in the desert versus remaining in the big city. She proved correct.

Bought the Palm Springs Hotel

They arrived when there were but 15 buildings in the entire village. Among them was the original Palm Springs Hotel whose owner, Welwood Murray, was more than happy to sell.

They contacted Lykken and suggested he might like Palm Springs too, so he came to Palm Springs to become one of the village's early and more notable settlers.

Dr. Florilla White, a medical doctor, was a dedicated horsewoman, a member of the Desert Riders, and often spent days in the mountains and canyons exploring with the Cahuilla Indian Lee Arenas or his brother Simon. She served as the village health officer during World War I.

Dr. White founded "The Nightingales" which began as a group of registered nurses she summoned from Riverside to come to Palm Springs to aid in the 1918 flu epidemic. Over the next several decades the volunteer group got involved in a number of medical projects.

It has been reported that her sister Cornelia White never wore skirts, even in that age of pompous petticoats and constricting whale-bone girdles. For 45 years she was seen all over the area in riding pants, leather puttees, fringed safari jackets and a sturdy jungle pith helmet. She was a small woman with a big appetite for adventure. Her hair was usually pulled back into a bun and parted in the middle.

Commenting on her everyday dress, writer Harry C. James noted about Miss Cornelia: "The common sense attire of a very modest woman in refinement and culture proved that an active outdoor life in chaparral country can be the life for a Lady."

Isabel less outdoorsy

In contrast to her two down-to-earth outdoors-loving sisters, Isabel White, who joined them in Palm Springs in 1915, always maintained a more dignified East Coast demeanor. Isabel married the Englishman J. Smeaton Chase in 1917, two years after he also arrived in Palm Springs. Chase had authored numerous books, most notably *California Coast Trails, California Desert Trails*, and *Our Araby*.

Chase died in 1923 and Isabel survived him by almost 40 years, living out her remaining years either in nearby Banning and her home near the Tennis Club. They are buried side by side in the old pioneer Welwood Murray Cemetery at the base of the mountain.

In 1915 Cornelia White bought a piece of property covered with orange trees at the corner of what was then Lime and Main streets (now Baristo Road and South Palm Canyon Drive) for $75. She sold it to the builder of the proposed Del Tahquitz Hotel in the mid-1930s for $7,000. Then a bank purchased the property years later for considerably more money.

Cornelia White hung on to the south end of the property origi-nally purchased from Murray

An elder Cornelia White personifies the spirit of adventure. *Photo courtesy Palm Springs Historical Society.*

(south of Tahquitz Canyon Way) until it was developed into La Plaza in 1936, still a main focal point in Palm Springs.

Dr. Florilla White died in 1943, and Cornelia disposed of their real estate holdings north of Tahquitz Canyon Way, except for her home, the original railroad tie house built by Welwood Murray. In 1944, she had it moved across the street where it remained until 1979.

Miss Cornelia also built a small house next to the current Welwood Murray Museum. Lykken later remarked that Cornelia had put her considerable building skills to work when she constructed that stone house as it was designed to be half buried in the ground for coolness. That building later became the custodian's house for the museum.

In April 1947 Cornelia deeded the property along Tahquitz Canyon Way between Palm Canyon Drive and Indian Canyon Drive for the Palm Springs Desert Museum. She requested no publicity and only retained a life tenancy on a portion of the property. The main floor gallery of what is now the Palm Springs Art Museum is dedicated to Cornelia White for her contribution to the museum's first original permanent location.

Miss Cornelia White was widely known for her love of adventure as well as her kindness and generosity. She died in September 1961 in Banning; her house was willed to the Palm Springs Historical Society and moved to the Village Green as an historical attraction. She is buried in the Welwood Murray Cemetery alongside her two sisters.

CHAPTER 17

Great-Grandmother Pilot
ZADDIE BUNKER

One of the most colorful of the Palm Springs pioneers was Zaddie Bunker, a can-do woman who became nationally famous as the "Great-Grandmother Pilot." Born in Missouri in 1886, she and her husband Ed Bunker came to the village of Palm Springs in 1914 in an old Maxwell car.

They first lived in a corrugated lean-to on Main Street (Palm Canyon Drive and Andreas Road) where Ed worked as a blacksmith. They both studied auto mechanics from handbooks and they opened Bunker's Garage which they made from sheet iron. They bought additional property and also built the Bunker Cottages.

Eventually Ed left Zaddie and their young daughter Frances. He relocated with his new wife up on the Palms-to-Pines Highway where he ran cattle out of the Bunker Ranch. Ed died in 1969.

Alone, Zaddie stayed in Palm Springs to run the garage and went on to become one of the village's most successful entrepreneurs and wealthiest landowners. His daughter Frances would later marry Earle Strebe, who built a theater on the site of the original Bunker Garage.

"First Fall Get-together" at El Mirador (left to right): Zaddie Bunker, Mrs. Fred Weigel, Mrs. Pearl McManus, Fred Weigel and Mrs. Harold Bell Wright. *El Mirador photo.*

Nellie Coffman's son George Roberson had been responsible for transporting mail and passengers from the train station to town. When he went off to World War I, those duties went to California's first female holder of a chauffeur's license, the indomitable Zaddie Bunker.

Zaddie ran Bunker's Garage, at the time the only place to repair motor vehicles, and at first there were only four cars in the entire village! Zaddie was a skilled mechanic, with her bib overalls often covered with grease as she would take off to the train station to pick someone up. She could, and did, take vehicles apart and put them back together again.

Zaddie's sisters

Two sisters of Zaddie's also relocated to Palm Springs. One, Henrietta Parker, who was married to a railroad brakeman, arrived at the Garnet train station, the earlier-named Seven Palms train station, in July 1914. In a 1988 The Desert Sun article, she recalled that Zaddie and her 7-year-old daughter Frances drove her down the dirt road called Indian Avenue, which was lined with pepper trees. Henrietta remained in Palm Springs her entire life.

The other sister, Lillian Goff, was the owner of a hotel on North Palm Canyon Drive, on the site of what would later become the El Morocco Hotel. Goff eventually left Palm Springs and relocated to Pasadena.

Zaddie and Henrietta together bought a lot across the street from Bunker's Garage that later became the village's first cinema. The garage itself was remodeled and turned into the first bank in Palm Springs and later, in 1929, became the popular Village Pharmacy. It was part of the block that was razed in 1967 for the Desert Fashion Plaza.

The Village Theater was built next door to the garage in 1932 by the Strebe family.

When Zaddie's daughter Frances married Earle Strebe, Zaddie and her son-in-law worked together on many real estate projects, building theaters, and leasing most of the downtown block to Irwin Schuman for the historic Chi Chi nightclub. Zaddie became quite wealthy and her grandchildren realized millions when the Bunker's Garage and Village Theater were sold.

From businesswoman to pilot

At an age when many people begin to enjoy the fruits of their labor with inactivity, Zaddie Bunker was just getting started. She went on to become known as the "flying grandmother."

She took flight instructions in San Bernardino, got her pilot's license at age 60, and "soloed" in 1952. She received her multi-engine rating at age 63. Still flying when she was a great-grandmother, her private plane, "Zaddie's Rocking Chair," had the name stenciled on its fuselage.

The press loved her and regularly reported on her exploits, like racing in the Powder Puff Derby. In 1962, at age 76, Zaddie won a cross-country airplane race from Dateland, Arizona, to El Centro, California, beating five male pilots.

At age 73, she had passed the tough physical for Air Force jet pilots, and became became an honorary Air Force colonel. She was allowed to pilot an F-100 Super Sabre jet, becoming one of the first women to break the sound barrier.

In 1959 the "Supersonic Great-Grandmother" went to Spain as part of President Eisenhower's People to People program and, according to The Desert Sun, "stole the hearts of city officials and 80 little orphan girls in Seville."

Also in 1959, she was a surprise honoree on the immensely popular Ralph Edwards "This Is Your Life" television show.

Once, while in Washington, D.C., for a race, Zaddie returned to her hotel to learn that then-Vice President Richard Nixon's secretary had been calling all afternoon. Nixon had wanted to meet the famous lady pilot and invited her over the next morning. It was a real thrill for the former desert town mechanic.

With her can-do attitude, she even applied for the Apollo moon flight when she was in her eighties. They let her have some time in the space capsule simulator, but she didn't get the bid. All who knew her felt she could have done it.

The remarkable woman who refused to acknowledge failure finally proved to be mortal; she died in 1969, one week shy of her 82nd birthday.

Zaddie Bunker, great-grandmother pilot. *Photo courtesy Palm Springs Historical Society.*

CHAPTER 18

Making a Difference
WOMEN PIONEERS

Dr. June Robertson McCarroll

The U.S. Government called upon a woman to be the first medical doctor to serve the five Indian reservations in the Coachella Valley. But for all of her medical accomplishments, she also became recognized as the person who originated the idea of painting a line down the center of the road to help prevent automobile accidents.

Born in Kentucky in 1867, Dr. June Robertson attended medical school in Chicago, where she was one of the few women to establish a practice, and became physician for the Nebraska State Industrial School. She came to the Coachella Valley in 1904, hoping the new theory of desert air would cure her husband's tuberculosis. They settled in a health camp near Indio and his health improved.

Meanwhile Indio's resident doctor had his fill of the desert environment and headed back east. Robertson was prevailed upon to fill the void of providing medical care to the growing number of settlers there. She grasped the challenge and initially tried to serve the entire area from Palm Springs to the Salton Sea by auto but the primitive roads (or lack of roads) forced her to revert to horseback.

The government also needed an Indian doctor in the desert and, in 1907, Dr. Robertson was also appointed to oversee the health of the Indians there. It took courage, aplomb, and diplomacy in dealing with illnesses and assuaging the authority and healing prowess of the various chiefs and medicine men. As an unneeded token of her authority she admitted to always carrying her "six-shooter in plain sight whenever on the reservation."

Dr. Robertson often performed surgery on kitchen tables and with rudimentary lighting and conditions, laying out and sterilizing her instruments as necessity demanded.

Her husband eventually succumbed to his illness, dying in 1914. In 1916 she married Frank McCarroll, the Southern Pacific agent. As other doctors settled in the area, Dr. Robertson retired from the medical profession, but became active in organizing and serving in various women's groups.

Her Department of Transportation legacy came about after her Model-T Ford was forced off the road by an oncoming driver hogging more than his share. After some thought, she determined a lot of accidents might be prevented if there was a line down the center of the road. In 1917 she even hand-painted a four-inch strip down about a mile of Highway 86.

The Riverside County Board of Supervisors tabled her idea in 1918, but undaunted, Dr. Robertson got the local Indio Chamber of Commerce and women's groups to endorse it. In 1925 California's highway department adopted the idea and the Department of Transportation credits the frontier doctor with originating the center stripe idea in California.

In October 2003 the City of Indio and the local history fraternity dedicated a monument with a plaque honoring Dr. June Robertson McCarroll. The stone marker is at the corner of Indio Boulevard and Smurr Street. While not based in the village of Palm Springs, she was known throughout the Coachella Valley.

Frances Stevens

Pioneer educator Frances S. Stevens is another who came to Palm Springs for health reasons and stayed to make a contribution to the bustling village. She had the same surname all her life, just spelled a little differently. Born Frances Stephens in Illinois, she attended Mt. Morris College, got a degree in literature from the University of Chicago and was a teacher in the Midwest before embarking on an adventurous trip to Colorado.

There she met and married cattleman Prescott Thresher Stevens, who jokingly taught her "the correct way to spell her name." The couple lived a frontier life, driving cattle throughout the Gunnison area and into Utah. Daughter Sallie Stevens Nichols was born to the couple in the Rocky Mountain wilderness in 1908.

In 1912, the Stevens family moved to Hollywood, California, relocating in 1914 to The Desert Inn in Palm Springs hoping the warm desert air would improve Frances' respiratory problems. She improved and immediately got into helping her newfound community. Frances and P.T. Stevens built a house in the 900 block of North Palm Canyon Drive, and also maintained a residence in Hollywood.

A former teacher, Frances soon got involved in education and served on the desert's school board. She joined the legacy of dedicated Palm Springs teachers, dating back to a Miss Annie Noble who taught part of the 1893-94 school year and an almost forgotten Miss Hogel, who taught six children in eight grades in 1911.

Mrs. Stevens was hard working and dedicated; one time she and colleague Rose McKinney got blasted in a sandstorm as they rode on horseback for several hours to the San Gorgonio Pass to recruit a teacher.

Frances and her husband P.T. Stevens, who became a developer in Palm Springs, donated the land and funding for what was to be known as the Palm Springs Desert School. Frances died before the school was completed in 1927; the school was dedicated to her—the Frances S. Stevens School.

The Palm Canyon Theater now graces the original school site and the neighboring park on North Palm Canyon Drive, which is constantly in use for art and cultural events. It is also dedicated to the pioneer educator. Three of Frances Stevens' grandchildren, the sons of Sallie Stevens and Culver Nichols, attended the school named for their grandmother. One, grandson Steve Nichols, became president of the Palm Springs Historical Society in 2003.

Katherine Finchy

Too often teachers recruited to Palm Springs did not last long, leaving because of the isolation and desert climate. Over 20 teachers worked with Palm Springs children from 1893 until 1922. That year the village was fortunate to receive two teachers, including one young woman who would spend the rest of her life in Palm Springs. Miss Katherine Finchy remained a Palm Springs educator for almost 30 years, retiring in 1951.

Finchy, born in 1893 in Minnesota, came to California where she majored in English and received her bachelor's degree at Biola College and a secondary degree from U. C. Berkeley. Thus, she was the desert's first high school teacher. She immediately identified with her students and many a village elder can recall being helped by Miss Finchy. One of her classes published the desert's first general newspaper in 1926, a year before the first issue of The Desert Sun.

Finchy went on to become the principal of the Frances Stevens School and then superintendent of the Palm Springs Desert School District. Active in numerous civic affairs, including the Palm Springs Historical Society, she also organized the Palm Springs Soroptimist Club and helped found other Soroptimist chapters.

Her presence made a lasting impression on Palm Springs. One of her former students later wrote,

> *Our teacher was Katherine Finchy—Miss Finchy—who
> was also the principal, disciplinarian, soft-ball referee, coach,*

and conductor of chin-ups and push-ups that were part of the physical fitness tests required by the Riverside County superintendent of schools....Miss Finchy was a perfectionist, albeit a gentle and understanding one. She taught us early the value of honest dispute and difference of opinion....

The Katherine Finchy Elementary School on Tachevah Drive was named in her honor. It was originally called the North End School, as Miss Finchy would not allow the school board to name it for her until she retired. Miss Finchy died in 1987 and her headstone at the Welwood Murray Cemetery proudly notes, "Katherine Finchy 1893-1987 'Teacher—Leader—Friend.'"

Harriet Cody

Harriet Cody was another woman who, following the untimely death of her husband, was able to make not only a living for herself and her young daughter, but a contribution to the growing village of Palm Springs.

Sometimes people who have succeeded in Palm Springs came from unlikely backgrounds. Harriet Cody was a proper, conservative, and beautiful Vassar graduate of Scottish ancestry who married the promising young architect Harold Bryant Cody in 1910. Harold soon contracted pneumonia and they left Philadelphia for a more temperate climate in Hollywood. Some claim that Harold's cousin was the famous cowboy turned showman Buffalo Bill Cody. Harold secured work and among his design projects was a remodel of Riverside's famous Mission Inn.

After Harold's condition worsened, they rented out their Hollywood home in 1916 and moved to the drier climate of Palm Springs. They initially lived in a small cottage next to The Desert Inn where Harriet was befriended by the magnanimous Nellie Coffman. Harriet later reminisced, "She is the soul of goodness, a woman who gave help to many, as she did to me, and yet left the recipient still in possession of her self-respect."

For a while Harold was able to contribute, even designing a grandiose home for Lois Kellogg, nicknamed "Fool's Folly." As his condition worsened, Harriet had to make ends meet. Trying to live on the Hollywood rent, they bought a tract of land with the last of their money. Then tenants got remiss with the rent and the Codys became desperate. Harriet quite literally became a horse trader and traded for an old gypsy camp wagon and two horses. She also traded the Hollywood house for 80 acres of land in Palm Springs which still did not provide sufficient income.

They camped out in a tent in Tahquitz Canyon and started renting out the horses, acquiring more along the way. Harriet Cody established the city's first riding stable at the corner of Palm Canyon Drive and Ramon Road. She bought more horses, including good quality ones from Lee Arenas, the popular Cahuilla leader. By the time her husband passed away in 1924, she had 35 horses. Harriet was an accomplished rider, and wore jodhpurs and monogrammed silk blouses advertising the stable when she went on promotional visits to The Desert Inn.

Harriet realized that real estate was an even better way to succeed than horses, and began to engage in several profitable real estate deals, including the South Palm Highlands. An income was thus secured for her and her daughter. She dusted off some of her husband's old plans and built the Casa Cody, an intimate inn in the Tennis Club district—175 South Cahuilla—that is still in existence.

Harriet's daughter, Patricia, married Bill Rogers, a cousin of humorist Will Rogers, and she ran the Casa Cody after her mother's death; after Patricia died the property changed hands several times. In 1986 the Casa Cody was purchased by Frank Tysen and Therese Hayes who have expanded and remodeled it. They bought property next door which was part of the Francis Crocker estate. On it was an older two-bedroom adobe house built in the years shortly before WWI.

Today the Casa Cody engenders a feeling of history, with 17 charming tile-covered rooms, and restful gardens draped in bougainvillea and citrus trees.

Many celebrities have stayed in Harriet Cody's inn over the years and their images permeate the place. Allegedly Charlie Chaplin lived in the cottage; General Patton stayed at the Casa Cody while training troops in the nearby desert. But the strongest image is that of the plucky founder of Casa Cody, a strong-willed Victorian lady who made the desert yield to her.

SECTION 4

❀

Establishing a Community

Palm Springs was a small village in the sun in the early 1900s. The dry desert air had attracted persons afflicted with respiratory ailments and a few modest sanatoriums had been catering to them. But the mild winters and therapeutic air of the desert was not the restricted domain of the ill.

With the close proximity to the Los Angeles/ Hollywood area it was inevitable that the spa village known as Palm Springs would be discovered.

Within a couple of decades it had become a resort destination, a fabled getaway for celebrities. A few visionary developers like P.T. Stevens who built the memorable El Mirador, and Charles Farrell and Ralph Bellamy who opened the Racquet Club changed the face of Palm Springs forever.

CHAPTER 19

Early Settlers Helped Build Town
THEY CAME TO STAY

David Manley Blanchard – First General Store

After John McCallum closed his small shop, there was only one place for the pioneers to buy supplies and that was the store established by David Manley Blanchard in 1898.

Blanchard was an auctioneer in Minneapolis who became inflicted with pneumonia, driving him and his family, a wife, daughter and son, to the warmer climes of California in 1897. In Los Angeles, his condition worsened and was diagnosed as tuberculosis, so after a brief time there, they came to Palm Springs hoping the warm, dry air would cure him.

He arrived in the middle of the drought years but was able to sustain his family. He rented a house for $15 a month, bought three burros, and got a job shuttling mail between the village and the train station at Seven Palms. Soon he opened D.M. Blanchard's Feed and Grocery Store. It was part of the old adobe stage station in the heart of the village. Even though there is no record, Wesley Black of Riverside, Blanchard's grandson, believes Blanchard actually acquired McCallum's store.

Blanchard became the Palm Springs postmaster as well as the village barber. He bought a square block downtown on Andreas between today's Palm Canyon and Indian Canyon Drives on which he built a small four-room hotel, a larger store, and several tent houses. The store was a simple board structure which he later expanded to fit his growing needs.

Along with groceries, he sold hardware and other supplies, including ice which he hauled from the train station on horse-drawn wagons. Most of his groceries came from Los Angeles, but the ice was produced in Colton and shipped in 200-pound blocks. Due to the heat, the huge blocks lost between 75-100 pounds of their volume in the journey.

Blanchard sold his enterprise to Carl Lykken and J.H. Bartlett in 1913, but not before establishing himself as a real Palm Springs pioneer who made a difference. It was a reciprocal arrangement. The desert climate cured Blanchard of his respiratory ailments completely, and he lived until age 69, dying in 1927, 30 years after his arrival.

Dr. Harry Lee Coffman – First Physician

The first Palm Springs physician licensed by the state of California to set up practice in the village was Harry Coffman, M.D. He and his wife Nellie started The Desert Inn and ran it together for nine years. Nellie became better known as she continued to run the famous resort for decades. The Desert Inn, however, was first a sanatorium and Dr. Harry Coffman played no small part in getting it established.

The son of Charles A. Coffman, Harry was born in Marysville, near Sacramento, California, on October 1, 1866. The family then settled on a 400-acre ranch in Ranchito, California—now Pico Rivera, between Los Angeles and Whittier—where Harry's father was one of the organizers of the Southern California Walnut Growers Association.

Harry managed the walnut groves for his father, and became enamored with the widow Nellie Norton Roberson who had a small son, George. Harry and Nellie wed on March 5, 1891, and after their marriage, he entered school in southern California. Deciding he wanted to become a doctor, Harry enrolled in a Philadelphia medical school, a city where he also interned. He received his medical degree in 1901.

Dr. Harry Coffman (far left) and group of villagers. *Photo courtesy Palm Springs Historical Society.*

In their early years together the young family lived on the walnut ranch. Together they had a son, Owen Earl Coffman, born in 1892.

Hearing of the recuperative climate in the desert and deciding to utilize their combined skills, Harry and his family moved to Palm Springs on October 16, 1909, where they immediately established The Desert Inn, a hotel and sanatorium. There, at the present site of the Desert Fashion Plaza, Dr. Coffman treated numerous patients who came to the desert seeking respiratory ailment cures.

In 1918, Dr. Coffman left Palm Springs and his family and went to Calexico to practice medicine. He also had a ranch in Cherry Valley before he moved to Alpine, California, where he cared for patients as a sanatorium doctor until his death in April 30, 1935. Dr. Harry was a pioneer humanitarian, a man of adventure, a successful businessman, and was the first to establish the medical profession in Palm Springs. He was buried in the old Welwood Murray Cemetery in Palm Springs.

George Ball Roberson Jr. – First Fire Commissioner

George Ball Roberson Jr. was the son of George Ball Roberson, a Dallas contractor and Nellie Norton Roberson Coffman. He was born in Dallas on July 5, 1888, several months after his father had perished in a fire.

George went to Santa Monica High School and the Arizona School of Mines, and came to Palm Springs with his family in 1909 where he remained an influential citizen for almost 60 years.

He helped his family manage The Desert Inn, served in World War I, and returned to become vice president of The Desert Inn Corporation, which he continued to operate with his step-brother O. Earl Coffman until it was sold in 1955. In 1919, Roberson opened the Coachella Valley's first automobile dealership, The Desert Inn Garage.

In addition to his entrepreneurship, Roberson always remained dedicated to civic responsibilities. The first fire commissioner in the early 1920s he was also on the first police commission, a member of the first planning commission and the first sanitary district, and helped secure water for Palm Springs. He helped plan The Polo Grounds, which later became

The Los Angeles Angels originally trained at Angel Stadium in Palm Springs.

Angel Stadium, and was a charter member of the Thunderbird Country Club and the Palm Springs Committee of 25, a group managing the O'Donnell Golf Club.

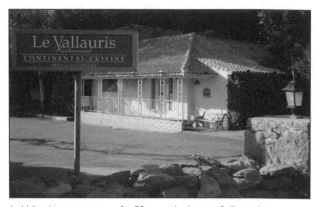

Le Vallauris restaurant was for 50 years the home of village pioneer George Roberson.

In 1924 George Roberson and his wife Alta built a family home along the south side of Tahquitz Canyon Way, west of Cahuilla Road. It was a stuccoed Mediterranean/ Spanish Revival home which the family lived in until the 1970s. George died in 1968 and Alta died in 1976. That Roberson family home was sold in the mid-1970s and remodeled to become the upscale Le Vallauris restaurant.

Owen Earl Coffman–Tramway Visionary

Owen Earl Coffman joined his family in the desert in 1910, after graduation from Santa Monica High School. He helped them run The Desert Inn and also served in WWI, where he was an ambulance driver/medic at the front in France. He returned to Palm Springs to become secretary-treasurer of the new corporation.

Coffman was a co-founder of the Palm Springs Aerial Tramway and served as first chairman of its governing body, the San Jacinto Winter Park Authority.

He founded the Palm Springs American Legion Post and served as its first commander. Incidentally, the post is now named for Lt. Owen Baylis Coffman, Coffman's son, who was killed in WWII.

Coffman was on the board of the Palm Springs Chamber of Commerce, was a founding member and first president of the Desert

Palm Springs Aerial Tramway sign.

Riders and founder of the Vaqueros del Desierto. He was also a founding member of the Palm Springs Desert Museum, the Committee of 25 (See chapter on Tom O'Donnell), and the Polo Club.

During two summers Earl managed the famous Ahwanhee Hotel in Yosemite National Park, and for nine years the North Shore Tavern at Lake Arrowhead.

Owen Earl Coffman married Helen Ann Baylis in 1917. Their children are Owen Baylis Coffman and Elizabeth Ann Coffman. They divorced in 1942 and Earl married Barbara Courtright in 1943.

Coffman died at the result of a stroke in a La Jolla convalescent hospital on August 17, 1967.

Carl Gustav Lykken – First Telephone

Carl Lykken was born in 1884 in North Dakota and went on to graduate from the University of North Dakota with a degree in mining engineering. He went to Sinaloa, Mexico, to survey land for an American colony which had settled there. He knew the White sisters— Florilla and Cornelia—and had left Mexico with them during the revolution. Soon after arriving in Los Angeles, Lykken followed their suggestion and joined them in Palm Springs.

He partnered with a J.H. Bartlett and together they bought David Blanchard's general store in 1913. They soon moved the entire operation across the street, now Palm Canyon Drive. The building with an arched roof covering the entrance was later the home of Celebrity Books and other businesses.

The partners originally called their store Lykken and Bartlett, but later it became known as the Palm Springs

Village pioneer Carl Lykken with Melba Bennett, founder of the Palm Springs Historical Society. *Photo courtesy Palm Springs Historical Society.*

Department and Hardware Store, and it continued to serve the community until 1979.

Carl took over the store by himself and perhaps is best known for acquiring and maintaining the village's first telephone—an extension from it went to The Desert Inn. His store also provided the town with a post office and for years its only telegraph service. Lykken himself served as postmaster, 1927-1930, and for years was the agent for Western Union. He had a dry battery connection to the telegraph at the Southern Pacific Railroad agent's office in Garnet, thus establishing the village's only contact with the outside world.

Lykken continued to serve the community in many ways for almost 60 years. A founding member of the Palm Springs Library Board, the Palm Springs Community Church, the Desert Museum and the Palm Springs Rotary, he was a charter member of the Polo Club and the Desert Riders. He founded the Palm Springs Police and Fire Protection Districts and served as president of the chamber of commerce and the local community chest. He was also a member of the Palm Springs Historical Society's Board of Directors.

Lykken married Edith Coombs in 1917, and in 1929 they built the town's first home with central heating on Mountain View Place in the Las Palmas area.

In the 1940s Lykken sold the business at 180 North Palm Canyon to Tom Holland who continued to run the Palm Springs Department and Hardware Store. Holland later sold to Newt Hotchkill and Murray Barrick. The store was bought in 1968 by John Doyle and Earl Stahl. Richard and Mary Beth Marek, who own "The Alley" leased the location in 1979 before moving farther south on Palm Canyon Drive.

Near the end of a lifetime of dedicated civil service, a Carl Lykken Day was celebrated in 1970. Over 150 well-wishers gathered at the Oasis Hotel to honor the pioneer citizen. In 1971, Lykken donated $10,000 for the construction of a new library and a wing is named in his honor.

Carl Lykken died on January 12, 1972, at the age of 87. Lykken loved to hike and explore the desert, so, in his honor, on June 26, 1972, the old Skyline Trail behind the Desert Museum was renamed the Lykken Trail. In May 1980 an expanded Lykken Trail opened following a dedication at the Desert Museum. Carl's wife Edith died in 1974.

Carl and Edith's daughter Jane Hoff has lived in Palm Springs all her life, serving on numerous civic activities, including the Palm Springs Historical Society's Board of Directors. In March 2003, at age 83, Jane was recognized by former Mayor Frank Bogert as the surviving pioneer who had been in town the longest.

Otto R. Adler—First Newspaper

Otto Adler, born in 1870, arrived in Palm Springs in 1914. Noting only one small place where the growing community could buy supplies, he established and began to operate a small grocery store out of a tent. He soon built a larger store and adjacent hotel, the Red Front Store and Hotel, which was north of The Desert Inn also on the west side of Main Street (now Palm Canyon Drive).

He put out a newspaper, the *Red Front Store News*, a four page, three-column-wide paper, which debuted on August 1, 1914, making it the first newspaper in Palm Springs. The two inner pages consisted almost entirely of promotions and sales of the Red Front Mercantile Store.

The big 1914 summer sale consisted of women's Union Suits, men's suspenders, towels, bulk cookies, Red Front coffee, cob pipes (your choice— 5 cents), buggy whips, lamp chimneys and more.

An ad on the back page highlighted the Red Front Hotel: "Open Every Day. One Block West of Post Office, Two Blocks North of Sanitarium. Screen Tent Rooms—50 cents. Open Air Dining Room, Chicken Dinner—50 cents. Meals at all Hours." And in reference to Adler's German heritage, the two words "Deutsche Kueche," meaning "German cooking," accompanied the meal sign.

The *Red Front Store News* was not a public newspaper with general advertising, but more a promotional paper for the Red Front. However, the newspaper still filled a void and covered the goings and comings and highlights of the citizenry.

For example: "Edward Bunker, the genial and thoroughly competent blacksmith and auto mechanic, is building a new garage. We wish him every success."

Or: "Sorry to hear Mr. Bisbee lost one of his valuable mules this week, just as he began shipping grapes and needed him. 'Inconsistency your name is mule.'"

The Red Front's name was changed to the La Palma Hotel and it grew into a charming two-story hotel with a shady tree-covered courtyard, stone pillars out front and the sign "La Palma Hotel—We Never Close," alluding to the fact that it was one of the first village businesses to remain open in the summer.

Adler was always active in civic affairs, serving on the chamber of commerce and helping with the development of Palm Canyon. He was also the head of the volunteer fire department.

In 1928, Adler leased the La Palma Hotel to Randall Sparks. Adler and his wife Louisa moved to Venice, California. Ray Bryant then took over the operation and ran the hotel, dining room, and Ray's Waffle Shop next door. The location became home to the El Rey and then the famous Chi Chi before it was renovated into what was originally called The Desert Inn Fashion Plaza.

Louisa died in 1933 and her grave marker in the Welwood Murray Cemetery has one of the most unusual epitaphs, "Louisa Adler 1873-1933 Died of Grief Caused by a Neighbor. Now Rests in Peace." Otto died in 1949 and is buried by her side in Palm Springs.

Raymond Cree – First School President

Raymond Cree, whose name became synonymous with education in the early years of Palm Springs, was born on August 19, 1875, in Des Moines, Iowa. His father brought the family (wife and four children) to settle in San Jacinto, California, in 1885, seeking relief from his asthma. There he established a brick business and the children attended school.

Raymond attended Chaffey College, then a part of USC and excelled in track, twice breaking the interscholastic world's record for the 50-yard dash. He taught seven years in the public school system, then attended Stanford University (1904-06) where he majored in public school administration.

In 1907 Raymond Cree became the Riverside County Superintendent of Schools, his work often taking him to Palm Springs. He served as county superintendent until 1920, with time out to serve in WW I in France. In 1915 he bought 65 acres of land in Section 29—north of today's Target store on East Palm Canyon Drive—in Palm Springs and began to grow Deglet Noor dates and grapefruit.

In 1920 he moved to Palm Springs permanently and was appointed the first president of the Palm Springs Union High School District. Due to his dedication to education, the Raymond Cree Middle School in Palm Springs is named in his honor.

As early as 1918 he spearheaded attempts to get much of the area surrounding the Coachella Valley set aside as national parks and monuments. Some of his ideas prevailed and visitors to Joshua Tree National Park have Cree in part to thank for that bit of protected wilderness.

Cree's wife Margaret who was a reporter and feature writer in Riverside, became a realtor and civic worker in Palm Springs. She died in 1946 at age 47.

Joshua Tree National Park.

Over the years Cree increased his real estate holdings and by the mid-1940s owned considerable land including a section which later became the site of the Thunderbird Country Club. (The Palm Valley School, now Kings School, is on part of his ranch.) Cree also helped Fred Markham subdivide Smoke Tree Ranch into Smoke Tree Colony. Cree, who had become president of the local Lions Club, remained active in Palm Springs real estate until his death in 1967 at age 92.

Dr. Jacob John Kocher – First Pharmacy

Dr. Jacob John Kocher was a physician and pharmacist who opened the village's first pharmacy in November 1917. He built an adobe building directly across the street from the main entrance of The Desert Inn and called his new drug and apothecary shop the "Mortar and Pestle." He even had a rock which had been used as a mortar on the porch in front of the store.

The "desert doctor," as he became known, opened for business in November 1917 and his guest book signatures included most of the local citizenry, both Indian and Anglo alike.

News of his ability as a doctor spread and he was increasingly called upon to perform surgery, deliver babies, and attend to the well being of the settlers.

Dr. Kocher and his wife Reta were both charter members of the original Palm Springs Presbyterian Church, first organized in March 1917 with 19 charter members.

Books were Dr. Kocher's passion and he helped found a private library. He also loved the valley and would often go out to the desert or the canyons to paint. The Kochers lived out by the Cree Ranch which later became Palm Valley School Road in Cathedral City.

When the Palm Springs Board of Trade was formed in 1918, Dr. Kocher became its first president.

Years later, in 1936, a "Stork Party" celebration was held for Dr. Kocher and many of the "babies" he delivered were in attendance, including the first non-Indian born in Palm Springs, Ted McKinney, his sister Barbara McKinney, Beatrice Willard, Elizabeth Coffman and Owen Coffman. The "Desert Doctor" was directly responsible for helping the Palm Springs legacy to continue.

CHAPTER 20

A Pioneer Family Legacy
THE ENDURING McKINNEY FAMILY

It was neither land speculation nor respiratory ailments that brought the McKinney family to Palm Springs. It was a specific job and the prospect of more work that attracted Oliver S. McKinney and his wife Rose McEuen McKinney.

The family stayed on and they became pioneers in helping establish Palm Springs, with four generations of the family now having made a mark on the town. Oliver was hired by Raymond Cree, Riverside County Superintendent of Schools, to dig a water well on his date ranch in Palm Springs. So the McKinneys dropped what they were doing, which was trying to establish a ranch on their Morongo Valley homestead north of Palm Springs, and relocated to the village.

The McKinney Family, 1934. Front row (left to right): Donald, Theil, Oliver, Rose and Arol.
Back row (left to right): Barbara, Willard, Glenn, Ted and Eldon. *Photo courtesy of Palm Springs Historical Society.*

Rose and Oliver McKinney arrived in Palm Springs in February 1916 with, according to Frank Bogert in *Palm Springs First Hundred Years*, "five children, a chicken coop, two tents and a Dutch oven for cooking."

The McKinneys were well suited for the challenge. Rose, the family matriarch, was born on February 13, 1886, near Independence, Missouri, and came to California in a covered wagon.

Oliver was born in 1877 and had served in the Spanish American War as an aide to Teddy Roosevelt. Oliver and Rose settled in San Jacinto, California, and were living in a miner's cabin in the Gavilan Hills south of Riverside where their first child, Marshall Glenn, was born in 1904. The family then established the Morongo Valley homestead. Oliver had by this time earned a reputation as a competent well driller.

Once in Palm Springs, Oliver found constant work and never looked back. He dug more wells, and then with his tripod hoist, found his services in demand for planting large palms, cacti, and other desert trees and plants for the growing number of estates and hotel resort properties.

The Desert Nursery

Oliver's landscaping work led to the Desert Nursery which the family owned and operated from 1925 to 1945. They had bought 10 acres of what now fronts the 600 block of South Palm Canyon Drive, (near the intersection of Indian Canyon Drive), in 1924 and originally opened a small campground. Then they developed it into a tourist court and mobile home trailer park. Along with the Desert Nursery, the McKinneys built 20 small rental units.

The Desert Nursery, established by the McKinney family, next door to the Builders Supply Company on South Palm Canyon Drive. *Photo courtesy Builders Supply Company.*

They also acquired an 80-acre farm in what is now the Deep Well section of Palm Springs.

First non-Indian children born in Palm Springs

The McKinneys had three more children in Palm Springs, establishing a couple of "firsts" along the way. Their son Ted, who was born January 11, 1919, was the first non-Indian child born in Palm Springs. Daughter Barbara McKinney Moore was the first non-Indian girl, born shortly before Nellie Coffman's two granddaughters.

The McKinney children attended the local one-room school, immediately doubling the student population from four to eight students. It has been said by many a pioneer that almost all the early Palm Springs children at one time or another were classmates of a McKinney.

The McKinney sons were Marshall Glenn, Willard A., Eldon, Ted, and Donald McKinney. Daughters were Arol Campbell, Theil Eastabrook and Barbara Moore.

Later, as adults, the five sons got together and re-established the family's Morongo Valley Ranch and ran cattle under the appropriate "5M" brand.

Willard had owned and operated McKinney's Market on South Palm Canyon Drive. He also owned the W.A. McKinney Construction Company.

Marshall Glenn, the oldest child, owned a Palm Springs blacksmith shop, leased it out, got his teaching credentials and was a teacher for 31 years. The former Eagle Scout also established a winery in Napa Valley. He became a Palm Springs historian publishing his memoirs in 1996 titled *Vanishing Footprints in the Hot Desert Sand, Remembrances of a 90-Year-Old Palm Springs Pioneer: Horse and Wagon Days on the Southern California Desert*. He died in 2002 at age 98.

Ted, who was born in the family trailer park, graduated from the University of Redlands in 1946 and served in the Army Air Corps. He joined the family business and was a Palm Springs real estate agent for 25 years. He served on the Palm Springs City Council for 12 years and was chairman of the Indian Planning Committee. He served on the board of the Palm Springs Historical Society, was the first president of the Jaycees, past president of Los Compadres, and a member of the Palm Springs Air Museum. He died in 1995 at age 76.

Eldon, born in 1909 died in 1967. Donald, born in 1928, died in 1981.

Arol, an accomplished rider, managed a stable and later moved to a ranch in Ramona.

Theil Eastabrook was a hair stylist, still practicing in her mid-nineties, operating out of her small shop in Morongo Valley. She has continued to make regular trips to Palm Springs to visit members of her family.

Barbara McKinney Moore continued to own and operate a car wash on the family's original land at 645 South Palm Canyon Drive. She called it the "Desert 100 Percent Hand Carwash and Nursery" alluding to the family's original business. She sold the car wash in 1998 to Larry and Patty Stearns who continue to operate it. No more "nursery" in the name though. Barbara died in December 2001.

The family matriarch Rose, who gave birth to and raised eight children in difficult conditions, still found time to serve her community. She was a founder and board member of the Palm Springs Historical Society, a member of the Soroptimists, and member of the Eastern Star.

The famous cat swindle

There's an interesting story from the 1930s about Rose and the famous actor John Barrymore. In the actor's biography, reference is made to Rose in the following unflattering manner: In Palm Springs, Barrymore was "…swindled out of $75 for a mangy cat by a hag in a roadside stand."

The truth, according to daughter Barbara, was that an unruly, drunken Barrymore, who had trouble standing up, saw the cat and demanded to have it. Rose told him it was not for sale. Barrymore insisted. Rose still said it was not for sale. Finally, upon his insistence, to end the matter she quoted the ridiculous amount of $75. To her surprise, he whipped out the money and took the cat. Sounds plausible and more likely.

Oliver died in 1956, and his wife Rose McKinney, died on May 30, 1968.

CHAPTER 21

They Spread the Word
WRITERS AND ARTISTS

Celebrities have been associated with Palm Springs from its very early days, and it was some of the early writers, artists, and photographers, several of whom became celebrities themselves, who extolled the merits of Palm Springs and gave world-wide fame to the village of the Agua Caliente Indians.

Many of these early California literary personas knew each other. Helen Hunt Jackson had written to John Muir requesting help and advice for her to spend her remaining months on earth in the High Sierras. He responded by calling on her in San Francisco but arrived too late as she had just passed away.

The writer George Wharton James hired Palm Springs artist Carl Eytel to illustrate his book, *The Wonders of the Colorado Desert,* on the desert. James and his fellow Englishman J. Smeaton Chase also died in the same year (1923). James had also corresponded with Jack London and Charles Lummis, as did John Muir. Photographer W.W. Lockwood and artist Carl Eytel often journeyed into the desert together.

They shared a sense of art and literacy; they shared mutual respect and admiration; but more importantly they shared a love of California, especially that area that became known as Palm Springs.

John Muir

By far, the most prestigious Scotsman who left his mark upon California was John Muir, a naturalist, author, founder of the Sierra Club, and the man most responsible for preserving the California wilderness. While usually associated with his work in the Sierras and mountain wilderness—Alaska's Muir Glacier is named for him—he also made an impact upon Palm Springs.

It was 1905 and his wife Louie Wanda Strentzel Muir had just died, leaving Muir with two daughters, Wanda, born in 1881, and Helen, born in 1886, along with the Strentzel family's orchards in Martinez, California.

Helen was frail, in poor health, and Muir had sought a healthful climate for her. His colleague and fellow writer, Charles Lummis, recommended Palm Springs.

That Muir appreciated the recommendation can be seen in this letter to Lummis, dated June 13, 1905:

> *Dear Mr. Lummis—*
>
> *You made no mistake in sending us here. The water is cool and delightful, as are the nights. The days [are] hot enough and dry enough to evaporate every disease and all one's flesh. On our arrival the first night we lay down under the olive tree in the sandy orchard, and the heat of the sand brought vividly to mind Milton's unlucky angels lying on the burning marl. But O the beauty of the sky evening and morning and how charming the old doctor and his wife. Helen is better already* [Muir's daughter]....
>
> *Faithfully yours,*
> *John Muir.*

The old doctor referred to was fellow Scotsman Welwood Murray. And the Muir visit is a Palm Springs legend. It appears that the telegraph from Muir to Murray requesting accommodation only arrived on the morning of their train arrival. It was summer and the Palm Springs Hotel was officially closed. But for someone so prestigious, one who has dined and camped with presidents, (not to mention another prominent Scotsman, the industrialist Andrew Carnegie), Murray knew he had to get busy.

All of the cottages, save one being used by another summer visitor, were dusty from recent sand storms and needed cleaning. Food had to be prepared, and the place was quickly in a whirlwind. A couple of Indians hastened to help clean, and the other guest, one Helen Lukens Gaut—daughter of Theodore P. Lukens, a grower and pioneer of Pasadena, California—was asked to accompany Willie Marcus and meet the Muirs at the train station. By remarkable coincidence, Miss Lukens was a friend of Muir's and she had previously been on outings with the family.

According to Helen Gaut in the October 1948 *Palm Springs Villager*, Mrs. Murray initially quickly prepared a simple dinner, and after that, Muir's older daughter Wanda sort of took over and prepared the groups' meals. Gaut noted, "During the meal the two opinionated old Scotchmen had a lively talkfest, exploding (sic) their theories, sometimes in cordial agreement, sometimes in heated argument."

Gaut added that Muir even made a comment chastising Murray for his pompous language, especially in talking to the Indians. For example, Muir heard Murray instruct the Indian Ramon on digging a tree hole, "You must make the excavations of greater radius at the lower extremities than at the upper, in order that the wide-spreading roots will have greater opportunity for expansion."

As the daytime temperatures hovered between 100 to 120 degrees, the group made daily forays into the nearby canyons for picnics. Then Muir, against Murray's protestations that it might be too arduous for Helen, decided to camp in Andreas Canyon, which they did for six carefree days.

After his Palm Springs visit, Muir returned to Martinez, and in 1907 found a desert place for Helen, this time in Daggett, near Barstow. Wanda returned to Martinez, and Helen married J. Buell Funk.

Muir was visiting his daughter and new grandson in 1914 in the cold high desert when he became ill with pneumonia. The great man who was born in Dunbar, Scotland, in 1838, died a few days later in Los Angeles on Christmas Eve, 1914. Glaciers, groves, peaks, trails and schools, all named Muir, honor the man who made a whole country take a look at its resources.

George Wharton James

George Wharton James was an author whose most highly acclaimed book *The Wonders of the Colorado Desert*, published in 1906, was inspired by, and in large part written in the Palm Springs area. James explored the desert on foot, and with burros, often accompanied by the book's mapmaker Lea Van Anderson and the artist Carl Eytel, whose 300 plus sketches helped render the book a masterpiece.

In the book's preface, along with acknowledging the help of Palm Springs pioneer Dr. Welwood Murray, James admits:

> *The desert itself, however, has been my chief inspiration. Upon its northwestern edge I have a camp of my own....Up in a canyon (Chino Canyon) on the northeastern slope of the great San Jacinto Range, where seeping water makes a 'cienega' and gives life to a good sized patch of grass; where someone, some-time, planted a fig tree, which has grown to rugged maturity and rich bearing; where there is a hot spring to bathe in, and a cold spring to drink from; sheltered on one side by one of the steepest and highest walls in the world, and on the other with an outlook over illimitable wastes of desert land, here is where I love to come to rest, think, and write.*

Born in Lincolnshire, England, in 1858, he emigrated to Nevada in the 1870s for his health and became a Methodist preacher there. He moved to Long Beach, California, where he underwent a messy divorce under all sorts of weird accusations from his incredibly insecure British wife. After he was kicked out of the church his three children returned with their mother to England.

James then convalesced body and spirit in New Mexico. He later traveled the country as a lecturer, did social work in Chicago, and returned to southern California in 1892, where he became social director for the Mt. Lowe Railway and Hotel. In 1895 James remarried a widow with two daughters, with whom he enjoyed the remainder of his life.

George Wharton James. *Photo courtesy Palm Springs Historical Society.*

In California he wrote *Traveler's Handbook to Southern California* (1894), *In and Out of the California Missions* (1905), *Through Ramona's Country* (1908), *California: Romantic and Beautiful* (1914), and much more.

With his rising fame, James gave lectures throughout the state, (primarily on California literature), wrote articles and pamphlets, and championed numerous causes.

He died in 1923 at the age of 65 in a northern California sanatorium at St. Helena. The tranquil Chino Canyon where James loved to "rest, think and write" would 40 years later become the setting for the Palm Springs Aerial Tramway.

Carl Eytel

According to J. Smeaton Chase in his 1920 book *Our Araby*, the artist Carl Eytel was a Palm Springs pacesetter:

> *It looks more than likely that ten or fifteen years from now a school of painters will have made Our Araby their province...A forerunner of the group I forecast has already*

been working with Palm Springs as his headquarters, Mr. Carl Eytel, whose knowledge of his field has been earned, as it were, inch by inch and grain by grain, and whose conscientious work gives a truer rendering of the desert than do sensational canvasses of the popular Wild West sort.

The first resident artist of Palm Springs, Eytel was born in Wurtenburg, Germany, in 1862, and educated in Stuttgart. He came to the U.S. in 1885 where he went to work for a German-speaking cattle rancher in Kansas. There he started drawing and his life-long interest with the American west commenced. Returning briefly to Germany to study art, he came back to the U.S. in 1898 and settled in Palm Springs.

With permission from the McCallums, and lumber built from settlers' abandoned houses, he built a small cabin beside the water ditch on the McCallum family property near the present Tennis Club. From there he roamed the desert in all directions, rendering the pen and ink drawing for which he became so well known.

Eytel, who did not make much money with his art, was beloved by the Palm Springs community. Nellie Coffman often invited him to "tea" to ensure he had enough to eat, and also bought him art supplies. He sold his drawings to anyone he could and was hired by George Wharton James to do over 300 of them for his book *The Wonders of the Colorado Desert.*

Carl Eytel wrote articles for the *Los Angeles Times* and also a German newspaper. His hundreds of pen and ink drawings helped publicize Palm Springs and the surrounding desert. A friend of fellow artist Jimmy Swinnerton, photographer W.W. Lockwood, writers George Wharton James, J. Smeaton Chase, and Edmund Jaeger, more importantly he was a friend of the local desert Cahuilla Indians, the Agua Calientes. Upon his death in 1925, at age 63, he was accorded the honor of being one of only two white men buried in the Indian Cemetery.

J. Smeaton Chase

Author and photographer J. Smeaton Chase came to Palm Springs in 1915 and married Isabel White, one of the White sisters, two years later. In 1919 he published *California Desert Trails*, and in 1920, *Our Araby: Palm Springs and the Garden of the Sun,* a small gem of a book that is still being sold regularly in Palm Springs gift shops and book stores.

Chase was born in 1864 in London, where his father Samuel Chase was a publisher and his brother worked in a bookstore. Chase came to California in 1890 and originally settled in a mountainous area of San Diego County. For a while he did social work in Los Angeles, but loved the out-of-doors and covered the length and breath of his adopted state. His first book *Yosemite Trails*, a combination guide book/nature essays, published in 1911, is still considered a High Sierra classic.

Then Chase wrote *Cone Bearing Trees of the California Mountains*, a tree-lover's handbook, enhanced by his own photos and line drawings by Palm Springs artist Carl Eytel. But it was Chase's third book, *California Coastal Trails*, (1913) a narrative of his horseback ride along the entire California coast, that won him broad acclaim and still inspires fans to retrace his route.

Chase died in Banning in 1923 and was buried in Palm Springs' Welwood Murray Cemetery. Never forgetting his English ties, he requested upon his death that a similar gravestone mark his death in England. So it was that his name was added to the family plot at the Old Bexley Churchyard in Kent, England.

His wife Isabel, who survived him by almost 40 years, is buried by his side in Palm Springs.

Edmund C. Jaeger

Edmund C. Jaeger, Professor Emeritus, Riverside City College, was renown as a botanist and desert authority. He came to California as a youngster in 1906 as his father's ailing health needed a change in climate.

A few years later he climbed Mt. San Jacinto and looked out across the vast desert. In the foreword he later wrote for the National Geographic Society's *Great American Deserts*:

> *...saw the desert spread out before me. I felt its richness and solitude—and beauty—tugging at me, and I vowed then and there that one day I would know it...*
>
> *For 30 years I was a Professor of Zoology at City College in Riverside, California, and I spent nearly every weekend and holiday camping in the desert with my students....*
>
> *I remember riding a burro into Palm Springs, at the edge of the desert, where I began teaching. There were 40 registered voters there, mostly Indians....*

That was in 1915 when Jaeger became one of Palm Springs' first school-teachers, initially teaching five children in a one-room school. Moving to Riverside, he became widely known and respected for his articles and books. Considered the dean of American desert naturalists, he became to the deserts what John Muir was to the mountains.

His landmark *The California Deserts* (1933), replete with original line drawings and maps drawn by the author, has undergone numerous editions and is still considered an excellent desert resource.

Palm Springs artist Carl Eytel entrusted his friend Jaeger to safeguard and keep his own numerous desert and Indian drawings. After Eytel died in 1925, Jaeger gave them to the Palm Springs Desert Museum.

In 1972, at age 85, Jaeger lamented that when he arrived in Palm Springs there was only one house on the road from there to Indio. "Today," he wrote, "about 100,000 people live along that road, and when you drive it, its hard to see open country on either side." Concerned about the burgeoning growth and off-roading in the desert, he added, "If we spoil our desert in pursuit of recreation, then there will be true recreation in the desert for no one."

Jaeger's writings inspired a vast legion of concerned people to champion setting aside significant portions of desert land for preserves and natural habitats. And of course, those five young students in Palm Springs in 1915 grew up with a healthy respect for the land upon which they lived.

Jimmy Swinnerton

James Guilford (Jimmy) Swinnerton (1875-1974) was a top cartoonist who worked for William Randolph Hearst in New York. He caught tuberculosis and in 1906 was sent by Hearst to the California desert for his health. He first arrived in Colton and by the following year became strong enough to venture to Palm Springs where he was one of The Desert Inn's first guests. He made his home in Palm Springs and became an ardent pro-Palm Springs booster, living there for the next 70 years.

America's first newspaper comic strip historically is credited to a strip called *The Yellow Kid* which came onto the New York newspaper scene in 1895. However, Swinnerton really should be given the recognition as by 1892, three years earlier, he had already been drawing comics and cartoons for the *San Francisco Examiner*.

Born in 1875 in Eureka, California, Swinnerton was a cartoonist who created *The Little Bears & Tykes, Little Jimmy, Canyon Kids*, and others. Later summoned to New York to work for Hearst's *New York Journal*, he also went on to national fame as a landscape artist, enjoying one-man shows across the country.

Jimmy Swinnerton and Palm Springs agreed with each other. When he arrived in 1907 he was given less than one year to live, yet he was 99 years old when he died in Palm Springs in 1974.

During 2003, two of Swinnerton's drawings were hanging in the Palm Springs Desert Museum, "Canyon Kiddies," a 1938 drawing of Indian children in the desert and "Untitled," circa 1930. His fine drawing titled "Little Colorado River Scene," which depicts a thunderstorm over the desert, was on display there during fall 2004.

W.W. Lockwood

W.W. Lockwood became known as the first professional photographer of Palm Springs. He arrived in 1911 with tuberculosis and stayed at Harry and Nellie Coffman's Sanatorium, The Desert Inn.

Lockwood took many wonderful photographs of the area and was often seen out exploring in the desert with the artist Carl Eytel. The two often covered the desert and nearby canyons on a mule-driven buggy in their quest for drawings and photos.

Stephen H. Willard

Stephen H. Willard was considered the finest scenic photographer of his era. Born in Illinois in 1894, at age two his family moved to Corona, California, where the photographer was raised. Steve's dad gave him his first camera at age 16, thus beginning a life-long avocation.

He photographed everything he could, from California's mountains to the deserts, including the area around Palm Springs. After serving in France in World War I, he traveled Europe selling photos he made into postcards for American troops still there.

He moved to Palm Springs and established his first studio, maintaining a summer studio in Idyllwild. He married Beatrice Armstrong in 1921, and in 1922 they built a house on Palm Canyon Drive, where he moved his studio. Willard exhibited his photos at The Desert Inn Gallery, and Beatrice ran the trading post in Palm Canyon where they also sold his photos.

They built a home on South Palm Canyon Drive in 1929 that they lived in until 1947. Their home became part of today's Moorten Botanical Garden and, with bubbling fountains, the lovely house is now often the setting for weddings and outdoor parties.

Willard loved the desert and made extensive trips all over California, Arizona, Utah, New Mexico, and the Sonoran Desert of Mexico. He also visited Israel and Africa's Sahara Desert several times.

In addition to straight photographs, Willard did hand-painted enlargements and experimented with various media. Mrs. Willard helped with the tinting. His photos, paintings and postcards were widely sold and he was one of very few people at the time to support himself as a full-time photographer.

Willard had a 1920 Chalmers automobile which he took out into the rocky desert roads and trails around Palm Springs to find and create his photographs. He helped establish Joshua Tree National Monument, now a national park.

The Willards stayed in Palm Springs until 1947 when they moved to the Owens Valley where Willard died in 1966. The love of the wide-open spaces was transferred to their daughter Beatrice (Betty), who became a leading ecologist. Willard's old studio on Palm Canyon Drive was demolished in 1989 to make way for John Wessman's La Plaza de las Flores project.

The Stephen H. Willard Photography Collection and Archive, consisting of over 16,000 original items, was donated to the Palm Springs Desert Museum by his daughter, Dr. Beatrice Willard. The museum featured a major six-month display of his California works in 2004. One of them, titled "Silent Interlude," taken in 1947, is particularly eye-catching. It is a beautiful tinted photograph of majestic Mt. San Jacinto rising above the desert floor.

Numerous Steve Willard photos are also owned by the Automobile Club of Southern California and have been on display in various museums.

The Willard House was built in 1929 by photographer Stephen Willard. It is now part of Moorten Botanical Garden.

Fred Payne Clatworthy

Fred Payne Clatworthy, born in 1875, was a lawyer turned color photographer. He photographed many of the western national parks, and his color photos for a 1923 *National Geographic* were among the first published by that publication.

He settled in Estes Park, Colorado, where he sold stock images and did custom work out of his Ye Little Shoppe. He was the official photographer for the YMCA of the Rockies and on their board of directors.

He and his wife Mabel and daughters Helen and Barbara eventually moved to Palm Springs, living in a home on Ramon Road.

In 1930, Clatworthy made an extensive photography trip into Mexico on assignment for the Southern Pacific Railroad and the Mexican railroad as well as some national magazines. He went down the west coast of Mexico to Mazatlan where he shot the colorful carnival, to Guadalajara where he photographed pottery and pottery makers, to Mexico City, and then following the trail of Cortez to Vera Cruz to some pyramids which were only discovered in 1922.

Clatworthy was long a proponent of the Palm Springs area; he died in 1953.

Gordon Coutts

Perhaps the most internationally famous artist to call Palm Springs home was Gordon Coutts (1880-1937). Another Scotsman to find his way to Palm Springs, Coutts was born in Aberdeen, Scotland He studied art in Glasgow, London, and Paris, and became best known for Moroccan figures, desert scenes, and nudes.

He lived in Sydney, Australia, for several years where he was a painting instructor at the Government School of Art. He was highly regarded in Australia where he often painted portraits of celebrities, and many of his finest works hang in Melbourne and Sydney museums. Others hang in The National Gallery in England, and some found their way to important American collections.

Internationally famed artist Gordon Coutts. *Photo courtesy G. Douglas Smith of the Korakia Pensione.*

He was a friend of Winston Churchill, and

painted a portrait of the steel magnate Andrew Carnegie.

The flamboyant red-headed artist traveled the world, leaving his strict Presbyterian home at an early age because his parents wouldn't let him paint on Sundays. He was already married and divorced when he met and married model Gertrude Russell of Ohio, 30 years his junior. They traveled together and settled for several years in Tangier, Morocco, where he painted Arab sheiks and other celebrities.

Coutts loved Morocco and would have remained but they visited Palm Springs, liked it, and returned. Coutts had bronchial problems he hoped would improve.

Entrance to Korakia Pensione reflects its Moorish inspiration.

In 1924 Gordon and Gertrude Coutts moved to Palm Springs and built their own Moorish castle, "Dar Moroc" at 257 Patencio Drive. With towers, Moorish arches and domes, keyhole shaped windows, huge doors, tiled fountains, and courtyards dripping with bougainvillea, oleander, palms, olive and citrus trees, the Dar Moroc was like a little bit of Tangier dropped onto the Palm Springs landscape. The villagers referred to it as "Coutts Castle."

At Dar Moroc, the Coutts hosted numerous dignitaries and artists, including Grant Wood (*American Gothic*) and Sir John Lavery, England's great portrait artist.

Gordon Coutts became one of Palm Springs' most revered and well-liked resident before passing away following a lingering illness in 1937.

Among his pallbearers was Fred Payne Clatworthy. He and Gertrude were survived by two daughters, Jean Granada Coutts and Mary Gordon Coutts.

The Dar Moroc has been transformed into the upscale desert hideaway, Korakia Pensione, a restful 29-room hotel. Neighboring properties were acquired by G. Douglas Smith, who established the Korakia in 1989. The Korakia has continued to attract artists and writers, including noted abstract painter Brice Marden, Pulitzer Prize winner Judith Thurman and John Irving. Mexico's famous writer Octavio Paz even reserved a room at the restful inn.

Coutts' daughter Jean, in talking about her father and the early days in Palm Springs, noted, "Before the movie colony took over, Palm Springs was an art colony like Taos."

John W. Hilton

John W. Hilton (1904-1983) was an accomplished desert painter who spent most of his life in the high desert community of Twentynine Palms. He also loved to paint the Palm Springs area and went on sketching trips with fellow artist Jimmy Swinnerton.

Born in Carrington, North Dakota in 1904, Hilton lived with his family in a farm shack. His parents became missionaries and took young John with them to China, where among his experiences was walking on the Great Wall of China.

Hilton moved to Los Angeles in 1918 and worked for a gem company. In the 1930s he moved to the desert and became a highly competent desert painter while at the same time operating a curio shop.

Among the books illustrated by Hilton are: *Sonora Sketch Book* (1947), *This Is My Desert* (1962), and *Hilton Paints the Desert* (1964). Among publications that featured Hilton illustrations are the *L.A. Times, Saturday Evening Post*, and *Desert Magazine*.

Hilton's first (he went on to have over 100 national shows) solo show was in Palm Springs in 1935. He was also an accomplished poet, musician, gemologist and miner. During WW II, he mined for calcite in the Anza-Borrego Desert. He became a friend of desert humorist Harry Oliver who began the annual Pegleg Smith Liars Contest. Hilton started a tradition at the contest of a bonfire into which he would burn his "mistakes" with great flourish.

Hilton died in 1983 on the island of Maui, Hawaii, where he maintained a home for the last decade of his life.

Edward S. Curtis

Edward Sheriff Curtis was the "Shadow Catcher," a photographer of the North American Indian from 1896 to 1930, covering and documenting various Indian tribes.

From 1905-1910 he worked among the Cahuilla in the Palm Springs area. He was a dashing, goateed young man, working under a broad-brimmed hat, and remaining dapper with turtle-neck sweater and a well-worn utility jacket.

Curtis not only photographed the Indian but also became their friend and benefactor. Numerous of his black and white photos, portraits and Indian life, hang in the Agua Caliente Tribal Museum.

He was recognized by the President of the United States for his work. In a letter to Curtis on December 16, 1905, President Theodore Roosevelt wrote, "I regard the work you do as one of the most valuable works, which any American could now do."

Curtis himself summed up his work thusly, "The passing of every old man or woman means the passing of some tradition, some knowledge of sacred rites possessed by no other, consequently the information that is to be gathered...respecting the mode of life of one of the great races of mankind, must be collected at once or the opportunity will be lost for all time."

CHAPTER 22

The Desert's Premier Golf Course
TOM O'DONNELL—OILMAN GOLFER

Visitors often ask Palm Springs residents about the Spanish-style house that sits on a ledge of the mountain right downtown. The nearby golf course below the house isn't quite as visible but the two landmarks are related and the man behind them both is Tom O'Donnell, an oilman who left lasting tributes to Palm Springs.

Tom O'Donnell (1870-1945) was a Long Beach wildcatter who got rich in oil fields in Los Angeles and Ventura Counties as well as Mexico in the years before WWI. It is said that he arrived in California from his native Pennsylvania penniless, but was worth millions when ailing health brought him to Palm Springs in the early 1920s.

He stayed at The Desert Inn and became a close friend of Nellie Coffman. O'Donnell bankrolled the expansion of The

Mr. and Mrs. Tom O'Donnell and Nellie Coffman. *Photo courtesy Palm Springs Historical Society.*

Desert Inn, and in exchange Nellie leased him the land on the hill behind the hotel. This became the first land lease in Palm Springs history not with an Agua Caliente member.

"Ojo del Desierto"

There the famous home "Ojo del Desierto" (Eye of the Desert) was built in 1925. The Mediterranean Revival home, designed by Charles Tanner, was designed to be consistent with the buildings of The Desert Inn below. The Desert Inn is gone now, replaced by the Desert Fashion Plaza and the Desert Museum, but the house on the hill is still an "eye over the desert" and a Palm Springs historical site. With red-tile roof, stucco

The famous "Ojo del Desierto" (Eye of the Desert) house, which overlooks downtown Palm Springs, was built in 1925 by Tom O'Donnell.

walls, broad porch and open second floor veranda, it still looks the same as it did in the 1920s.

Even though O'Donnell suffered from respiratory ailments—one report indicated he had tuberculosis—he still kept active. He sat on several presidential commissions and was a founding member of the American Petroleum Institute.

But O'Donnell loved golf, and with no course in the desert, he was often seen swinging clubs and practicing shots in the lawns between The Desert Inn's cottages. For a wealthy man, he did the next obvious thing—he built his own course! With his house finished, he bought 33 acres of land against the mountain immediately to the north—specifically for his own golf course.

Later expanded to 40 acres, the private nine-hole O'Donnell Golf Course opened for the winter 1926-27 season. O'Donnell spent over $200,000 (1926 dollars) bringing in Bermuda and rye grasses, fertilizer, shrubs, bushes, sand, and palm trees. He added large tamarisk trees to enshroud the course in privacy.

Designing by wedge and iron

Today's golf courses are laid out by leading pros and expert course designers. Not here. O'Donnell got a few buddies, including Captain J. F. Lucey, a Texas oilman, and John Kline, who remained the groundskeeper for years, and they laid out the course themselves. After seeing how far they could drive and chip, they placed the greens at distances they felt comfortable with.

Their system worked well enough to create a challenging par 35 (9 holes) traditional course. The hardest hole is a par-5 472 yards, while the easiest is a par-4, 274 yards. It is considered a tight course with fast greens.

The private O'Donnell Golf Course became an exclusive club and has limited membership through the years to about 250 with charter limits at

300. Membership has included some of the city's most prominent names, including Bob Hope and Kirk Douglas, with many other celebrities playing the course as guests. Presidents Eisenhower and Ford have played the O'Donnell Golf Course. As the desert's only enduring golfing venue for decades, tournaments at the intimate course attracted golfing's top stars, including Ben Hogan, Ken Venturi, and Babe Didrickson Zaharias.

O'Donnell did more for Palm Springs than open the first golf course. He also bought shares in the Whitewater Mutual Water Company and got involved in numerous civic ventures. He coordinated the drive to raise $26,000 to build the Welwood Murray Memorial Library, personally donating $10,000 of that amount; he helped establish the Palm Springs Desert Museum and the first hospital. During the depression he had a road built up the side of the lower slopes of Mt. San Jacinto to the location of long-time Easter Sunrise services. While his plan was originally to build another home there, the road helped provide employment for residents. But his greatest gift to the city was his golf course.

Tom O'Donnell loved his course with a passion. After his health deteriorated so much in the late 1930s, he considered closing it, but constantly visited it and sat around even though he couldn't play. When he saw his friends enjoying themselves so much, he decided to keep it open. He wanted to donate it directly to the city but was afraid they might be tempted to use it for something else, like a park or a civic center.

The O'Donnell Golf Course.

Committee of 25

So the shrewd businessman figured out a way to make it happen. In July 1944, less than a year before he was to pass away, he leased the golf course land for 99 years to 25 Palm Springs friends and home owners. A lease proviso stipulated that if the land was to be used for anything other than a golf course it would require a unanimous approval of the 25. He later deeded the land to the city subject to that 99-year lease. The Committee of 25 became the board of trustees of the course, and has included some prominent Palm Springs pioneers and merchants as well as a few celebrities, including Bob Hope.

O'Donnell received a huge tax break, and the city continues to this day to receive rent annual payments and a use tax, and it appears the O'Donnell Golf Course will be around another 40 years. True to O'Donnell's figuring, attempts were made by organizations and civic leaders on several occasions to break the lease, for various reasons, but the lease structure prevailed.

Tom O'Donnell died at age 74 on February 28, 1945. Services were held at noon, March 2, on his beloved golf course with many prominent citizens in attendance. Mrs. O'Donnell died in 1969 at age 89.

Precursor to 100 Courses

While a golf course briefly was open at El Mirador in 1929, it would be 20 years before the valley received its second permanent golf course, the 9-hole Cochran-Odlum course—expanded to 18 holes in 1974—on Floyd Odlum's Ranch in Indio. Over the next few decades golf courses sprang up like wildflowers after a wet winter:

> 1926 —- O'Donnell Golf Course
> 1929 —- El Mirador Golf Course
> 1947 —- Cochran-Odlum, Indio
> 1949 —- Shadow Mountain (pitch and putt)
> 1951 —- Thunderbird Country Club
> 1953 —- Tamarisk Country Club
> 1957 —- Indian Wells Country Club
> 1957 —- El Dorado Country Club
> 1959 —- San Jacinto (now Whitewater Country Club)
> 1959 —- Bermuda Dunes
> 1959 —- Palm Springs Municipal (public)
> 1959 —- Shadow Mountain
> 1961 —- Westward Ho

1962 —- Canyon Country Club
1962 —- Palm Desert Country Club
1962 —- Salton City Golf Course

During 1960's and early 1970's, four more were added:
Annenberg (private),
La Quinta Country Club,
Biltmore Hotel Course (1963),
Riviera Hotel

By the late 1970s the Palm Springs area boasted over 40 golf courses, making it the world's number one desert playground.

During the year 2001, the 100th golf course opened in the desert, giving the Coachella Valley floor the appearance of a green quilt from the air. By 2004 there were 106 courses. It started with a can-do oilman who built that first course hard against the San Jacinto Mountains in downtown Palm Springs. And thanks to his shrewdness, it will be there at least until the year 2043.

Early aerial view of El Mirador Hotel shows it was one of the first resorts in the desert. *Photo courtesy Palm Springs Historical Society.*

CHAPTER 23

El Mirador Draws The Celebrities

P. T. STEVENS/WARREN PINNEY

Of all the famous "in spots" in Palm Springs through the years, perhaps the El Mirador Hotel was the most renowned. It certainly attracted the Hollywood celebrities, political dignitaries, and prominent visitors. Their presence at the El Mirador helped establish and perpetuate a Palm Springs image of glamour, romance, and carefree fun in the sun.

The El Mirador opened with a flourish on New Year's Eve 1927 with a gala $15 per head opening party. Celebrities were immediately attracted to the new resort and the biggest movie stars of the era all spent time there. Guests during the first two months alone included: Mary Pickford, Douglas Fairbanks, Lillian Gish, Kenneth Maynard, Pola Negri, Eddie Cantor, and Gloria Swanson.

The legendary El Mirador was the brainchild of Prescott Thresher (P.T.) Stevens who formed a company with Alvah Hicks and other developers in 1926 to build the sprawling luxurious hotel just north of downtown Palm Springs. It featured a 68-foot tall Renaissance-inspired bell tower which dominated the landscape and offered a view over the entire valley. The hotel was aptly christened El Mirador, the Spanish term for "The Lookout."

P.T. Stevens

In addition to his memorable El Mirador Hotel, P.T. Stevens ensured the village of a steady supply of water, and gave back much to the community including donating land and funds for educational purposes.

A successful Colorado cattleman born in 1846, P.T. married a former teacher from the Midwest, Frances Stephens. Because of her respiratory problems, in 1912 the couple divested their Colorado holdings and relocated to California, first settling in Hollywood. They later moved to Palm Springs for the dry, warm therapeutic air.

They stayed at The Desert Inn while building a home in the 900 block of North Palm Canyon Drive. The astute P.T. immediately began buying up land, primarily on the northern end of town. He also invested in Hollywood real estate. By 1920 he had considerable Palm Springs holdings and the water rights that went along with them.

P.T. bought several thousand acres from the Southern Pacific Railroad, to the east and north of the village, embracing much of the alluvial fan from Chino Canyon, adding a great source of mountain water. He also bought shares in the original Palm Valley Water Company.

Prescott Thresher (P.T.) Stevens (center) examines date crop with others in King Gillette's Gardens. *Photo courtesy Palm Springs Historical Society.*

Whitewater Mutual Water Company

In 1927 he formed the Whitewater Mutual Water Company to insure a steady supply of water to the village. The company piped low-cost water from Whitewater Canyon, around Windy Point, to fill the village's agricultural needs. Much of the more established residential neighborhoods in Palm Springs, like Las Palmas, still utilize this water source today. Stevens also developed and was the principal owner of the Palm Springs Water Company.

He helped fellow pioneer Alvah Hicks subdivide, develop, and sell some 20 acres owned by Hicks. Together Stevens and Hicks sold much of the Las Palmas land for residences. And together they built the El Mirador.

P.T. Stevens also built the desert's second golf course and first 18-hole course at El Mirador. It opened in 1929 and was open to the public with low greens fees. Stevens had enlisted long-time aide Lawrence Crossley to design and build the course. As Stevens declared the golf course a non-profit venture, he turned over all net proceeds to a Los Angeles children's group. It was a noble gesture but the timing was anything but providential. The Great Depression arrived just months later and there were not enough golfers to sustain the course, so it closed.

The Depression was tough on Stevens. The hotel itself, while projected to cost about $750,000, exceeded $1 million. By 1931 Stevens was forced to sell to bondholders for $327,000, literally wiping him out. He died just months later in 1932.

Warren Pinney

The bondholders then hired Warren Pinney, a Los Angeles lawyer, to reorganize their venture and protect their interests. Under the 1931 reorganization, San Diego businessman and leading investor Ralph Lacoe assumed majority ownership interest, and Pinney took over as general manager.

When Pinney was presented an opportunity to pull the popular desert resort out of the debilitating Depression ennui, he did so with flair. Largely due to his guidance, the El Mirador Hotel continued to attract the Hollywood crowd, politicians, business leaders, and statesmen from around the world.

Mr. and Mrs. Warren Pinney with Warren Pinney Jr. *Photo by Maurice Terry.*

Pinney recreated a resort so sumptuous that its competitor The Desert Inn had to notch up its own legendary version of gracious hospitality and offer more amenities.

Pinney installed many attractions at the El Mirador, creating a professional staff, including polite and courteous bellboys smartly dressed in white shirts, ties, and double-vested maroon suits complete with the "El Mirador" monogram, gold trim, and shiny brass buttons. They resembled that decade's famous Phillip Morris pageboy icons.

The hotel's South Pacific Room offered fine dining on maroon-trimmed dishes complete with the El Mirador tower logo. Island-inspired meals, which ranged from $2.00 to $3.25 included Curried Lobster Malayan Style, Mandarin Duck, Beef Tomato Cantonese Style, and Pork with Chestnuts and Green Peas.

The hotel swimming pool, at 75-feet long, was the biggest around, had a see-through underwater window, and featured both high and low diving boards. Johnny Weismuller and Esther Williams were among the legions of celebrities to swim at the El Mirador. High diving exhibitions featuring daredevils diving from 100 feet helped delight the guests.

Visitors frolic in the pool at the El Mirador during its heyday. *Photo courtesy Palm Springs Historical Society.*

In addition to the pool, the hotel offered tennis courts, hiking and riding excursions, bicycles, buckboard rides, archery, golf, and even an early sauna that looked like a space capsule and was affectionately nicknamed the "sweat box."

Pinney hired Tony Burke to handle publicity and promotions. With his photos of celebrities strolling across the El Mirador grounds (which became legendary in themselves), Burke helped create the special air that pervaded the El Mirador clientele. He later included many of his photos in a book of his experience, *Palm Springs, Why I Love You,* and went on to become a prominent real estate agent in the valley.

During the 1930s, in addition to the top Hollywood names like Ginger Rogers, Al Jolson, Clara Bow, and Columbia Pictures mogul Harry Cohn were aviation's Howard Hughes, Jack Northrup, and Alan Lockheed.

Popular New York Mayor Jimmy Walker came, as did New York Governor Herbert Lehman who wanted his photo taken with young Shirley Temple. California Governor James Rolph Jr., and newspaperman George Randolph Hearst were guests.

Mr. and Mrs. Adolph Spreckles spent time at the El Mirador each winter and visitor Albert Einstein once entertained a few guests there by playing the violin for them. Writer/adventurer Richard Haliburton added his presence to the long list of literary personalities who have spent time in Palm Springs. In all, the decades before the war were heady times in Palm Springs.

El Mirador becomes Army Hospital

With World War II, the carefree years came to a screeching halt. General George Patton was sent to the Coachella Valley to train troops for the desert war in North Africa. A new airport was built by the Army Corps of Engineers and leased to the Army Air Corps to house the 21st Ferrying Command Group from Long Beach. The government also needed an army hospital for war casualties and bought the El Mirador, converting it into the Torney General Hospital, named for Brig. Gen. George H. Torney, U.S. Surgeon General 1909-1913.

Once expensive El Mirador guest cottages quickly became hospital wards; the renowned Coral Room was turned into the nurse's lounge, and the Tennis Court Club was converted into the Officers Club.

After the war years, like a phoenix rising from the ashes, the El Mirador rose from its drab military bearing to resume its importance as a desert resort for two more decades. A Chicago group formed a company which spent over $2 million to remodel the hotel and it finally reopened in 1952. The celebrities returned to an even larger, more opulent hotel than before, and the big names of the fifties and sixties discovered the El Mirador to be as hedonistic as did their counterparts in the thirties.

P.T. Stevens was not around to see the El Mirador settle into its place of continuous importance. Even though he lost on the deal, he and his wife Frances gave much back to Palm Springs, including land and equipment for the Frances Stevens School, named for his wife, an educator.

After P.T. died in 1932, daughter Sallie Stevens Nichols and her husband Culver Nichols, who inherited the water company, developed residential property on the site of the old golf course on the other side of the El Mirador.

Pinney's son, Warren Pinney Jr., who early on helped his father at the El

Mirador, went on to become vice president of an oil company in Dallas. His sister Phyllis moved to Thermal in the east Coachella Valley.

After its 21-year second resurgence, the El Mirador finally closed its doors as a hotel in 1973.

Desert Regional Medical Center

After closing a chapter of Palm Springs history, the renowned El Mirador Hotel became the Desert Regional Medical Center. A smaller hospital actually began in 1948 as Palm Springs Community Hospital, a 33-bed single building on the grounds of the El Mirador Hotel. In 1951 that building became the Desert Hospital. With much expansion in the 1970s after the closing of the hotel, the hospital is now known as the Desert Regional Medical Center and offers full medical services.

The El Mirador Tower became one of the most recognizable landmarks in Palm Springs. While the hotel is long gone, that tower still graces the Desert Regional Medical Center. Actually, however, the tower you see is a facsimile.

After conversion to a hospital, the main hotel building and landmark tower were left standing, but a July 1989 fire destroyed them completely. To recreate a link with the past, the tower was accurately reconstructed from the original plans in May 1991.

The El Mirador Hotel is gone, but residents and visitors, in seeing that tower, are reminded of an important venue in the legacy of Palm Springs. The reassuring "lookout" is still there.

The El Mirador tower, today part of the Desert Regional Medical Center.

CHAPTER 24

A Legacy of Commitment
ALVAH HICKS — MASTER BUILDER

In a sense, Alvah Hicks was an unlikely real estate investor and water company president. But he was hard-working, astute, and opportunistic, and ultimately left a legacy not only of development and commitment to the village of Palm Springs, but also of sons and grandchildren who continued the Hicks prominence.

Alvah Hicks was a master carpenter, born in 1884, who relocated from New York to Los Angeles in 1912. The following year he came out to Palm Springs, not for health reasons like so many of that decade, but for the simple opportunity for work.

With his wife and two small sons Hicks first established a homestead north of town, and soon found building and contracting work everywhere. He started buying Palm Springs area land and became a general contractor. Known for quality work, he quickly found many new settlers wanting the finest in desert residences. With the assistance of P.T. Stevens, he bought 20 acres of land in town, subdivided it, built quality homes, and promptly sold them.

His work was in demand. In 1921 he began construction on a lavish Moroccan style home for Lois Kellogg, the wealthy and beautiful socialite daughter of an ambassador who had relocated to the desert from Chicago. Harold Cody was architect of that elaborate project (nicknamed Fools Folly) and when Cody died in 1924, work stopped and the home was never finished.

The Alvah Hicks family (left to right): Milton, Alvah, Harold and Tess. *Photo courtesy Palm Springs Historical Society.*

Las Palmas Homes

In the 1920s and 1930s Hicks built some of the finest-quality desert homes to date, including the Ingleside Inn (which is still in operation) and the Cloisters, which became Liberace's opulent home. He is responsible for building 20 of the finest homes in the Merito Vista and Las Palmas areas, which he had subdivided. The Las Palmas area would become home to many titans of industry and celebrities and is still the city's most exclusive area.

In all his real estate dealings, one anecdote stands out. In 1934 Hicks sold 53 acres to actor Charlie Farrell so he could build his Racquet Club. Farrell paid Hicks $66 an acre for the parcel. Not bad until you consider that Hicks bought the land for $5 an acre, and it was in the windy north end of town. Not a bad profit!

Palm Springs Water Company

Realizing that in the desert, water is the most valuable commodity, Hicks acquired numerous water rights. In the mid-1920s he bought control of the Palm Valley Land and Water Company started decades earlier by village pioneer John G. McCallum. Later he founded the Palm Springs Water Company into which he invested vast amounts of time and effort to insure that the water flowed freely. The company was worth $6 million when, in 1968, it was sold and became the current Desert Water Agency.

In 1926, Hicks also established the area's premier hardware store, Palm Springs Builders Supply on Sunny Dunes Road, just off Palm Canyon Drive. Builders Supply Company is the oldest continuously operated business in Palm Springs. It is still going strong and is well visited by the area's contractors. Builders Supply Company, with a second store now operating in Desert Hot Springs, was sold by the family in 1960.

In 1937 Alvah Hicks became president of the 46th Agricultural District and helped plan the desert's original Date Festival and Horse Show. Alvah and his wife Teresa Ann (Tess) Hicks were both prominent civic leaders. Hicks served on the city's first city council and helped with the city's incorporation. He served on numerous boards and was a founding member of the Desert Riders and the Polo Club. Teresa died in 1942 and Alvah Hicks died in 1944; both are buried in the old Welwood Murray Cemetery.

Mr. Golf

Their son Milton (Milt) Hicks (1914-1966) took over the Builders Supply Company and became known in the desert as Mr. Golf, a title he acquired not only because of his intense love of the game, but his enthusiastic sharing of that passion. He was the chairman of the famous Bob Hope Desert Classic.

Son Harold Hicks (1909-1997) went on to village prominence. He was involved in insurance and real estate, selling numerous properties in the Las Palmas area. He became chairman of the committee to incorporate the city of Palm Springs, was a member of the Committee of 25 overseeing the O'Donnell Golf Course, and was president of the water company from 1942 until it was sold in 1968. Harold moved to Santa Barbara where he spent his remaining years.

A New Generation

One of Harold's children, Jim, continued to serve the village of Palm Springs. Jim Hicks took over his father's real estate business and eventually became president of the large Eadie Adams Real Estate Company. The leadership role was nothing new for him. From student body president at Palm Springs High School, Jim went on to become president of: the Palm Springs Jaycees, the Palm Springs Chamber of Commerce, the Desert Water Agency board of directors, the Downtown Development Advisory Commission, and the O'Donnell Golf Club. He was also a member of the planning commission. Jim's wife Carole is an artist and they have four children.

From when that master builder Alvah Hicks first set eyes on Palm Springs and started to help develop the village to the present day, there has continuously been a member of the Hicks family adding to the Palm Springs legacy.

CHAPTER 25

Racquet Club Becomes
Hollywood Haven
CHARLES FARRELL/RALPH BELLAMY

The Palm Springs Racquet Club, which became a legendary watering hole of the stars, was actually founded by a couple of Hollywood actors in 1934 and was still in operation almost 60 years later.

Charlie Farrell, who would star in 46 motion pictures and a successful television series, and his pal Ralph Bellamy, who appeared in 103 films, over 400 stage plays, and a number of TV appearances, built the Racquet Club because they needed a place to play tennis.

They both loved the desert and had rented homes in Palm Springs, which unfortunately did not allow for hotel guest privileges at the village's only courts, those at The Desert Inn and the El Mirador. So they cut a deal with Warren Pinney, manager of the El Mirador, who allowed them to use the courts, but only if no guests wanted to play. It was better than nothing.

In winter 1932 the two actors were out riding horses in a windswept area of the desert about a mile north of the El Mirador. They saw a "for sale" sign and contacted the owner (Alvah Hicks) who sold them 53 acres for their future speculation. They paid him $3,500.00, or about $66 an acre.

The pair continued to play tennis at the El Mirador but Pinney was forced to kick them out because too many paying guests complained that Farrell and Bellamy were hogging the courts. It has even been reported that actress Marlene Dietrich was one of the complainants.

Over a drink they commiserated and finally came to an idea that they would build a court on their "worthless" desert acreage. So they contracted the David Company from Los Angeles to come down and build them a court. While under construction, the contractor suggested that if they wanted another court, it would be cheaper then as all the equipment was there and it would just be more concrete. They said okay and also added a fence and a three-sided spectator shelter. That original shelter grew into today's main clubhouse that faces the #1 court.

The courts were ready for Christmas Day, 1933, and the pair began charging their friends $1 to play, all day if they wanted. That first day, they had taken in $18.

In time they added two more courts, a restroom, a couple of bungalows and a swimming pool. According to Farrell, "I guess you might say that the Racquet Club started in a haphazard way and grew in the same crazy, mixed-up fashion. Nothing was ever really planned. We just built, added on, or changed as we saw the need."

By spring of 1934, they had invested $78,000 in their venture and wanted to share the expense. So they sent invitations to 173 of their Hollywood friends offering membership for $50 in the new Palm Springs Racquet Club.

They only got four replies. Undaunted, they made a fancier batch of invitations, this time *raising* the offered membership to $75.00. They sent invitations every two weeks, raising the price of membership each time, until the cost to join was $650. The higher prices worked and created such a demand a waiting list had to be formed.

Grand Opening

The Grand Opening was December 14, 1934, and by this time featured four tennis courts, now sheltered by eucalyptus trees, swimming pool, kitchen, dining room with dance floor, and the famed Bamboo Bar that is still there today. The Bamboo Bar (or Lounge), designed by film director Mitch Leisen, was reputedly the world's first bar constructed from bamboo. The tables, chairs, and trim are also made of bamboo. It is said that the Bamboo Lounge is where the Bloody Mary was invented.

In 1936, Farrell and his wife Virginia left for England where they spent two years working on movies. They left Ralph Bellamy and his wife Catherine in charge of the Racquet Club. Ralph's background was in acting, not business, but it was immediately obvious they were hemorrhaging profits. After some long-distance consulting with Charlie and getting professional investigative help, he caught the bartender and some waiters in a scam that was ripping off the club.

They hired western cowboy actor Frank Bogert, who had been working at the El Mirador, to be general manager. According to Bellamy, "...one of the smartest things we ever did was hire Frank Bogert as general manager of the club. He was more than a manager. He did everything but count the money and keep the books." Bogert managed the club from 1938-1942.

Bellamy was so busy at the Racquet Club he was missing out on some acting roles, so when Farrell and his wife returned from Europe in 1938, it was decided that they would buy Bellamy out so he could devote more time to his acting career.

Every year the Racquet Club grew, with guest cottages added, and additions and improvements constantly made. The spacious and secluded "Members Only" facility became a haven for the Hollywood elite, and the membership roster was a veritable "who's who" of tinseltown. The biggest movie names were there as well as the aspiring actors and starlets.

For instance, a few months after it opened, a 29-year-old pilot and movie producer who would become the world's most famous recluse flew to Palm Springs and was in the Bamboo Bar talking to Charlie Farrell. That's when a 17-year-old English actress under contract at Paramount named Ida Lupino walked past Farrell and his guest, the incomparable Howard Hughes. Hughes was immediately smitten and asked Farrell for an introduction. Enamored, Hughes then spent the next few days buying meals for Miss Lupino and her mother who accompanied her. He later even flew over to Catalina Island to see Ida who had gone there with her mother.

At Catalina, Hughes and Miss Lupino danced a bit and then he took her for a plane ride, but according to author Terry Moore and Jerry Rivers in *The Passions of Howard Hughes* he realized that she was young enough to be "jailbait" and returned her intact, frustrating his infatuation.

Over the next few decades almost all of the popular movie stars of the time frequented the Racquet Club: Humphrey Bogart, Jack Benny, William Powell, Jane Russell, Bob Hope, Lucille Ball, Desi Arnaz, Rita Hayworth, Errol Flynn, Gene Autry, Marilyn Monroe, Cary Grant, Lana

The white lattice entrance to the Racquet Club and its Bamboo Lounge.

Turner, Betty Davis, Barbara Stanwyck and her husband Robert Taylor, and many more. Spencer Tracy, before he moved to Old Las Palmas, lived in Bungalow #19 all winter.

The stars could be seen swimming in the pool or playing tennis during the daytime, and holding court in the exclusive Bamboo Lounge at night. Many studio photo shoots were done on premises and Farrell was astute enough to allow younger undiscovered rising actors and actresses to mingle with the established stars. In fact, it is said that photographer Bruno Bernard "discovered" a starlet named Norma Jean Baker (Marilyn Monroe) poolside at the Racquet Club. Hollywood agent Johnny Hyde met her there at the shoot and the rest is history.

Charlie Farrell

There is no movie actor's name more closely related to the City of Palm Springs than Charlie Farrell. For decades after the opening of the Racquet Club, Farrell was called "Mr. Palm Springs," a title he earned as a businessman, city promoter, councilman, and mayor. Farrell served as mayor from 1948-1953, at a time when his personal acting career had resurged to new heights on the small screen in the immensely popular *My Little Margie* series in which he played Gale Storm's father.

Born Charles David Farrell in Walpole, Massachusetts, on Aug. 9, 1900, he majored in business administration at Boston University. He then went to Hollywood and got into the motion pictures, starting with the silent film *The Cheat* in 1923, mesmerizing the audience in the 1927 silent movie *Seventh Heaven* with Janet Gaynor and ended his big screen career with his 46th movie *The Deadly Game* in 1942.

In 1931, he married Virginia "Ginnie" Valli, a beautiful Hollywood star, who helped him manage the Racquet Club and encouraged him to invest in real estate. Farrell served in World War II and was an excellent tennis player.

Farrell was known as a most cordial host to his guests at the most exclusive and prestigious club in Palm Springs. The charm exuded from both Farrell and his wife definitely contributed to the success of the Racquet Club.

Ginnie died in 1968 and Farrell lived out his remaining years at their home on Tachevah Drive and Miraleste in Palm Springs. He died on May 6, 1990 having made a lasting impression on Palm Springs. A statue of Farrell was dedicated in front of the Palm Springs International Airport in 1999.

Ralph Bellamy

The Grand Marshal of the Palm Springs Golden Anniversary parade in 1988 was Ralph Bellamy, whose major role in the founding of the Racquet Club was recognized by the city.

Bellamy was born in Chicago on June 17, 1904, and at age 17 he ran away from home to join a Shakespearean repertory company. Over the next nine years he played 375 roles for some 15 stock companies. He debuted on Broadway in 1929 *Town Boy*, and began his movie career in 1931 with the movie *Secret Six*. In 1933 alone he appeared in 10 of his lifetime's 103 films.

He was nominated for an Motion Picture Academy Award in 1937 (for *The Awful Truth*) and again in 1960 (for *Sunrise at Campobello* in which he played FDR). He received Broadway's Tony Award in 1958 and a Lifetime Achievement Oscar in 1987. Younger audiences might remember him from *Oh God, Trading Places*, and *Coming To America*.

Bellamy died in Santa Monica on November 29, 1991, at the age of 87. Bob Hope called him "...a hell of a man with a great sense of humor." Mousie Powell, widow of actor William Powell and longtime Racquet Club habitue, noted that Bellamy was instrumental in having so many people come here. Former general manager Frank Bogert, who went on to become Palm Springs mayor twice, said, "Ralph was a real person, not a phony-baloney."

After the stars

Farrell sold his interest in the Racquet Club in 1959 for $1 million, but he continued to manage it. But the heyday of the Racquet Club had passed. While many of the Hollywood crowd stayed on as members, others had died or drifted away as their individual stars had waned.

In 1977 Hotel del Coronado Resorts bought the Racquet Club and refurbished and enlarged the facilities. Condominiums were added in the 1980s as were a variety of private villas that sold out fast.

In 1989 the club was turned into a public facility and non-members could enjoy the rooms, restaurant, and amenities. Rental cottages included the Dorothy Lamour House (1 bedroom and private pool), the Albert Frey House (3 bedroom and indoor pool), and the Clark Gable Cottage (#61). By 1990 the Racquet Club, then owned by M. Larry Lawrence, was again for sale, for $10 million at that time.

In January 1992 some 30 Racquet Club villas were auctioned off. Purchase price of the 1,400 square feet units included one year membership of the facilities, which then included 12 tennis courts and a health club.

In 1999, the 11-acre Racquet Club was purchased by Sign of the Dove, a Canoga Park based company that operated eight upper-end retirement assisted-living centers in the state. The hotel's parent company then spent over $1 million remodeling it.

The restaurant and famed Bamboo Lounge remained open to the public and offered various promotions, like in 2001 and 2002 when it offered a Friday evening seafood buffet, that was excellent but didn't draw the numbers hoped for.

On June 1, 2002, the legendary Racquet Club was transformed by the Sign of the Dove company into the valley's first gay and lesbian retirement community, reflecting the changing demographics of Palm Springs.

That project never really got off the ground and the restaurant and other facilities closed, leaving just the private homes and bungalows occupied by their individual owners. The tennis courts and non-private areas were padlocked and fell into disrepair.

In November 2004, the Racquet Club property was sold to Scott Jones of Lake Arrowhead and Michael Mueller of Los Angeles for $4.2 million, and they are planning to restore the historic site.

A lot of famous people have walked through the white lattice archway entrance to the Racquet Club over the years and many careers were made or broken at the small horseshoe-shaped Bamboo Lounge. The Palm Springs Racquet Club has survived almost seven decades and, thanks to a couple of tennis-loving Hollywood stars, became a real Palm Springs institution.

CHAPTER 26

Theaters Come to Town

EARLE C. STREBE

The honor of receiving the number one star in the Palm Springs Walk of Stars went to a person hardly known outside of Palm Springs, Earle Strebe. That singular honor went *not* to a top name entertainer like Bob Hope or Frank Sinatra, both of whom were also immortalized in concrete along Palm Canyon Drive, but to one who brought entertainment to town.

The initial year of the walk in 1992 found seven inductees who contributed to the fame that is Palm Springs: Bob Hope, Ginger Rogers, Ralph Bellamy, Charlie Farrell, Ruby Keeler, William Powell, and Earle Strebe. Yes, the number one star, that one honoring Earle Strebe, is directly in front of the historic Plaza Theatre, 124 South Palm Canyon Drive.

And that's where it belongs too, in front of the theater established by Strebe. While not *in* the motion pictures, he was responsible for bringing them to the people and his Palm Springs Plaza Theatre was one of eight that he owned and operated.

Born in 1906 in Indiana, Earle Strebe came to Palm Springs during the 1926-27 winter after one year at Butler University where he was unable to fulfill his basketball scholarship due to an enlarged heart.

He was playing football on the grounds of The Desert Inn when owner Earl Coffman came out, talked to young Strebe for a while and offered him a job on the spot, that of bellman/night clerk. Strebe went on to perform numerous duties at The Desert Inn, including those of waiter and bookkeeper.

Movies in the lobby

Strebe began showing movies to guests in the lobby with an old Bell and Howell projector, and soon made a deal with Coffman to operate the business of showing movies to the public in the hotel. As his audiences grew, Strebe moved the "theater" venue to Frances Stevens School. In fact, teacher Katherine Finchy helped collect tickets.

He built the town's first movie theater just south of the Frances Stevens Park, across Alejo Drive. According to former Mayor Frank Bogert, "Everybody went every night. There wasn't much to do at night."

In 1930, Strebe married Zaddie Bunker's daughter Frances Bunker, who was then 24 and had just graduated from Los Angeles Osteopathic College and began practicing medicine in Palm Springs.

Through the years Strebe became a businessman and developer and helped Zaddie manage her properties. But his primary love was the movies. In 1932 he built the Village Theater in downtown Palm Springs, an enterprise which kept in business until 1980.

In the 1920s and 1930s some movie stars went to nearby Lake Arrowhead for the summer and Strebe followed them and built the first movie theaters in that town too. Over the years he would open eight movie theatres throughout southern California. He owned three in the mountains—Lake Arrowhead, Crestline and Big Bear—one at the beach, the short-lived Rancho Theater, the El Paseo Theater, the Village Theater (aka Palm Springs Theater), and the jewel of his chain, the Plaza Theatre in downtown Palm Springs.

Plaza Theatre attracts top premieres

The state-of-the-art Plaza Theatre on South Palm Canyon Dr. opened on December 12, 1936, with the premiere of *Camille* starring Greta Garbo and Robert Taylor. The enigmatic Garbo herself attended the opening incognito, wearing blue jeans and a shawl over her head. Before the showing, it is alleged she went to Strebe's office and introduced herself but requested that Strebe respect her anonymity and that he not announce her presence, a request with which he complied.

The Plaza Theatre became the venue for a number of world premieres, including the musicals *My Fair Lady* and *Music Man*. The Plaza was a popular theater during the 1940s for famous stars to do their broadcasting. Jack Benny, Bob Hope, and Amos 'n' Andy all did radio shows from the Plaza, bringing national attention to downtown Palm Springs.

The historic Plaza Theatre served Palm Springs well for decades and it was finally abandoned in 1989. That's when Riff Markowitz set about to renovate the place and open the Fabulous Palm Springs Follies, a lively high-stepping show that brings folks in by the busloads (See "As Young As You Feel").

City Council Member

Over the years, Strebe was quick to open his theaters for community activities and charity events. He was also eager and willing to help his community, heading the chamber of commerce, and serving on the Palm Springs City Council. An unassuming and modest man, Strebe was extremely well liked. "He was the nicest guy you could have ever met," reflects Bogert.

Earle's brother George Strebe and wife Ethel owned The Doll House, among the most famous restaurants and night clubs in the valley.

Along with his theaters, Earle Strebe owned and managed much of the property in downtown Palm Springs, and was instrumental in a great deal of the town's development.

He died in 1994 at the age of 88 at home after a long bout with cancer. He and Frances were together for 64 years and lived in the same Palm Springs home for 50 years. She died in 1996 at age 89. They had three daughters, Geska Strebe Miller (deceased), Dorothy Ann Strebe Strozier, and Susan Strebe Porter (deceased).

Of his death in 1994, entertainer Phil Harris of nearby Palm Desert said, "He always had the theaters and he was always active in promoting Palm Springs. He did a lot for that town. He was a beautiful man."

SECTION 5

Desert Resort Comes of Age

Palm Springs became a city in 1938 and continued to grow in importance over the next few decades. The desert resort became a venue for movie makers; it harbored troops during WW II; and it welcomed more and more celebrities who came to stay and establish homes in the area.

It even influenced the architectural world with the sleek new style that would be called Palm Springs Modern.

Palm Springs leaders also culminated a dream by building a state-of-the-art tramway from the desert floor to the rugged mountaintop.

CHAPTER 27

Palm Springs Becomes a City

ORGANIZED IN 1938

What originally began as an agricultural community in 1887-1894 soon became better known for its restorative powers. The dry warm desert air did wonders for any number of respiratory ailments: tuberculosis, asthma, pneumonia, and various other bronchial conditions. Indeed many of those who established the town came to improve their condition or that of a family member.

While the health benefits of Palm Springs were still evident, by approximately 1915-1918 many in town felt their village had more to offer. A "sanatorium" appealed specifically to the ill. But a "desert resort" had much broader appeal. In an attempt to attract a more diverse guest list, for example, during those years Nellie Coffman had dropped the "and Sanatorium" from The Desert Inn's name.

People from all walks of life were converging on the fledgling community to experience the desert oasis first hand. For a while the town went through another transition, becoming an important artist colony, with famous artists, photographers, and writers settling and working here. Indeed, many still do.

By 1918, there were 40 Palm Springs residents on the voter registration rolls. Many of those were family members: for example, Otto and his wife Louisa Adler, six residents named Bunker, four Coffmans, two Lykkens, Oliver and Rose McKinney, and the White sisters.

With visitors attracted to Palm Springs and businesses booming, several of the leading citizens banded together in 1918 and formed the Palm Springs Board of Trade, a forerunner to the chamber of commerce.

Among those serving on that first board

Palm Canyon Drive in 1934. *Photo courtesy Palm Springs Historical Society.*

of trade were pioneer settlers whose stories are told in this book: Carl Lykken, Cornelia White, George Roberson, Oliver McKinney, P.T. Stevens, and Ed Bunker. Dr. J.J. Kocher was president.

By the time the board of trade was established, the village had just established direction as a resort destination, albeit one with lots of citrus trees and a climate that also was good for respiratory ailments. Just don't call it a sanatorium.

The Palm Springs Chamber of Commerce was actually around for years in some form before actual incorporation. In 1932 it was already called the chamber, and Frank "Pop" Shannon, the owner of a small apartment house, served as secretary-manager. Culver Nichols, son-in-law of P.T. Stevens, served several times as president, including the year it was incorporated, after Palm Springs officially became a city.

Becoming a city

While the board of trade and the chamber of commerce were of considerable help to business interests, more organization for the village as a whole was needed. By the mid 1930s many felt that Palm Springs might do better to incorporate, creating local services and gaining greater control over municipal matters like zoning and planning.

According to the book, *Palm Springs First Hundred Years* by former Mayor Frank M. Bogert, a 30-member committee headed by temporary chairman Frank Bennett was formed in November 1936 to study the possibility of incorporation. Among the village's prominent citizens serving on that committee were Ralph Bellamy, Phil Boyd, Earl Coffman, Alvah Hicks, Culver Nichols and Warren Pinney.

Harold Hicks was selected as permanent committee chairman and at a meeting on August 14, 1937, the committee established city boundaries, divided the city into seven wards and drew up the incorporation petition.

By 1938 there were 910 registered voters in Palm Springs and on election day, April 1, 1938, 442 voted for cityhood and 211 against. A councilman was elected for each ward: Phillip L. Boyd, Dr. Bacon Clifton, Alvah Hicks, Robert Murray, Austin G. McManus, Frank Shannon, and John W. Williams.

Phil Boyd was selected to serve Palm Springs as its first mayor. Boyd was a local banker who included Deep Well Ranch in his real estate holdings. Boyd became an influential member of the desert community, also serving as a California state assemblyman, a patron of the arts, and a regent of the University of California. As assemblyman, he labored long and hard for the Palm Springs Aerial Tramway.

Boyd and his wife Dorothy B. Marmon, of the Marmon Car Company in Indiana, were wed in 1926 at The Desert Inn. The Boyds later donated several thousand acres to the Living Desert and the U.C. Riverside Deep Canyon Research Project in Palm Desert.

Boyd was the first of a list of illustrious citizens who have served as mayor of Palm Springs. Until 1982 the mayor was selected from among the council members. Mayors were:

Name	Term Began	Term Ended
1. Phillip L. Boyd	April 18, 1938	April 21, 1942
2. Frank V. Shannon	April 21, 1942	April 18, 1944
3. Eugene E. Therieau	April 18, 1944	April 9, 1946
4. Clarence E. Hyde	April 9, 1946	April 20, 1948
5. Charles Farrell	April 20, 1948	July 31, 1953
6. Florian G. Boyd	July 31, 1953	Nov. 13, 1957
7. Gerald K. Sanborn	November 13, 1957	April 15, 1958
8. Frank M. Bogert	April 15, 1958	January 24, 1966
9. George Beebe Jr. (pro tem)	January 24, 1966	April 19, 1966
10. Edgar L. McCoubrey	April 19, 1966	April 24, 1967
11. Howard Wiefels	April 24, 1967	March 1974
12. William A. Foster	April 1974	March 1977
13. Russell J. Beirich	March 1977	April 1980
14. John F. Doyle	April 1980	April 1982
(First Elected Mayor —1982, 2 year term)		
15. Frank M. Bogert	April 1982	April 1984
16. Frank M. Bogert	April 1984	April 1988
(Term to four years beginning 1988)		
17. Sonny Bono	April 1988	April 1992
18. William Kleindienst	April 1992	November 2003
19. Ron Oden	November 2003	

The Palm Springs City Hall itself is a great example of Mid-century Modern architecture. Originally designed by noted architect Albert Frey in 1952, later additions were made by Robson Chambers and E. Stewart Williams. The logo at the entrance is the city's motto, which reflects the subservient goal of the city employees, "The People Are The City."

CHAPTER 28

Prominent Palm Springs Women
LEADERS IN YEARS OF GROWTH

While the first Palm Springs city council was comprised entirely of men, women were still very active in businesses, civic improvements, and even politics. In 1948, 10 years after incorporation, a woman was elected to serve on the city council.

Ruth Hardy

The first elected female Palm Springs City Council member, who served from 1948-1960, was Ruth Hardy, a businesswoman from Indiana, who became best known for developing the historic Ingleside Inn.

The inn was originally a two-acre estate built in the 1920s by Alvah Hicks for Carrie Birge, the widow of the manufacturer of the Pierce Arrow motorcar. Mrs. Birge made several buying trips to Europe to furnish the place. It was said that the value of the antiques was greater than the land and building combined.

After Carrie Birge left the United States for Paris, her son Humphrey and his wife Ethel took over the estate. Their daughter, Caroline, ended up marrying Harold Hicks, son of the contractor who built the estate and himself a prominent Palm Springs businessman.

In 1935 Ruth bought the old estate and turned it into an exclusive first class hotel, beginning by inviting special paying guests into her home. She retained much of the original elegant furnishings and antiques, including a bed allegedly slept in by Queen Isabella and a priceless bust of Petrarch's Laura. The rooms all had fireplaces and Hardy later added bungalows.

During Hardy's rein over the Ingleside, she hosted many famous guests: opera star Lily Pons had her own suite each season for 13 years before she bought her home. Industrial magnates and royalty joined the likes of Howard Hughes, J.C. Penney and others at the Ingleside. Greer Garson, Margaret O'Brien, Salvador Dali, Elizabeth Taylor, and Lowell Thomas were also guests.

Old-timers recall Hardy serving free champagne to her guests any days the sun didn't shine. She also was a tinkerer and once made a workable air conditioner out of odd parts.

The savvy hotelier Hardy was a fan of city pioneer Nellie Coffman, another native of Indiana. She respected the older innkeeper's ability and, allegedly "practically followed Nellie around to get ideas."

The famed Ingleside Inn continues to be a discreet getaway.

As an elected member of the Palm Springs City Council, Hardy held the post with distinction for 12 years. She is known as the person responsible for the $1 million planting and lighting of palm trees along Palm Canyon Drive, a decision that gave the young city much of its charm and character.

Ruth Hardy died in 1965 at the age of 73 and is interred in the Welwood Murray Cemetery. Ruth Hardy Park adjacent to the old Movie Colony area is named in her honor.

To this day, The Ingleside Inn is still one of the most exclusive hotels in Palm Springs. In 1975 Mel Haber bought the hotel and spent $500,000 in renovations and in adding the upscale Melvyn's restaurant.

The Ingleside has continued to attract the rich and famous, including actor/Governor Arnold Schwarzenegger, Donald Trump, Frank Sinatra and many, many more. It is now a historical site.

The Ingleside Inn has once been listed as one of the U.S. 10 best dream resorts on the Robin Leach TV show "Lifestyles of the Rich and Famous" and Melvyn's restaurant was named one of the world's 10 best restaurants by the same show.

Melba Berry Bennett

Melba Bennett distinguished herself not only as a prominent Palm Springs civic leader, but as a writer and author of some distinction. She is probably best known as the definitive biographer of the California poet Robinson Jeffers. That biography, *The Stone Mason of Tor House*, published in 1965, won the 1966 Silver Award from the Commonwealth Club of San Francisco.

All told, from 1932 to 1965 Bennett authored six books, two volumes of poems, and 19 heavily researched treatises about the Famous Libraries of Europe. She also penned the popular *Palm Springs Garden Book* (1957).

In Palm Springs, author Bennett was best known as owner and operator of a nationally famed resort and an untiring civic leader.

Mrs. Bennett was born in 1901 to a well-to-do long-time California family. Her father Henry Berry owned, along with some of California's finest trotting horses, the Los Angeles Angels and San Francisco Seals baseball teams of the Pacific Coast League.

Bennett was graduated from Stanford University in 1922 and had eloped with Frank Henry Bennett while in her junior year. After graduation, they went to Los Angeles where Frank was a realtor and they arrived in Palm Springs in the late 1920s. In 1932 they became part-owners, along with Phil Boyd, and managers of Deep Well Guest Ranch, a dude ranch on the south end of town (East Palm Canyon Drive), which they ran for 16 years.

During World War II, Melba Bennett became chairman of the Red Cross Nurses Aid program and chairman of the local USO. During the summer, she invited military guards and other night personnel who couldn't sleep during the day because of the extreme heat a place to cool off. The summer of 1942 was the hottest in many years, with temperatures hovering around 120 degrees for two months. She also made the swimming pool facilities available to servicemen.

By October 1942 the citizens of Palm Springs chipped in supplies and money to have a swimming pool constructed on the Army post.

Frank Bennett served in both wars, becoming a Captain in World War II. In the 1930s he was on the first citihood incorporation committee. Frank was the first president of the Desert Hospital Board and a board member of the Desert Museum. Both Frank and Melba were involved in many civic activities including chairing numerous social events.

Melba was one of the early organizers of the Desert Circus, an annual gala city-wide western-type celebration with parades, hoe-downs, and entertainment begun in 1934 to help raise money for the Agua Caliente Reservation. Melba was responsible for running the Desert Circus stage show, called the Village Insanities and Village Vanities.

She loved Palm Springs and was enthusiastic about helping it develop. Founder (1955) and president of the Palm Springs Historical Society, she was active on the board of directors of the Palm Springs Desert Museum, the Palm Springs Unified School District board, the Welwood Murray Memorial Library Board of Directors, the Child Development Center, which she helped found, the garden club, and the Desert Riders, along with various other involvements.

The Bennetts, as hosts of one of the city's few stables, were both instrumental in the Desert Riders, a large group of Palm Springs cowboys and friends who liked to spend weekends on the nearby desert trails. Founded in 1930, the Desert Riders is the oldest club in Palm Springs and counted many of the early pioneers and settlers as members. Charter members, both Melba and her husband Frank served as president of the Desert Riders.

Melba Bennett's library was donated to the Desert Museum after her death in 1968. Frank, who was born in 1898, died in 1973. Both were interred in the Welwood Murray Cemetery in downtown Palm Springs.

Patricia Moorten

Patricia Moorten made her place in the desert by becoming so firmly attached to it, that when Palm Springs locals thought of cacti, succulents, and other desert plants, they automatically thought of Pat Moorten, owner and founder (with her husband Slim), of Moorten Botanical Gardens on South Palm Canyon Drive.

The Moortens not only provided the desert landscaping for many of Palm Springs' rich and famous homeowners, but were responsible for landscaping the route of the Palm Springs Aerial Tramway. During the 1950s, they were also called upon to create a desert setting for a new amusement park in Orange County that would be known the world over as Disneyland.

The Moortens were the right people for Walt Disney to hire for the job. Pat Moorten had become a can-do woman in Palm Springs who knew what she wanted. According to "The Patricia Moorten Story" by Christopher Griffin in *Profile Weekly Magazine*, "I knew what I wanted to do from the time I was quite young," Patricia Moorten says, "As a young girl I had built a very fascinating garden in Ohio, but I maintained that someday I would build a botanical garden of desert plants."

The fact that Ohio is virtually quite barren of desert flora didn't stop Patricia. She just waited until she was 17 years old and hopped on a train that brought her "out west" in 1937.

She settled in Los Angeles to study botany and horticulture at both USC and UCLA, making frequent forays out into the deserts. She once told *The Desert Sun*, "For me, the desert plants were the greatest challenge; they're the highest form of plant life on earth."

In a day when few women were accepted in the professional world, Patricia became a research botanist. While working at a botanical garden in Santa Monica she met Chester "Cactus Slim" Moorten, a desert landscaping contractor and designer. Patricia knew about Slim and his work with desert plants and arranged to be introduced on his next visit. Their passion for deserts brought them together and they married in 1940.

Slim was a real western character, a former orphan from the Pacific Northwest who, as a young man, lived by trapping, hunting, and fishing. Then in 1927 he went to Hollywood. He was tall, very thin, and had an ability to force his body into all sorts of weird contortions. He was hired on the spot by Mack Sennett Studios where he became one of the original

Keystone Kops. He worked in numerous silent movies and early talkies, but his poor diet, lean frame, and long hours did not help the tuberculosis which he had contracted and he was given three months to live.

Slim immediately moved to the desert and started mining gold in what is now Joshua Tree National Park. Moorten's Mill site is still an attraction there, a short walk from a parking lot. His health improved and he settled in Palm Springs where he began selling plants in 1938. In fact, Slim lived until 1980.

As more and more celebrities established homes in Palm Springs, the Moortens were called upon to create landscaping, including clients Frank Sinatra, Bing Crosby, Red Skelton, Lily Pons and Walt Disney, with whom they developed a close association. In addition to all their work at Disneyland, they were consultants for Disney's *The Living Desert* movie.

In 1957 they established Moorten Botanical Garden in Palm Springs. Called Desertland, Moorten has over 3,000 varieties of desert plants and the world's first "Cactarium." The nature trail passes cacti and plants from all the American deserts. Several TV shows have been shot on the grounds and the lawn of the Moorten home is used regularly for weddings and special events.

The Moorten home itself is a historical landmark, built in 1929 by the Willard family who settled in Palm Springs in 1913. Nature photographer Stephen Willard, wife Beatrice, and daughter Dr. Betty Willard, lived in the home until 1947.

Patricia developed an international reputation for her work. She wrote the highly regarded *Desert Plants for Desert Gardens* and, with her husband, traveled the world giving presentations and designing landscaping. For example, they were invited by Hilton Hotels to do the Hilton grounds in Cairo, Egypt.

Pat Moorten was on the first tram car to ascend Mt. San Jacinto on July 23, 1963, becoming the first woman to ride the famous tram.

Palm Springs pioneer Pearl McManus was a friend of Patricia's and liked to walk around Desertland. When she heard that Walt Disney had hired the Moortens to plant cactus gardens in Frontierland, she accompanied them to see the new plantings in place. Patricia later indicated she felt that "Auntie Pearl" used that as an excuse to see the new Magic Kingdom.

According to son Clark, 61, who now runs Moorten

Moorten Botanical Garden on South Palm Canyon is a favorite wedding locale.

Botanical Gardens, "My mom is a walking encyclopedia about Palm Springs." Now 84, she still greets visitors in her lovely desert garden setting. She and Slim both were honored with stars on the "Walk of Stars."

Elizabeth Coffman Kieley

The second non-Indian girl born in Palm Springs (after Barbara McKinney) was Elizabeth Coffman Kieley, daughter of Earl and Helen Coffman and granddaughter of Dr. Harry L. and Nellie N. Coffman, founders of The Desert Inn.

In 1941 Elizabeth married F. Thomas Kieley Jr. who also became a prominent Palm Springs citizen who has served on many boards, clubs and charities, but Elizabeth has made her own mark on Palm Springs.

She is a pioneer member of the Palm Springs Historical Society, which has been in operation since 1955. On the board of directors for 38 years, she has served that organization as chairman for a whopping 35 years.

Elizabeth stepped down from her historical society duties in November 2003. In a goodbye message printed in the society's newsletter *Whispering Palms*, she modestly noted, "With your help, the Society has achieved most of the goals set by our founder Melba Berry Bennett in 1955....Under Steve Nichols, our capable new chairman's direction, we shall continue to grow and provide preservation and service to our community."

Elizabeth Kieley served on the Palm Springs Library Board for six years and has been a member of the Palm Springs Desert Museum for 30 years.

She was instrumental in establishing the Village Green on South Palm Canyon Drive and the preservation of both the Cornelia White House as well as the original McCallum adobe.

Named "Historian of the Year, 1987" she has a star on the Palm Springs Walk of Stars. She has four children and eight grandchildren.

Katherine Siva Sauvel

While most of the biographies in this book are the Anglo settlers of Palm Springs, several Cahuilla women made a major impact on the development and growth of the people of the area. One of those is Katherine Siva Sauvel.

The respected tribal elder was born in 1920 on the Los Coyotes Reservation. With her father, Juan C. Siva, as her inspiration, she set out to achieve at an early age. Upset that speaking Cahuillan was forbidden at the authorized government school, he entered her in Palm Springs Elementary

School at age eight, the only Indian in attendance. She later became the first Indian to graduate from Palm Springs High School.

Sauvel has spent a lifetime preserving the Cahuilla customs and traditions and is noted for helping explain those traditions to non-Indians. A political leader as well, she has served as a member of the Los Coyotes Tribal Council and as its chairperson.

She also has served on the Native American Heritage Commission and the Riverside County Historical Commission, which honored her as Historian of the Year for 1987. That year she was also named the State Indian Museum's Elder of the Year.

With noted Indian researcher and author Lowell John Bean, in 1972 Sauvel co-authored *Temalpakh: Cahuilla Indian Knowledge and Usage of Plants*, a "highly readable volume and the foremost work of its kind currently available" according to the book *People of Magic Waters* by John R. Brumgart and Larry L. Bowles.

She has co-authored other scholarly books, co-founded and has served as long-time president of the Malki Museum, and has also translated Cahuilla oral literature into English on National Public Radio.

In 1993 she was inducted into the national Women's Hall of Fame and the following year the National Museum of the American Indian of the Smithsonian Institution presented her with the first Art and Cultural Achievement Award for her lifelong commitment to the preservation and advancement of the native community and culture.

At a 2002 symposium of the Coachella Valley Archaeological Society held at the Palm Springs Desert Museum, then 82 year-old Sauvel talked about the receding native Cahuilla language and culture. After listing only a handful of Cahuilla speakers still fluent, she advocated that elders increase their efforts to teach young people on the reservation.

In 2003 La Sierra University awarded Sauvel an honorary Doctor of Humane Letters in recognition for her lifetime of work to preserve Native American languages and culture.

A leader like Sauvel deserves a rightful place among those Palm Springs denizens who have "made a difference," having been recognized by proclamations from not only Riverside County, but the California State Senate and California State Assembly as well.

On the 40th anniversary of the founding of the Malki Museum in 2004, the Malki Museum Press published a two-volume work on the life of Dr. Sauvel entitled '*Isill Héqwas Wáxish: A Dried Coyote's Tail*. Today she lives on the Morongo Reservation, the home of her late husband Mariano.

CHAPTER 29

Frank Bogert, Cowboy/Mayor
THE COWBOY BEHIND THE CITY

This oldster looks incongruous in Palm Springs today among tourists and snowbirds who are bedecked in t-shirts, shorts, and sandals. He looks like the quintessential aged cowboy, craggy countenance, loping stride, 10-gallon hat, boots, bolo tie, and thick belt buckle. But unlike the rhinestone cowboys and western dancehall wannabe's, this 95-year-old cowboy is the real thing—and so versatile his leadership was instrumental in shaping the world-renowned resort of Palm Springs.

Being a cowboy is part of his Colorado heritage he never shed, but Frank M. Bogert has been much more than a cowboy. He did more for the city of Palm Springs over the past three-quarters of a century than any man, or woman, or three men together, might have.

And his interests and abilities have seen Bogert cram a lot into his years. He's been a rancher, an actor, a naval officer in World War II, a resort hotel manager, publicist, accomplished photographer, author, publisher, real estate agent and developer, and politician who has led the city of Palm Springs for decades. He was mayor twice (1958-1966 and 1982-1988), and has greeted, dined with, rode with, and befriended more celebrities, royalty and presidents than one can imagine.

Born the youngest of eight children in 1910, this independent son of a Mesa, Colorado, cattle rancher came to Palm Springs in 1927 and in addition to riding the local trails, went to UCLA, and got a job with RKO as a cowboy actor and stunt man, eventually appearing in 26 westerns, including John Wayne's first film, *On the Trail*.

Former Palm Springs mayor Frank Bogert and author Greg Niemann.

Almost an icon

The head of Paramount was all set to sign Bogert up in the starring role of Hopalong Cassidy. However, in the final interview, the mogul learned that Bogert ran a string of horses at Lake Arrowhead. As his young daughter had previously fallen off of a horse at Lake Arrowhead, the producer felt Bogert might have been responsible and called off the deal, casting Bill Boyd as "Hoppy" instead, thus granting Boyd the accompanying unprecedented fame with a generation of youngsters.

Hoppy's prominence created the movie star memorabilia mania, spawning over 2,000 products bearing his image. Boyd, by the way, lived in nearby Palm Desert for two decades before his 1972 death. The city commemorated him in January 2004 with a Hopalong Cassidy Day and named a trail in his honor. Bogert, who counted Bill Boyd as a friend and had also ridden the local trails with him, was in attendance.

In Palm Springs, Bogert worked at the Tennis Club, becoming a close and lifelong friend with village pioneer and owner Pearl McManus.

Bogert was a publicist and photographer for the El Mirador Hotel and extolled the merits of Palm Springs through articles, public speeches and photos. His lens captured the reigning celebrities of the time, including: Mary Astor, Amos 'n' Andy, Edgar Bergen, Claudette Colbert, Jackie Cooper—with whom he also went riding—Bing Crosby, Marlene Dietrich, Walt Disney, Dorothy Lamour, the Ritz Brothers, Robert Taylor, Shirley Temple, Rudy Vallee, and Jane Wyman.

Former California Governor Edmond G."Pat" Brown, former Palm Springs mayor Frank Bogert, and cowboy singer Gene Autry.

Ralph Bellamy and Charlie Farrell hired Bogert in the mid-1930s to be general manager of the Racquet Club, a job he performed with resolve and flair. Once, while effectively squelching a row caused by a mobster's bodyguard, Bogert was summarily placed on a "hit list." A message arrived saying Bogert should be out of town by nightfall or he would be killed. "I was worried sick for Frank...but he was not frightened at all," admitted Bellamy in *The History of the Racquet Club of Palm Springs* by Sally Presley Rippingale. Bogert wasn't cowed, did not leave town and, fortunately for him and Palm Springs, nothing ever happened.

Bogert served with distinction in the U.S. Navy during World War II, seeing plenty of action in the South Pacific, including Guadalcanal and Iwo Jima, and rising to the rank of Lieutenant Commander.

Bogert developed Thunderbird

In 1946, Bogert bought a section of land from Raymond Cree for $34,000 that he developed into the Thunderbird Dude Ranch. It later became the site of the Thunderbird Country Club, and Bogert became general manager. Early homeowners/members there included Lucille Ball and Desi Arnaz, industrialist Leonard Firestone, Bob Hope, Bing Crosby, Mary Pickford, Dean Martin, and Jerry Lewis. Bogert's kids grew up playing with many famous offspring, and Bogert and Lucy Ball grew so fond of each other they described their relationship as brother/sister.

Bogert went on to manage the El Mirador and then, in 1957, Desi Arnaz built a hotel at the new Indian Wells Country Club down the road and hired Bogert to manage it for a while.

In Palm Springs, Bogert was the first manager of the Palm Springs Chamber of Commerce. He also served on the first Tramway Authority, and under his time as mayor, the city acquired the Palm Springs Airport and developed city hall and the police department. He was responsible for the creation of the Airport Fountain, dedicated to honor the many contributions of Pearl McManus.

As mayor, Palm Springs official, and friend of many celebrities the world over, Bogert has been photographed greeting and cavorting with many luminaries, including: Mary Pickford, Clara Bow, Ginger Rogers, Dinah Shore, Rita Hayworth, both Prince Phillip and Prince Charles, other foreign dignitaries and U.S. Presidents Kennedy (1962), Truman (1953), Nixon (1962), Johnson (1964) and those presidents who have helped popularize Palm Springs: Eisenhower, Ford, and Reagan. He often rode horses with President Reagan and went bowling with Clark Gable. He's met more celebrities than any dozen Hollywood gossip columnists have; the pesky paparazzi would have done well to follow him around.

President Kennedy visits Palm Springs. *Photo courtesy Palm Springs Historical Society.*

In the 1970s Bogert became a real estate partner of Muriel Fulton, forming Fulton and Bogert. Fulton had been practicing real estate in Palm Springs since 1933, and she was a past president of the board of realtors.

Bogert published the *Palm Springs Villager*, the forerunner to *Palm Springs Life*, the definitive magazine of the Coachella Valley.

He lived the history

In 1987 as Palm Springs' most well-known and admired citizen, Bogert wrote *Palm Springs:First Hundred Years*, a 288-page coffee table book published by Palm Springs Heritage Associates. With many photographs of the Cahuilla, early pioneers, and leaders, it is obvious that Bogert has "lived the history" more than any single person.

The book became so scarce that the Palm Springs Public Library with assistance from the Palm Springs Historical Society revised and updated the historic book. Released in March 2003 with a presentation and formal signing, the library was packed to meet the straight-talking and non-pretentious Mayor Bogert.

Seeing the ocean of well wishers, Bogert quipped, "Hell, there were only 10 people at my first book signing, and all they wanted to do was see if their picture was in the book."

The laconic wit then introduced several other Palm Springs pioneers and thanked those who made the new edition possible, especially then city librarian Margaret Roades and Sally McManus, director/curator of the Palm Springs Historical Society.

His dry call-it-as-he-sees-it humor was still delighting Palm Springs residents in February 2005, when he did a brief stand-up tribute to the city at the 50th anniversary of the Palm Springs Historical Society.

Bob Hope's tribute

In a preface to Bogert's book, Bob Hope wrote in 1987, "I've been going to Palm Springs off and on for the past fifty years and every time I looked up Frank Bogert was mayor again. And I've never missed seeing him around there—even during the days of the 'Chi Chi' and 'The Desert Inn.' He was always doing something for the community and he's never stopped."

Among Bogert's contributions, he has served on the President's Commission on American Outdoors, on the California State Board of Tourism and the California State Trails Commission. He's been director of the Palm

Springs Water Agency, the Riverside Board of Equalization, and the Riverside County Flood Control. He's been president of the Desert Circus, the Palm Springs Desert Museum, and the Palm Springs Rodeo Association.

A well-decorated cowboy and noted professional rodeo announcer, the bi-lingual Bogert was honored by the Mexican Charro Association with their top award, the Golden Spur. He rides with the prestigious Rancheros Vistadores, an elite group that included President Ronald Reagan. He is past president of the Desert Riders, numerous equestrian organizations, and is still president of the Desert Trails Coalition.

Bogert was married to Janice Bibo, daughter of early pioneer Ruth Bibo, who ran the Acoma Indian Gift Shop. He has three daughters: Cindy Lamm, Donna Higueras and Denni Russell. Donna and her husband José Higueras, a world class tennis player from Spain, have two children, Jordi and Jenna.

Bogert's current wife Negie has been by his side in recent decades, including a 1984 visit to the Reagan White House. Bogert, in introducing Negie at the Palm Springs Library signing, said, "I imported her from Mexico, and I'm going to keep her."

A full-size bronze statue of Bogert, Palm Springs' most famous

Frank Bogert's daughter Denni helps him sign books.

cowboy, astride a galloping horse, is in front of the Palm Springs City Hall. A likeness of the statue graces Bogert stationary.

The people of Palm Springs were better served by the man who could have been immortalized as "Hoppy."

CHAPTER 30

Celebrities Create Desert Homes
THE MOVIE COLONY/OLD LAS PALMAS

Hollywood celebrities have been flocking to Palm Springs for R&R ever since the village first began to grow. Early on, many stayed at The Desert Inn; then the El Mirador also began to "pack 'em in." By the time Charlie Farrell and Ralph Bellamy opened the Racquet Club in the early thirties, Palm Springs, only 100 miles from Hollywood, became an easy and comfortable place to unwind and relax among their own.

The "tonic" that was Palm Springs was so effective that many stars decided to forsake the hotels and have their own homes in the desert oasis, albeit in most cases a second, or seasonal home.

There seems to have always been celebrities living in town, or in one of the neighboring communities like Rancho Mirage and Palm Desert. Even today, entertainers Suzanne Somers and Barry Manilow and author Sidney Sheldon are among the many recognizable names who are Palm Springs residents.

While most celebrities merely maintained seasonal homes for relaxation and social events, others became more a part of Palm Springs. For some important residents, the mere power and status of their names lent a favorable impact on the area. Stars like Bob Hope, Frank Sinatra, Dinah Shore, Donald O'Conner, Kirk Douglas, William Powell, and William Holden created enormous good will with their continued presence.

Others invested in businesses in the area; for example actor Alan Ladd (Shane) owned the Alan Ladd Hardware at South Palm Canyon Drive and Ramon Road as well as the Spanish Inn on North Indian Canyon Drive.

And at different times cowboy Gene Autry and TV producer Merv Griffin were both the owners of the former Givenchy Spa Hotel in town, now The Parker Meridien. Then singer Sonny Bono, who owned a restaurant on North Indian Canyon Drive, became mayor.

Gathering steam in the 1930s, celebrities sought restful enclaves for their "homes away from home." Accommodating them in that decade were builders and developers like Alvah Hicks and P.T. Stevens who subdivided properties and constructed exclusive hideaways for the "rich and famous."

As Palm Springs was small and the neighboring communities not developed yet, many of these old estates were built near downtown Palm Springs, either in Old Las Palmas, west of Palm Canyon Drive, sheltered by the mountains, or in what became known as the Movie Colony, east of Indian Canyon Drive and north of Alejo Road. South of Alejo Road, and to the east was Section 14, land belonging to the Agua Caliente Indians.

Old Las Palmas

Old Las Palmas, as defined by Palm Springs realtors today, comprises approximately 275 properties west of Palm Canyon Drive, north of Alejo Road, east of Via Monte Vista and south of Stevens Road. The area south of Via Lola has also been known as Merito Vista.

Today Celebrity Tours runs a regular route through the area on air-conditioned busses. The following are some homes pointed out, even though many of those under 60 years of age might never have heard of some of the former celebrities:

From the south, at the northwest corner of Belardo Road (501 Belardo) is the Casa de Liberace, 20-year home of former flashy pianist Liberace. Wladziu Valentino (Lee) Liberace bought the old Cloisters Inn in 1967 and renovated it in his particular flamboyant style. He died there in 1987, and the property has new owners, but a signature candelabra and the sign "Casa de Liberace" still grace the entrance today.

The next corner (222 Chino Drive) was the former residence of Clark Gable. At the end of Chino Drive, actor George Hamilton's signature in wet cement can still be seen in his driveway at 591 Patencio Road. Mary Pickford and Buddy Rogers reputedly lived at 701 Patencio.

Across the street (481 Merito Place) was the home built by Hoot Gibson and later owned by opera star Mario Lanza. Songstress Lena Horne lived at 465 Merito Place, and comedienne Lily Tomlin sold the home her mother had been living in at 443 Merito Place in 2003—the

The former home of flamboyant pianist Liberace is across from the O'Donnell Golf Course on Alejo Road.

new owners named the house the "Lilly Pad" in her honor. Also on Merito Place were Lawrence Harvey (300), and Rod Taylor (271).

Around the corner on Mission Road was the home of drummer Buddy Rich (775) and the former home of Spencer Tracy and Katharine Hepburn (776). Las Vegas hotel owner and MGM head Kirk Kerkorian owned the home at 735 Prescott Drive.

The final home of cowboy singer Gene Autry was at 328 West Mountain View Place. His widow Jackie Autry still owns it.

George Hamilton scribbled his name in wet cement in front of his Patencio Road home.

At 432 West Hermosa Place, Dinah Shore's second desert home changed hands again during 2003. Elizabeth Taylor used to stay across the street at 417 Hermosa Place. Universal Studios/MCA chief Lew Wasserman owned the home that used to be 295 Hermosa Place. It was razed after his 2002 death. Producer Samuel Goldwyn retired to 334 Hermosa Place, a property he had earlier rented. The nearby movie mogul Sam Warner's estate at 1050 Cahuilla Road also fronts Via Lola.

Writer Sidney Sheldon still lives at 425 Via Lola, and owns other homes in the area. Kirk and Anne Douglas sold their home at 515 Via Lola in 2001 to be closer to family in Santa Barbara. Former Arkansas Governor Winthrop Rockefeller lived at 467 Via Lola during the 1960s. Eddie Foy of the vaudeville troupe lived at 350 Via Lola.

Popular novelist Harold Robbins had his home at 601 Camino Sur modified for the wheelchair he was confined to following a 1980 stroke. He wrote several books from the wheelchair. Among his earlier homes was one around the corner at 990 North Patencio Road.

Tony Martin and Cyd Charisse lived at 697 Camino Sur. Sultry actress Kim Novak rented the home at 740 Camino Sur in the 1960s. George Nader lived at 893 Camino Sur.

Peter Lawford owned the home at 1295 Via Monte Vista, and Dean Martin bought the one at 1123 Via Monte Vista. Crooner Rudy Vallee lived at 484 West Vereda Norte and mega-star of the thirties William Powell and his wife "Mousie" bought the home at 383 West Vereda Norte in 1941; Mousie lived in it until her 1997 death.

Elvis and Priscilla Presley honeymooned at 1350 Ladera Circle in 1967 before they bought their Little Tuscany home. Trini Lopez lived full-time at 1139 Abrigo Road. Debbie Reynolds used to live at 670 Stevens Road, producer Howard Hawks lived at 501 Stevens Road, and actress Carolyn Jones lived at 368 Stevens Road.

The former Donald O'Conner home is at 700 Via Las Palmas, and 1950s actor Alan Ladd with his wife Sue owned the home at 323 West Camino Del Norte. The star of 150 movies, Ladd died in that home in 1964. Also on West Camino Del Norte were homes of Howard Hughes (335) and Mary Martin (365). Famous ventriloquist Edgar Bergen lived at 1575 North Via Norte.

Little Tuscany

Just to the north of Las Palmas is the area known as Little Tuscany, approximately 210 properties west of Palm Canyon Drive all the way to the mountains.

At the corner of Kaweah Road and Stevens Road (1441 Kaweah Road) was the guest house owned by Liberace and often used by his brother George. Jack Benny owned the home at 424 West Vista Chino, while on the next street Zsa Zsa Gabor reputedly owned the home at 595 West Chino Canyon Road.

Farther up the canyon, 845 West Chino Canyon Drive was a house owned by Elvis and Priscilla Presley. In addition to Graceland, it was the only other home owned by the "King" at his death.

Also in Little Tuscany lived composer Frederick Lowe (815 Panorama Road), George Randolph Hearst (701 Panorama Road), designer Raymond Loewy (600 Panorama Road), and Zsa Zsa's sister Magda Gabor (1090 Cielo Drive).

The Elvis Presley home on Chino Canyon in Palm Springs was the only home Presley owned besides Graceland.

The Movie Colony

While old timers refer to the area as "behind El Mirador," a realtor coined the phrase "Movie Colony" as many old time stars had elected to own homes in the area east of the El Mirador Hotel. Eddie Cantor lived at 720 Paseo El Mirador, across the street from the old hotel. Band leader Lawrence Welk lived at 730 Paseo El Mirador until the late 1970s. Writer Truman Capote owned the home at 853 Paseo El Mirador. Songstress Keely Smith, former wife of Louie Prima, still lives at 1055 El Mirador.

Former Mayor Charlie Farrell lived out his years at 630 Tachevah Road at the corner of Via Miraleste. Billionaire Howard Hughes and second wife Jean Peters lived at 1451 North Paseo de Anza in 1957. Hughes then moved to a small nondescript home at 1185 Pasatiempo Road to hide out from the press and conduct his mega-deals.

Bob Hope, whose futuristic Southridge home is a valley landmark, also owned homes in the Movie Colony, one which he bought in 1941 at 1014 Buena Vista Drive, and another at 1188 El Alameda Drive. The Hopes raised their family at the El Alameda home. Nearby were Hedy Lamarr (1232 El Alameda Drive), and Bing Crosby (1011 El Alameda Drive).

Woolworth heiress Barbara Hutton and husband Cary Grant lived at 796 Via Miraleste, and producer Darryl Zanuck was known for hosting great parties at 346 Tamarisk Road. Frank Sinatra's first desert home was at 1148 East Alejo Road—it now it faces Colusa. Tony Curtis and Janet Leigh lived at

Palm Springs looking east, with the downtown area on the far right. Area in foreground (below dark horizontal line which is Palm Canyon Drive) is Old Las Palmas/Merito Vista. *Photo from the early 1940s.*

641 North Camino Real and another of Jack Benny's homes was at the end of Avenida Palos Verdes (987).

Dinah Shore and husband George Montgomery built the home at 877 North Avenida Palos Verdes in 1952. Cary Grant and his second wife lived nearby at 928 Avenida Las Palmas. Al Jolson lived at 570 Via Corta.

These are just a few of those who have called Palm Springs home over the years. Many other celebrities, some well known and others whose stars have waned with the times, have made Palm Springs a home-away-from-home. Some have settled in the Tennis Club area a little farther to the south, or in the Mesa area off of South Palm Canyon Drive.

Actor Steve McQueen and Ali MacGraw lived at 2203 Southridge Drive, just below Bob Hope's large house. Actor William Holden lived in the Deep Well area at 1323 South Driftwood Drive.

Sonny Bono lived in the Mesa area (294 Crestview Drive), and current Mesa residents include actress Suzanne Somers (385 Alta Vista Road), and singer Barry Manilow (2196 South Camino Barranca). Manilow also owned homes in the Las Palmas area.

Palm Springs continues to attract the celebrities. Television personality Huell Howser, who has done a series of shows on Palm Springs, moved to town permanently in 2003 and is often seen talking to visitors along Palm Canyon Drive.

Some celebrities have bought homes in nearby communities like Rancho Mirage, Palm Desert, and La Quinta. Then there are many other celebrities who just continue to come to the desert resort for a little R&R, staying at secluded hideaways like the Korakia Pensione, the Ingleside Inn, or the La Mancha at Avenida Caballeros and Alejo Road.

CHAPTER 31

Big Names Bring World Attention
HOPE/SINATRA/SHORE

Of all the celebrities who played in Palm Springs and established residence in the desert oasis, only a handful were responsible for the tremendous impact on making the name "Palm Springs" known around the world.

Presidents Dwight D. Eisenhower, Gerald Ford, and Ambassador Walter Annenberg certainly qualified, and President Ford still lives in Rancho Mirage. His wife helped establish the Betty Ford Clinic.

Among the Hollywood people, three big names stand out even among other mega-stars for their continuous contributions to Palm Springs and the surrounding desert areas: Bob Hope, Frank Sinatra, and Dinah Shore.

Bob Hope

When Bob Hope passed away in 2003 at age 100, after almost a century of entertaining the world, numerous mourners placed floral wreaths atop the star on Palm Canyon Drive that bears his name.

Bob Hope was more than an entertainer, he was an institution, bringing joy and laughter to millions, yet his favorite place of all was Palm Springs.

Palm Springs' first and foremost honorary mayor, Hope first visited Palm Springs in 1937 and bought his original home at 1014 Buena Vista in the Movie Colony in 1941. He also owned another home nearby, at 1188 El Alameda. He still owned both at his death in July 2003. He often used the El Alameda home rather than staying at his formal residence, the futuristic Southridge home that has become a valley landmark.

The huge building shaped like Darth Vader's helmet resting on a Southridge hill at the south end of town is the landmark most residents and visitors recognize as the "Bob Hope house." Also described as a Flying Saucer, the huge home is 28,000 square feet and was primarily used for entertaining. The home features a par 3 fairway and golf green. The actual house you see was not the original as it was burned to a skeleton frame in July 1973 and totally rebuilt.

His annual Palm Springs Bob Hope Golf Classic begun in 1964 has become one of the major draws to the Coachella Valley. It is perhaps the desert's largest fund-raiser, dispensing millions of dollars over the years to over 130 non-profit organizations. The Bob Hope Classic Ball is one of the premiere social events of the year.

Hope donated 80 acres of land in 1966 (worth over a half million dollars at the time) to develop the Eisenhower Medical Center on what is now Bob Hope Drive in Rancho Mirage. In addition, his golf tourney through the years has provided millions of dollars for the Eisenhower Medical Center.

Bob Hope's name will be passed on to future valley generations with the Bob Hope Cultural Center (theater) in Palm Desert and the fact that Bob Hope Drive is one of the Coachella Valley's main thoroughfares.

The comedian loved the desert. Hope even spoke to a graduating class of Palm Springs High School who presented him with an honorary diploma. This man, who has 54 honorary doctorate degrees, a Peabody Award, the Special Oscar, an Emmy, and the Congressional Gold Medal, among other honors, told the delighted young audience that he really cherished the honor.

He's even showed up unannounced at the Plaza Theatre to throw a few one-liners to a surprised Fabulous Palm Springs Follies audience. He loved to walk and even in his 80's was spotted walking down Palm Canyon Drive.

While his primary residence was in Toluca Lake where he passed away, his love of Palm Springs helped make the desert oasis a household word.

Frank Sinatra

In the waning days of their marriage, Frank and Nancy Sinatra designed a $150,000 air-conditioned home at 1148 East Alejo Drive in Palm Springs. They signed the papers in late October 1948 and an impatient Sinatra paid triple costs to have it completed for a New Year's party. The modern 4,000 square-foot home, called "Twin Palms" was designed by noted architect Stewart Williams, featuring lots of glass walls and high ceilings.

Frank kept the Palm Springs house after the divorce settlement, along with a 1949 Cadillac convertible and his musical compositions. Years later, a new owner of the house was doing some renovating and, so the story goes, found some of Sinatra's original work.

That Palm Springs home has been sold several times since, in 1997 for $1.1 million, in 2004 for $2.05 million, and to a Newport Beach designer in March 2005 for $2.6 million.

Sinatra was married to Ava Gardner, whom he allegedly met at the Chi Chi in Palm Springs and divorced a few years later in 1956. Throughout the

1950s Sinatra entertained often and long at his Palm Springs house.

He later built a large compound on what was originally called Wonder Palms Road in nearby Rancho Mirage. Later the road name was changed to recognize the star. The Sinatra compound's address is now 70588 Frank Sinatra Drive in Rancho Mirage.

He campaigned hard for his friend John F. Kennedy in 1960 and immediately after the election beefed up the security in the compound, added a large guest house with a dining room capable of seating 40, and added a heliport anticipating Kennedy turning the Sinatra compound into the Western White House. But because of Sinatra's ties with organized crime, Kennedy prudently chose to stay at Bing Crosby's desert estate instead, forever irritating Sinatra.

In 1976 Frank married Barbara Marx, who formerly was wed to Zeppo Marx, one of the famed Marx Brothers.

After his father's death in 1969, Frank Sinatra raised $805,000 to endow the Martin Anthony Sinatra Medical Education Center adjoining Desert Medical Center, the old El Mirador, in Palm Springs.

During 1980, Sinatra campaigned for friend Ronald Reagan, who named him chairman of his inauguration gala. That year he raised another $1.3 million for the Desert Medical Center, for which the grateful U.S. Representative Jerry Lewis addressed Congress naming Frank "America's number one entertainer and philanthropist."

Frank and Barbara Sinatra continued to spread their wealth around to Palm Springs benefactors, the Desert Medical Center being one of them. Barbara Sinatra has the Children's Center at Eisenhower Medical Center named after her. Among numerous honors, the one Frank cherished most was the Presidential Medal of Freedom presented by President Reagan at the White House in 1985. Frank died in 2001 and Barbara continues to be a major benefactor in the Palm Springs area.

Dinah Shore

Dinah Shore, by hosting what evolved into the premiere women's golfing event, immediately gave status, credibility and prominence to the LPGA. Born in Tennessee, the popular singer, entertainer, and TV variety show hostess, back in 1972 kicked off the Dinah Shore Classic, originally known as the Colgate Dinah Shore Winners Circle. It became the Dinah Shore Nabisco LPGA Championship Tournament in 1982.

Today called the Kraft Nabisco Championship and in its 33rd year, it still attracts the top LPGA competitors, including three-time winner and Hall of Famer Annika Sorenstam.

Dinah and husband George Montgomery built their first Palm Springs home in 1952 in the Movie Colony area at 877 Avenida Palos Verdes. Then they moved to the estate at 432 Hermosa in Old Las Palmas. That home sold during 2003 for approximately $3 million only to undergo extensive remodeling. Once the Dinah Shore Classic was up and running, Dinah had moved to Mission Hills Country Club, the site of the tourney.

Dinah Shore passed away in 1994. Dinah Shore Drive, named in her honor, a major east-west thoroughfare between Palm Springs and Palm Desert, even includes a Dinah Shore Bridge over the Whitewater riverbed.

Her husband, the former actor George Montgomery, was an accomplished artist and sculptor, and there is a room full of his art in the Palm Springs Desert Museum.

Both Dinah and George have been honored with stars on the Palm Canyon Walk of Stars. The Dinah Shore Classic continues to be a major Palm Springs event and attracts many people to town in a party atmosphere.

Streets named for desert icons

The Coachella Valley has a few other streets and thoroughfares named for entertainers and celebrities. There's Gerald Ford Drive in Rancho Mirage, Fred Waring Drive in Palm Desert, Buddy Rogers Drive in Cathedral City, Ginger Rogers Road in Rancho Mirage, and Gene Autry Trail in Palm Springs.

Actor Kirk Douglas, who lived in Palm Springs for 50 years, was once offered to have a street named after him in Rancho Mirage. According to an article in *The Desert Sun*, his son Joel Douglas, who still lives in Palm Springs, said his dad declined, saying, "No, I live in Palm Springs. Palm Springs is my home."

The legendary actor was finally recognized by Palm Springs when the city changed the name of Airport Road to Kirk Douglas Way. A dedication ceremony, with numerous celebrities in attendance, was held on October 17, 2004 at the newly named road near the Palm Springs Airport.

Hollywood legends Dinah Shore and Kirk Douglas, both long-time Palm Springs residents, share a light moment on the dance floor. *Photo courtesy Palm Springs Historical Society.*

CHAPTER 32

The Palm Springs "Studio"
MOVIES MADE IN THE DESERT

Not only did the "stars" of movies discover Palm Springs, but so did the producers and moviemakers. Since 1915, numerous movies, television shows, commercials, and videos have been filmed in the desert oasis with the dramatic mountain backdrop.

That first movie filmed in Palm Springs in 1915 was *Lone Star Rush* and was directed by early Palm Springs homeowner Edmund Mitchell. The cast and crew were hosted by Nellie Coffman at The Desert Inn.

Later, about 1919, an old William Fox western was filmed in Palm Springs. In 1920, the incomparable Rudolph Valentino, America's heartthrob

Villagers crowd around an early movie company filming in Palm Springs. *Photo courtesy Palm Springs Historical Society.*

of the silent movies, filmed a French Foreign Legion movie in several locations in and around Palm Springs. His most famous movie *The Sheik* was also shot in the southern California desert.

In 1922, *The Covered Wagon* with Ernest Torrence was filmed near Palm Springs, prompting many other silent films to follow suit. Also in 1922 silent screen vamp Theda Bara starred in the popular *Salome* filmed near Palm Springs.

Many more movies were being made in the go-go decade of the 1920s. One was filmed on the grounds of The Desert Inn, providing spectator entertainment for the village children. In 1923 Torrence starred in another Palm Springs made film about an African safari.

In 1925 William Powell and Shirley Mason starred in *Desert Gold*, filmed in several valley locations.

During the 1930s Amos 'n' Andy began broadcasting their popular daily radio show from the El Mirador Hotel.

Lost Horizon

Lost Horizon, directed by Frank Capra, was filmed in Palm Springs during the winter of 1935-36. An engaging movie, *Lost Horizon* was written by James Hilton in 1933 and is the story of five people who come across the mythical and elusive Shangri La, where people never age in a Tibetan valley. The waterfall they encounter, that is the essence of the unspoiled Shangri La, is the waterfall of Tahquitz Canyon.

A dramatic scene called for a horse and rider on top of the falls, but there was no trail to get the horse up there. So the movie people enlisted the aid of the McKinney family, owners of Desert Nursery. They had hoists and winches to move large palm trees, so they just winched the horse up.

In 1938 Paramount Pictures came to Palm Springs and filmed the first jungle movie ever made in Technicolor, *Her Jungle Love* with Dorothy Lamour and Ray Milland. Unmindful that Palm Canyon south of Palm Springs is not a jungle, the movie people took care of that by transplanting $20,000 worth of rare tropical plants, trees and vines.

About the filming, Mary Jo Churchwell in *Palm Springs, The Landscape, The History, The Lore*, reported: "At the same time, the tourists came like they had never come before, a great goggling crowd more attracted to the jungle made by Hollywood than the canyon made by nature. For six weeks the film crew struggled to keep them out of the shots."

During the 1950s, several episodes of the hit TV show *I Love Lucy* starring Lucille Ball, Desi Arnaz, William Frawley, and Vivian Vance were filmed around Palm Springs. The movies *The Shores of Tripoli* and the religious themed *The Big Fisherman* with Howard Keel were filmed in the valley in the fifties.

In 1962 the big screen comedy *It's a Mad, Mad, Mad World,* with a host of stars, was filmed around Palm Springs. The opening scenes were shot on a curvy highway in the Coachella Valley.

That same year (1962) a movie was filmed in Palm Springs *about* Palm Springs. *Palm Springs Weekend* starred Connie Stevens, Stephanie Powers and Robert Conrad as teenagers having fun in the desert city.

During the 1960s, numerous TV production scenes were shot in the valley, including *The Dating Game, I Spy* with Robert Culp and Bill Cosby, a Merv Griffin special, *Mannix,* and *The FBI.* Several of these featured scenes aboard the new Palm Springs Aerial Tramway.

In the 1970s, the James Bond flick *Diamonds Are Forever* featured a scene from a Southridge home.

Movies partially filmed in the valley during the eighties included: *American Gigolo, Fraternity Vacation, Less Than Zero, Lethal Weapon 2, Rain Man,* and *Pacific Heights.* Also for television, Robert Wagner and Stephanie Powers filmed numerous scenes for *Hart To Hart* at the La Quinta Resort Hotel and other valley sites.

Residents as extras

By the 1990s, movie and television people came to town several times a year to set up shop. Some were central to the town, like the TV series *PS— I LUV U* starring Connie Selleca, and another Spring Break picture *A Death in Palm Springs* which featured 200 residents as extras.

In 1993 the TV movie *Indian Wells,* which was based on a Joseph Wambaugh novel, was filmed here. Wambaugh, a former LAPD cop, is a Coachella Valley resident who has written two novels with a Palm Springs setting: *The Secrets of Harry Bright* and *Fugitive Nights.*

A Charlie Sheen movie *Terminal Velocity* was filmed around the Palm Springs windmills in 1993.

Even the TV series *Rescue 911* came to town to film a re-creation of a fallen hiker. Scenes were filmed at the Moorten Botanical Garden and in the Indian Canyons.

In 1997, the movie *City of Industry* was filmed in Palm Springs and was about a big diamond heist that took place in Palm Springs.

During 2001 the movie *Twentynine Palms* was filmed in the Movie Colony of Palm Springs. That same year some indoor scenes from the new *Oceans 11* movie with George Clooney, Brad Pitt, and Julia Roberts were actually filmed in an Old Las Palmas home.

In a way, the movie business has gone full circle. Old Las Palmas and the Movie Colony are the sections of Palm Springs where the early stars came to escape the movie business. Now the spotlights, cameras and current stars of the movies and have come back to those same areas to make movies for new generations.

Movie making in Palm Springs is big business these days and looms to get even bigger. During 2004, 88 film permits were issued by the city of Palm Springs to film at locations like Palm Canyon Drive, the Indian Canyons, the windmills, the Palm Springs Aerial Tramway, Palm Springs International Airport, and even City Hall.

Among the 88 filmings were two feature films, *Phat Girlz* and *Alpha Dog*, the NBC TV series *Average Joe*, an MTV series *Newlyweds: Nick and Jessica*, the televised Miss Teen USA pageant, other television shows and documentaries, and numerous commercials.

According to Palm Springs Mayor Ron Oden, "We've always known that Hollywood comes here to relax and play, but it's pretty obvious that they come here to work, too."

Oden added that the total economic impact to Palm Springs alone during 2004 was more than $7.2 million.

CHAPTER 33

Design – Palm Springs Style
MID-CENTURY MODERN ARCHITECTURE

It was the perfect marriage: desert designers working with natural and simple materials—rock, steel, glass and concrete—and new desert dwellers eager to have the "outdoors brought indoors" through the dramatic innovations of those designers.

During the 1950s and '60s, a new architectural design style erupted that was fervently embraced in the city of Palm Springs. Now called Mid-century Modern or to many even "Palm Springs Modern," the bold horizontal lines, large high windows, and spacious airy block designs became hallmarks of desert design.

Whether you fly into the Mid-century-inspired Palm Springs International Airport or drive into town on Highway 111 passing the original Tramway Oasis Gas Station, you're quickly inundated in the style of architecture called Palm Springs Modern. A number of innovative architects were involved in the transformation, but perhaps the biggest name is that of Albert Frey.

Albert Frey

Albert Frey was a Swiss architect who studied under the famous Frenchman Le Corbusier, famous for his Chapel at Ronchamp. Frey designed the Fer a Cheval apartment building in Boitsford near Brussels in 1924, a fine example of what he called "minimalist functionalism." He came to America in 1930 and moved to the Coachella Valley in 1939.

Frey met Charlie Farrell and Ralph Bellamy and did additions on their Racquet Club for them. He began work on his own house in 1941, doing additions over the next 10 years. Frey designed the Cahuilla Elementary School in 1941 and the Katherine Finchy Elementary School in 1948-49.

In 1946 Frey was commissioned by Raymond Loewy, a famous industrial designer, to build his Palm Springs house. The site was so rocky that the rocks were incorporated into the design. A swimming pool containing several boulders, for example, even extends into the living room.

A decade later in 1956, Frey solved the rocky site problem for client Laura Carey differently. He lifted the house on steel tubes to rest on the rocks, resembling a lunar landing probe which appears to float over the landscape.

In 1963, Frey was commissioned to design the Palm Springs Aerial Tramway Valley Station. He built the modernistic building directly over the creek bed, like a bridge.

He also designed the soaring-roof Tramway Gas Station built by Sallie and Culver Nichols in 1965. Working with Robson Chambers, Frey built a lightweight structure supported by only a few steel tubular pillars. The roof is a hyperbolic paraboloid of steel I-beams and corrugated metal roofing.

The station closed in 1997, was purchased in 1998 and refurbished for the Montana St. Martin art gallery. It closed in 2002 and the historic building reopened in November 2003 as the City of Palm Springs' official Visitors Center.

The "tramway gas station" designed by Albert Frey, is now the Palm Springs Visitors Center.

Frey's second home, Frey II, was built on a steep and rocky hillside above downtown Palm Springs in 1963. He used boulders (one large one separates the living from sleeping areas) and also used eight-inch steel I-beams to support a corrugated aluminum roof. The walls are almost all glass with the dramatic roof overhang providing shelter from the sun.

Of over 200 lifetime projects, Albert Frey's favorite was the Palm Springs City Hall, a terra-cotta colored block modernistic building with formed metal screens and sleek, clean lines. Originally built in 1952, additions were made through the years by John Porter Clark, Robson Chambers, and E. Stewart Williams.

After Frey's 1998 death, his house, Frey II, was willed to the Palm Springs Desert Museum.

John Porter Clark

A partner of Frey's, John Porter Clark is known for several innovative modernistic buildings in Palm Springs in addition to his work on the city hall.

Clark designed the Welwood Murray Memorial Library which opened in February 1941. In 1948, Clark was mostly responsible for the Owen Baylis Coffman American Legion Post #519 on Belardo Road.

William F. Cody

William F. Cody was 26 years old when he arrived in Palm Springs in 1942 as architect for The Desert Inn. The USC School of Architecture graduate later made a number of contributions to the architecture of the desert.

A typical example of Mid-century Modern is the unassuming Del Marcos Hotel at Baristo and Belardo which was designed by Cody in 1946. (For some time it was called the San Marino Hotel, but is now back to its original name.) It has large sliding glass windows, private patios and lots of horizontal lines.

Cody built his own interesting home on Desert Palm Drive in 1950 for wife Winifred and their children. Now owned by a designer who used to work with Cody, the home features several block segments surrounding gardens and a patio. Huge glass panes "bringing the outside in" actually forced the owner to tape a sign on one at a recent viewing lest someone try to walk through the glass

Cody's largest Palm Springs project was the Palm Springs Spa Hotel commissioned by the Agua Caliente Band of Cahuilla Indians to occupy the grounds of the original "hot springs." At the corner of Indian Canyon Drive and Tahquitz Canyon Way, the hotel, casino and several hot mineral pools were assembled by Cody in his typical modernistic fashion. Large concrete blocks, long narrow pools and a surrealistic sculpture were typical of his signature. The Spa Hotel has had several design modifications through the years.

Cody also designed the El Dorado Country Club in Palm Desert and St. Theresa Church in Palm Springs.

John Lautner

In 1968 architect John Lautner designed the Arthur Elrod House, a large concrete building on a rocky ridge. A huge concrete dome spans a massive 60-foot diameter living room with glass windows that look out over the desert. The result resembles a spaceship and set the stage for Lautner's more famous and visible landmark, Bob Hope's house.

In 1972 Lautner designed the Bob Hope house on Southridge, which is easily seen from Highway 111 (so tourists can enjoy it too). It is so modernistic that it is said that Bob Hope, when first viewing the model, quipped, "Well, if they come down from Mars, they'll know where to go."

Richard Neutra

One of the most honored architectural gems of Palm Springs is the Edgar J. Kaufman House designed by Austrian architect Richard Neutra. In 1935 Kaufman hired Frank Lloyd Wright to design what became known as "Fallingwater," a Wright masterpiece in Bear Run, Pennsylvania. For his Palm Springs house in 1946, Pittsburgh retailer Kaufman chose Neutra over Wright.

Near the west end of Vista Chino (470), Neutra used geometric quadrants that spin the rooms out over the rocky landscape in a pinwheel design. A second floor roofed aerie, which is really not a room as zoning ordinances prohibited a second story, is a masterpiece compromise that offers great views. The "gloriette" as Neutra called it, is an open outdoor living room with adjustable vertical aluminum shutters.

Singer-songwriter Barry Manilow lived in the historic Kaufman home for years and penned 25 consecutive top-40 hits there.

Donald Wexler

Donald Wexler came to California after receiving his architecture degree from the University of Minnesota in 1950. He honed his skills working under both Richard Neutra and William Cody. Wexler built seven experimental 1960s homes constructed of steel and glass (3200 block of Sunny View) that were recently designated as historic sites, and he was called upon to design the Palm Springs International Airport in 1966.

Wexler worked closely with the two airlines that were operating in Palm Springs at the time and came up with large expanses of glass affording newly arrived travelers a dramatic view of the mountains and city. The airport has been expanded numerous times since and now resembles a brilliant white Bedouin tent perched atop a modern glass and steel structure.

Wexler, still active in Palm Springs, also built Mid-century Modern homes for Kirk Douglas and Dinah Shore in the Las Palmas area.

Williams, Williams, and Williams

The Spanish Eclectic style shopping center La Plaza, in the 100 block of South Palm Canyon Drive, with shuttered windows, white stucco walls and red clay roofs, is a far cry from the Mid-century Modern architecture. However, its architect and his sons made quite an impact on Palm Springs.

In 1931, Julia S. Carnell, owner of the National Cash Register Company in Dayton, Ohio, bought Miss Cornelia White's 3½ acres downtown and summoned Dayton architect Harry J. Williams to design La Plaza. La Plaza, one of the state's first multi-use shopping centers, opened in 1936 and is still the heart of the village.

With his sons, E. Stewart and Roger, they remained to form the architectural firm, Williams, Williams, and Williams.

E. Stewart Williams

The Williams firm became one of the busiest and enduring of the Palm Springs architects. In 1948 it was called upon by Frank Sinatra to design "Twin Palms," the first valley residence owned by "old blue eyes." With vaulted ceilings and walls of glass, it offered unobstructed views of the San Jacinto Mountains.

In 1952 they designed the two-story Oasis Commercial Building (with its open atrium and expansive use of glass and stonework) at the corner of Palm Canyon Drive and Tahquitz Canyon Way. The building was actually an expansion of the historic Oasis Hotel built in 1925 and housed their offices.

One of E. Stewart Williams' favorite buildings was his 1960 design for Santa Fe Savings at 424 South Palm Canyon Drive. It features a flat roof and gold anodized perforated metal screens shielding large, full-length glass walls.

Also in 1960, Williams designed the Coachella Valley Savings at 499 South Palm Canyon, now Washington Mutual. Reverse concrete arches sweep upward toward a flat roof. It originally had a floating staircase over a reflecting pool.

Williams designed the Tramway's Mountain Station. With a totally different terrain from the desert floor, the more rustic design of Williams differs dramatically from Frey's Valley Station design. The Mountain Station actually anchors the top of the tram, and to better provide visitors with unparalleled views, Williams used huge glass frames.

Williams had a challenge when confronted with a 35-foot height limit in the design of the Palm Springs Desert Museum in 1976. To fit the museum's Annenberg Theater in those confines, Williams had the theater and the

Palm Springs Art Museum, originally called the Palm Springs Desert Museum.

outdoor sculpture garden placed below grade. The building features concrete and volcanic cinders matching the nearby mountains as well as vertical fluting of the concrete walls.

E. Stewart Williams was called out of retirement in 1996 to design the museum's Steve Chase Art Wing and Education Center.

George and Bob Alexander

While big-name architects were designing special upscale homes and buildings, it took Los Angeles developer George Alexander and his son Bob to bring the Mid-century Modern style to the masses. Between 1955 and 1965 the Alexanders built 2,200 homes in several Palm Springs tracts.

Designed for the middle class or as second or seasonal homes, the homes were praised for their simplicity. Resting on concrete slab floors, posts and beams support gently sloping roofs with wide overhangs. The open floor plans, broad expanses of glass, and distinctive style soon became known simply as "Alexander Homes."

The most glamorous of the Alexander neighborhoods was Vista Las Palmas, a subdivision between Old Las Palmas and the mountains to the west. The homes were a little larger there, but still modest. For example, a few Alexander homes there have a fourth bedroom and go up to 2,500 square feet. Elvis and Priscilla Presley spent their honeymoon in an Alexander home on Ladera Circle in Vista Las Palmas.

Most Alexanders are only about 1,200 square feet and many smaller ones can be found in the other tracts: the Twin Palms area off South Palm Canyon

Drive, the Racquet Club Estates by Indian Canyon and Racquet Club Road, and the Ramon Rise Estates southwest from Ramon Road and El Cielo Drive.

Designed as seasonal homes, with open beam ceilings, the houses have virtually no insulation to temper the hot summer sun. Plus, the kitchens are small since it was felt people would be eating out rather than cooking. Regardless, Alexanders have been a hot commodity lately and even though all sorts of improvements and transformations by newer owners have been made, an experienced eye can readily spot an Alexander.

Back to the Fifties

It's not just the Alexander homes that are a hot commodity. By the mid-1990s, a wave of nostalgia for anything Mid-century was sweeping the country. Posters of icons Lucille Ball, Marilyn Monroe, and James Dean flooded gift shops around the country.

Palm Springs and its plethora of Mid-century Modern architecture was nirvana to die-hard Modernism buffs. Here they could buy the whole house and design it in all its former modernistic glory.

Even old designers like Donald Wexler have come back to update their traditional Mid-century Modern designs. In late 2003, Wexler finished Tropicana, four post-and-beam glass houses off Palm Canyon Drive and Merito Place that were snapped up quickly by aficionados. The homes feature a steel and glass entry, eight-foot doors and windows throughout, as well as glass walls soaring 13 feet. They just don't throw rocks around there.

A company called Modern Living Spaces, LLC is currently building a tract of inexpensive Mid-century Modern homes in an area north of Palm Springs.

There is so much interest in Mid-Century Modern that several local organizations, including the Palm Springs Preservation Foundation and the Palm Springs Modern Committee, now host an annual Palm Springs Modernism Show in February.

A number of antique shop owners along North Palm Canyon Drive who used to sell baroque and French provincial furniture decided to adapt and adjust. Many shops are now filled with free-form Formica coffee tables, shiny steel fixtures, bright orange Danish modern chairs, lots of Naugahyde, and the synthetic plastics that were so popular in the decades following World War II. What goes around comes around.

CHAPTER 34

The Real Cable Car to the Stars
PALM SPRINGS AERIAL TRAMWAY

The most dramatic attraction in Palm Springs is one unforgettable ride, straight up the mountain from the desert sands to the mountain forest.

The Palm Springs Aerial Tramway, already the world's largest single span vertical cable car ride, was outfitted during summer 2000 with the world's largest, most state-of-the-art rotating cable cars. The two 80-passenger cars slowly revolve, affording visitors not only a tense and exciting view of up-close rocky crags, but an all-encompassing 360 degree panorama of the valley floor.

The tram ride from Palm Springs' Chino Canyon to Mt. San Jacinto whisks you in elevation from the 2,643 foot Valley Station to the 8,516 foot Mountain Station, a climb of over a mile, in 14 minutes. The total route by cable is only two miles, making it one of the world's steepest.

The Palm Springs Aerial Tramway passes through five distinct and unique life zones or ecosystems, from the Sonoran desert through the creosote scrub community, the chaparral, the montane coniferous forest, to the subalpine coniferous forest atop Mt. San Jacinto.

There are five towers on route, and as you near one, you can feel the car move up a little more vertically, then a little bump, and a slight drop and sway, all to the audible apprehension of the occupants.

It's hard to say which is better, the journey or the destination, because both are outstanding.

The Palm Springs Tramway boasts the world's largest rotating tram car.

After almost touching a steep mountain from a cable car, you disembark at Mountain Station, a welcome relief especially when it is only 80 degrees and it's a blistering 120 on the valley floor—it's quite typical to note a temperature range of 30-40 degrees or more, much like going from Mexico to Alaska in 14 minutes, which in essence is what you've just done.

Winter provides skiing and playing in the snow atop the mountain, but it's more popular during the summer months because the Mountain Station is the gateway to the 13,000 acre Mt. San Jacinto State Park and Wilderness Area. There are 54 miles of hiking trails, primitive campgrounds, refreshing streams and verdant valleys. The trails range from short walks nearby vista spots to more ambitious overnighting and summiting the various peaks.

In less than an hour one can hike to some beautiful desert vistas where the green Coachella Valley seems a stark contrast to the light beige desert beyond. Palm Springs residents with keen eyes can spot their homes below.

On the mountain there's an adventure center, a ranger station, and also mule rides available. The Mountain Station also features a restaurant, cocktail lounge, snack bar, gift shop, natural history museum, and a theater showing a documentary film on the history of the tramway.

A dream that never died

The tramway was the fulfillment of a dream that never died, and one that took 28 years to fruition. It was in the summer of 1935 when two Palm Springs men were driving to a Kiwanis meeting in Banning. Electrical engineer Francis Crocker mentioned to Carl Barkow, publisher of *The Desert Sun*, that it sure would be nice to take people up to the top of the mountain to cool off. Crocker immediately envisioned a tramway up the sheer cliffs to the snow-capped summit.

Thus "Crocker's Folly" was born and he set about garnering support. He enlisted the aid of The Desert Inn manager O. Earl Coffman, son of area pioneer Nellie Coffman, who became chairman of the committee to make it happen. Together the pair, along with the energetic Frank Bogert, got a lot of local enthusiasm, but ran into political roadblocks. Early on they were also opposed by environmental groups fearing the construction would threaten wildlife.

The objective was to create a Mt. San Jacinto Winter Park Authority who would then generate the funding and plan the massive effort. The bill to establish the authority was vetoed by Governor Culbert L. Olson in 1941, and then in 1943 Governor Earl Warren let a similar bill die, shelving the plans during the war.

Governor Warren did sign a third bill in 1945 and a seven person governing board was appointed: O. Earl Coffman (Chairman), Frank M.

Bogert, Francis E. Crocker, Virgil O. Davidson, V.W. Grubbs, James G. Nusbaum, and Stanley J. O'Neill. Henry Lockwood was the general counsel who helped keep things moving.

No public money spent on project

While right-of-ways were being acquired from private and Indian lands, and designs were considered, funds were being raised through the sale of bonds. Not one cent of public money went into the project, and of the approximately $8 million raised in bonds, all was paid by 1995.

Swiss engineers with the experience of scores of tramway systems behind them were called upon. O. Earl Coffman spent two years in Switzerland to observe and evaluate trams and negotiate with the Van Roll Company for the equipment. The original two cars, and even the two new ones, were built in Switzerland and shipped to Palm Springs.

From an engineering standpoint, the project became the "eighth wonder of the world." As only the first tower is accessible by road, helicopters flew some 23,000 missions over 26 months, without mishaps, to construct the other towers and ferry the men and materials for the 35,000 square-foot Mountain Station.

The Mountain Station was designed by E. Stewart Williams, who had already achieved fame as one of the Mid-century Modernists. On the mountain however, he developed a more rustic, outdoors look adhering to the state park guidelines.

The noted modernist Albert Frey, using man-made materials, designed the Valley Station which accentuates its marriage with nature by spanning the creek. The Valley Station was named an historical site by the City of Palm Springs.

The Palm Springs Tramway Valley Station was designed by Albert Frey to sit directly over a creek bed.

Completed in 1963

It didn't take long for the negative term "Crocker's Folly" to go by the wayside. Instead Francis Crocker is now known as the "Father of the Tram." His dream was completed in 1963 with the inaugural ride on September 14.

The tram has been ridden by governors and senators, presidents and princes, not to mention scores of other celebrities from the sports and entertainment world.

It has been featured in television and in movies. Episodes of *Mission Impossible, Mannix, General Hospital*, and *Beverly Hills 90210* were all filmed there. In *The Six Million Dollar Man* actor Lee Majors actually did his own stunt work crawling around outside on the cables.

The Royal family of Monaco rides the Palm Springs Aerial Tramway — Prince Rainier Grimaldi III, Princess Grace, and their children. *Photo courtesy Palm Springs Historical Society.*

A Hollywood tribute to the tram actually occurred on opening day when many celebrities marked the event by hosting parties in their Palm Springs homes. Among them were Walt Disney and comedian Red Skelton.

Not widely known is that Crocker himself was not present for opening day, having previously resigned in a dispute with members of the Mt. San Jacinto Winter Park Authority.

If Francis Crocker is considered the "Father of the Tram," then O. Earl Coffman must surely be considered the "Godfather." It was the dedicated and persistent Coffman who traveled far and wide lobbying politicians in Riverside, Los Angeles, San Francisco, Sacramento, and even Washington, D.C. Coffman, that guiding light behind the Palm Springs Tramway, died in 1967. The originator himself, Crocker, lived until 1992.

The Palm Springs Aerial Tramway has been embraced by the local citizenry and the public at large. As one of the top attractions in the Palm

Springs area, tourists still flock to the tram all year long, and currently there are about 350,000 to 400,000 riders each year. Over 13.5 million people have enjoyed the tramway experience over the 40 years of its existence.

Palm Springs pioneers at top of Tram (left to right): Carl Lykken, Zaddie Bunker and her sister Henrietta Parker, Katherine Finchy, and Zaddie's daughter Francis Bunker Strebe. *Photo courtesy Palm Springs Historical Society.*

A 40th anniversary party was held at the Valley Station in September 2003 and fares were reduced 40 percent. City dignitaries mingled with tourists and well-wishers at the festive event.

The cars depart every half hour from 10 a.m. Monday through Friday and from 8 a.m. on weekends and holidays.

At night from the Mountain Station as the lights twinkle from the Coachella Valley at your feet, the vast panorama of stars above set against a black velvet sky provides a peaceful feeling. That song about San Francisco where a cable car takes you to the stars—right state, wrong town. If you want a cable car to the stars, head for Palm Springs, where you can really appreciate a man's vision. The only "folly" in Palm Springs is the upbeat variety show "Fabulous Follies" downtown.

CHAPTER 35

First Black Resident Helps Indians
LAWRENCE CROSSLEY

When the Agua Caliente Indians needed a friend and ally, they found one in Lawrence Crossley, a successful Palm Springs businessman who came to town in 1924 and quickly realized he was the first and only black person to live there.

Undaunted by his minority status, and following in the footsteps of his mentor and boss Prescott T. Stevens, Crossley just forged ahead, buying property, investing, and attaining such a stature he was in a position to help others, something he had the compassion to do.

Born on a Mississippi farm, Crossley was raised in New Orleans and went to California in 1924, going to work for P.T. Stevens as a chauffeur and handyman. After a month in Palm Springs, he sent for his Creole wife Martha and their daughters Margaret and Yvonne. Martha became the Stevens' maid and cook.

Developing into Stevens' right hand man, Crossley invested in the El Mirador Hotel, built the El Mirador Golf Course, and took over the Whitewater Mutual Water Company as manager. He invested in Palm Springs and surrounding area and would own a trailer park in Cathedral City called Tramview a full two decades before the tram was built.

Crossley also owned a laundromat, a restaurant, the Crossley Courts—now part of Ramon Trailer Park on Ramon Road—as

Lawrence Crossley. *Photo courtesy Palm Springs Historical Society.*

well as a 20-acre subdivision. The subdivision was originally built for black families and the streets are named for Crossley's family members. Today Crossley Road is the name of the main road in the part of town he developed.

A "kindred spirit"

Crossley was successful and he accomplished much. He chose to spend much of his time with the Agua Calientes. The Indians took to him like no other, sensing the "kindred spirit" of another non-white and recognizing the sheer sincerity and generosity of Crossley.

During those decades, most of the Agua Calientes were living in Section 14, the downtown Palm Springs section allotted to them. There they still had not realized any specific land nor benefits awarded them by the federal government and mostly lived in tents and shacks made of available materials: cardboard, pieces of tin, irregular pieces of wood, and branches.

Their only sources of revenue were the small fees charged for use of the hot springs at the southeast corner of Section 14, and fees for entrance into the canyons. Occasionally, some would find work for movie companies shooting westerns and needing "Indians."

Crossley was genuinely touched by their plight and, over the years, was taken into their confidence. Crossley spent time with the Indians, talking to them in their homes, comforting them, helping them, and learning their rites and culture from them.

Martha Crossley, who shared her husband's zeal and compassion, was also highly regarded by the Agua Calientes. She regularly participated in their rites and helped provide food and other supplies to those most needy.

The "round house" was the special gathering place of the Agua Caliente tribal leadership, and Crossley was the only non-Indian invited in to discuss tribal matters, much to the awe of whites who were barred from entering.

Friends with the Chief

Chief Francisco Patencio, who was also a strong medicine man, became one of Crossley's closest friends. Crossley learned much from Chief Francisco and was even permitted to witness a few fascinating and unexplainable incidents of telepathy that the chief occasionally experienced.

For example, once, in the middle of a conversation, Chief Francisco became still, stopped talking, then got up, saying, "He needs me," and started running into a canyon an hour and a half away. There they found an Indian man who had fallen and broken his leg!

Chief Francisco also shared with Crossley the secret of "blood tea," a bright red drink made from certain mountain plants and secretly blended together. Wanting to share this particular product with others, Crossley formed a company and marketed it as Nature's Desert Mystery Tea. His company also produced a facial clay.

Liaison with the Indians

By 1953, about the time Crossley determined that he wanted to do even more for the Indians, attorney Hilton H. McCabe had been assigned by Governor Earl Warren to be judge of the newly opened branch court in Indio. Once on the job, the inequities rendered the Indians of Palm Springs became the dominant theme of his life.

McCabe's task, as he saw it, was to rescue these "millionaire-poor" Indians from decades of denials, delays, and inattention that had relegated their lives to the substandard squatting existence on Section 14. One of his first tasks was to find someone to serve as Indian liaison, and no one was better equipped than Lawrence Crossley.

With Crossley's help, Judge McCabe's tireless efforts of chipping away at bureaucracy and red tape, assuaging naysayers and special interest groups, began to unfold progress for the Indian. The 1876 treaty and granting of Section 14 to the Agua Caliente Band of Cahuilla Indians signed by President Ulysses Grant was at last beginning to have meaning.

The Indians were finally granted that which was promised them. Each tribal member was finally and actually awarded property and cash from a fund.

New businesses were able to lease land from the Indians in Section 14 and the beautiful new Spa Hotel opened on the site of the original hot springs. On hand at its opening in November 1962 were Eileen Miguel, head of the Agua Caliente Band of Cahuilla Indians, U.S. Grant IV, grandson of the president who signed the original treaty, and Judge Hilton H. McCabe.

Lawrence Crossley had passed away the year before, but not before preparing and presenting a petition to Judge McCabe, signed by 41 Agua Caliente Indians, thanking him for his tireless efforts that finally ended almost 100 years of inattention and inactivity regarding the tribal lands.

Both the Crossley daughters were well liked in high school and both married wealthy Los Angeles businessmen. Crossley left a legacy in Palm Springs of which they can be proud.

SECTION 6

✺

Palm Springs –
A Late Century Revival

As newer communities were being developed to the southwest, the economic center of the Coachella Valley shifted with it and Palm Desert and Rancho Mirage became the new valley hubs. By the 1960s and 1970s Palm Springs itself was no longer the center of attention, as the city had not kept up with the times. Down, but not out, the city of Palm Springs spent the latter part of the 20th Century reviving its illustrious image.

CHAPTER 36

Cities of the Coachella Valley
NEIGHBORS OF PALM SPRINGS

Sometimes people say they live in Palm Springs when they don't. Usually the reason is because of the name association and popularity of Palm Springs.

Residents, when out of the area, often encounter people who claim to know someone in Palm Springs. The resident then discovers the address to be in Desert Hot Springs, or Cathedral City, or someplace else. Because so few people outside of California have heard of some of the valley cities, many other valley residents simply say "Palm Springs."

This book is primarily about the city of Palm Springs proper. But there are nine cities and a few other communities in the Coachella Valley that are often referred to collectively as "Palm Springs." Some are newer cities that are still undergoing growth and expansion, and others, like Indio, are old and established. In addition to the nine cities, there are several smaller communities like Thousand Palms and Bermuda Dunes near I-10, and farther southeast the agricultural towns of Thermal and Mecca.

Highway 111, which runs northwest to southeast, bisects eight of the nine cities, most of which are completely south of Interstate 10—parallel to, and a few miles north of Highway 111. The exception is Desert Hot Springs which is entirely north of I-10, and directly north of Palm Springs.

Desert Hot Springs

Appropriately named, Desert Hot Springs is famous for natural hot mineral waters that surface throughout the town. Nestled up against the Little San Bernardino Mountains and the Joshua Tree National Park boundary, the town grew as numerous spas and resort hotels developed around the natural bubbling springs.

The town was homesteaded in the early 19th Century by Cabot Yerxa, who spent 40 years building his now famous Indian Pueblo. Yerxa then subdivided and sold property to create the town. Desert Hot Springs incorporated in 1963 and has a population today of 17,700.

While the town itself is not much, there are several large resorts in the area, including the Miracle Springs Resort and Spa, Mineral Springs Resort, the Desert Hot Springs Spa Hotel, and the upscale Two Bunch Palms.

Miracle Springs offers pools and spa services and has meeting and banquet facilities. Mineral Springs Resort features a hotel and Nirvana Spa, numerous massage and spa packages, a fitness center, and restaurants.

Desert Hot Springs Spa Hotel features 50 guest rooms around a central courtyard and eight natural hot mineral pools, ranging from 70 to 104 degrees. It also offers massages and other therapeutic services.

Two Bunch Palms is literally a hedonistic oasis of tranquility where cell phone usage is even restricted in public areas. This exclusive resort which has a history of privacy, discretion, and tranquility was described by *Sunset Magazine* thusly, "It is a unique, if somewhat decadent, perspective on the universe."

The unique Yerxa home in Desert Hot Springs was built by a promoter of the hot springs.

Palm Desert's El Paseo.

Cathedral City

This appears to be a misnomer because there is no cathedral, nor is the sprawling "city" much of a city, but the town was named for Cathedral Canyon, a solemn canyon in the cove to the south of town.

Formerly a reputed gangster hideaway, Cathedral City once was known for several gambling joints, numerous bars and a laid-back mentality.

Cathedral City incorporated in 1981 and has enjoyed continuous growth to a current population of 48,600. A new downtown has been created in the last decade, including a new city hall, movie theaters, parking structure, and a library. Phases II and III of the city's plan are in the works and will transform about 70 more acres in downtown into residential, retail, and commercial areas.

Today the section along Highway 111 boasts an entertainment plaza with a 270-seat, six-story-high screen IMAX theater and the popular Mary Pickford Theatre with 16 screens. Nearby are the Cathedral City Auto Center and numerous builder supply houses, mostly along Perez Road. On Date Palm Drive are Sam's Club, Wal-Mart, and other retailers.

It's primarily a live-in town, one that each holiday season has several neighborhoods attracting crowds to see outdoor lighting displays. Family oriented Cathedral City boasts ball fields, miniature golf courses, parks, and other amusements.

Rancho Mirage

The Thunderbird Country Club, which opened in 1951 and was the first 18-hole golf club in the entire valley, virtually gave birth to the city of Rancho Mirage.

By the 1960s, famous people living in Rancho Mirage included: Edgar Bergen, Jack Benny, Bing Crosby, Lucille Ball, Desi Arnaz, Ginger Rogers, Perry Como, Esther Williams, Sammy Davis Jr., Danny Kaye, Dean Martin, Dinah Shore, Frank Sinatra, and the Marx Brothers.

Ambassador Walter and Lenore Annenberg welcomed presidents, kings and world leaders to their Rancho Mirage estate. The popular local philanthropists once even made a $25 million gift for the Eisenhower Medical Center. Even today the "City of Presidents" is home to former President Gerald Ford and his wife Betty, who started the Betty Ford Center at Eisenhower Medical Center.

Along with the several exclusive developments named Thunderbird, the area along Highway 111 is known as "Restaurant Row." The River complex is a relaxing shopping/dining destination. Along the same street the city also sponsors a Cancer Survivor's Park complete with bronze sculptures, walkways, and a waterfall.

Rancho Mirage incorporated in 1973. Today's year-round population is 15,518, and the city's median household income is almost $60,000.

Palm Desert

Due to its central location in the Coachella Valley—where the Palms to Pines Highway meets Highway 111, the city of Palm Desert has evolved into the economic and demographic hub of the valley.

"Palm Desert" came into being with the opening of a post office there on July 14, 1947, two years after "Mr. Desert" Randall Henderson relocated his *Desert Magazine* from El Centro to a 40-acre site on a virgin desert cove.

He built a $260,000 Pueblo Indian style building which housed the magazine, plant, art gallery, bookshop, and museum. The town grew up around it.

Needing a post office to serve the magazine, Randall and his brothers Clifford and Phil kicked a name around, wanting to keep the word "desert" and came up with Palm Desert.

Incorporated in 1973, Palm Desert is today home to the area's main regional shopping mall—Westfield Palm Desert Town Center; the desert area's most upscale shopping street—El Paseo Drive, which is considered the Rodeo Drive of the desert; the College of the Desert; the McCallum Theater; a new branch of the California State University/San Bernardino; and The Living Desert.

The Living Desert is an outstanding zoo and botanical garden stretching over 1,200 acres with 400 desert animals including desert bighorn sheep on a natural hillside setting. Approximately 300,000 guests a year also enjoy over 1,500 species of desert flora. The Living Desert, started in 1970 by biologist Karen Sausman, is a nonprofit organization supported by numerous grants and donations.

The Palm Desert Chamber of Commerce celebrated its 50th anniversary in December 2004. Palm Desert has the world's largest golf cart parade.

Indian Wells

One of the fastest growing cities in California with the valley's highest personal income ($108,663), Indian Wells was once known for several local watering holes carved out of the limestone bedrock by the Indians.

When the Desi Arnaz Western Hills Lodge opened in 1957 in what is now Indian Wells, it was the only valley hotel built on a golf course. After a long and interesting history, that original hotel is now the Indian Wells Resort Hotel, still a beautiful and luxuriating place. The city now also boasts several other world-class resorts, including the Tuscany-inspired Miramonte Resort, the classic Hyatt Grand Champions, the spacious Renaissance Esmeralda Resort, and the second largest tennis stadium in the world.

The impressive new Indian Wells Tennis Garden, which opened in 2000, has been home to the annual Indian Wells Tennis Masters Series presented by Newsweek. The main stadium has seating for 16,100 fans on three levels with 44 luxury suites. Two other stadiums have seating for 8,000 and there are a total 20 championship tennis courts, two clay courts, a seven-acre village site and 50 acres of parking.

The Pacific Life Open, held at the Indian Wells Tennis Garden over two weeks in March, draws the sports' largest names and has a tremendous economic impact, bringing over $100 million to the area. The world's sixth largest tennis tournament, the Pacific Life Open attracted 280,652 fans in March 2005, a record.

Indian Wells incorporated in 1967 and has a population of only 4,430.

La Quinta

In the early 1900s a rancher named Norman "Happy" Lundbeck homesteaded near what is today known as Point Happy, site of the Cliffhouse Restaurant.

Then in 1926 at a site to the south of the point, Walter Morgan built a lovely Spanish revival estate replete with 20 individual casitas and called it La Quinta Hotel, "la quinta" meaning "country house" or "inn" in Spanish. The beautiful old dowager of an inn has from its early days attracted famous people seeking privacy and luxury. Industrialist Cornelius Vanderbilt even wrote, "If far from the madding crowd you want to be, there's no better place than the exclusive La Quinta Hotel."

Now called La Quinta Resort, the 45-acre resort features scores of private walled casitas, 25 secluded pools, a fitness spa, 22 tennis courts plus a tennis stadium, conference facilities, two top golf courses—Dunes and Mountain, and privileges at some of the city of La Quinta's world-class courses.

La Quinta's famous six courses of PGA West were designed by the sport's top names: PGA West Arnold Palmer Private Course, Jack Nicklaus Private Course, Jack Nicklaus Tournament Course, Greg Norman Course, the Tom Weiskopf Private Course, and the TPC Stadium Golf Course.

The La Quinta Art Show, held each March, is an outdoor, juried show with mixed art forms that attracts over 250 pre-eminent artists and many art lovers from all over. Formerly held at the Polo Grounds, the premier event now has its own site, the Civic Center Campus, where ponds and streams provide a restful backdrop to fine art.

La Quinta incorporated in 1982 and has a current population of 32,500. Highly dependent on the tourist dollar, the city of La Quinta is going through a transition with new business areas being developed and more golf-oriented housing constructed. The area's first Kohl's Department Store opened in La Quinta in March 2005.

Indio

Indio was an Indian village before Lt. Robert Williamson surveyed the region in 1872 for the government. As the halfway point between Yuma and Los Angeles and being near Indians who could supply construction labor, the area was chosen for a railroad depot. Originally called Indian Wells, the name was changed in 1877 to Indio, Spanish for Indian, to avoid confusion with other locations.

Indio was surveyed and a town site map filed in 1888 with the San Diego County Recorder. In 1893 as part of the newly designated Riverside County, Indio became one of the 12 townships, and by 1896, it had 50 inhabitants. In 1890, the United States Department of Agriculture (USDA) sent date palms from Algeria to the region, and in 1904, the USDA established a date experiment station near Mecca.

The date went on to become a major crop for the Coachella Valley. Today 95 percent of all dates grown in the United States are grown in the valley, generating about $100 million in agricultural revenue. Dates are a very healthful fruit, being fat-free, cholesterol-free, sodium free, and a good source of fiber.

The Coachella Valley Water District was formed in 1917, eventually leading to the construction of the All-American Canal that brings Colorado River water to the valley.

Indio incorporated as a city in 1930 becoming the valley's first city when it had a population of 1,875. The 2004 population was 59,100; with considerable new construction in the south end of town, it is projected to exceed 100,000 within 20 years.

Today Indio is known as the City of Festivals, hosting three Native American powwows, the big International Tamale Festival each December, the Southwest Arts Festival, and the Riverside County Fair and National Date Festival in February. Indio also hosts many sporting events including the famed Skins Golf Game and the Indio Desert Circuit.

Indio is also one of the largest gateways to Joshua Tree National Park and is the site of the Fantasy Springs Casino, with more casino activity planned.

Coachella

The agricultural city of Coachella, considered the "Gateway to the Salton Sea," is at the southeastern edge of the valley for which it is named. From the confluence of the I-10 and Highway 86 southward, Coachella sprawls across several Indian reservations and is home to the Spotlight 29 and the Augustine casinos.

In 1901 it was a small community at Highway 111 and Avenue 50 called Woodspur—trains used to pull off on a spur and collect wood. Originally covering 2.5 square miles when the city incorporated in 1946, Coachella now encompasses 32 square miles.

Its agricultural roots are still evident today with Highway 111 called Grapefruit Boulevard. There's also a Cantaloupe Avenue. Vast date orchards are still evident and packing sheds still rise above the flat landscape.

Today Coachella's population of 27,000 is heavily Hispanic with a youthful median age of 22.8 years according to the 2000 Census. Over 60 percent of the population own their own homes.

It's the sun

There's something for everyone in the Coachella Valley, whose nine cities are also increasingly called the Palm Springs Valley. The valley has over 110 golf courses, world-class tennis courts, thousands of swimming pools, great restaurants, and scores of top-notch resorts. By the way, when the sun shines 350 days a year, most people don't really care what town they're in.

La Quinta Resort

CHAPTER 37

The Beat Goes On

SONNY BONO AND PALM CANYON DRIVE

By the 1970s Palm Springs was but a façade of its former self. The glitz and glamour of decades of celebrity had vanished. Fashionable shops, art galleries, and upscale restaurants had vacated downtown Palm Springs, opting for the newer "in towns" of Palm Desert and Rancho Mirage. The remaining businesses on Palm Canyon Drive were relegated to souvenir and T-shirt shops and inexpensive restaurants catering to a less discriminating tourist.

To further illustrate the downtrend, the Westfield Town Center, Coachella Valley's largest shopping mall, opened in Palm Desert in 1983, further relegating Palm Springs to backwater status.

By this time "Spring Break" had invaded Palm Springs in the form of thousands of students hell-bent on partying with a no-holds-barred mentality and the town's image suffered even more. Each year brought progressively more of the young people who cruised Palm Canyon Drive until traffic was at a standstill. One Palm Springs police officer said it took two hours to go two miles.

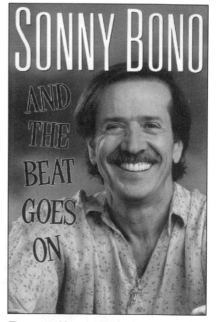

Drunk and rowdy, and their testosterone soaring amid scores of nearly naked girls, the crowds quickly got out of control. In 1986 there were 80 people arrested for attacking the Palm Springs Police and looting. The spring bacchanal had cast an ugly eye on the village of Palm Springs.

Back in 1969 the city had to enlist the aid of four other law enforcement agencies and they went into nearby Tahquitz Canyon to rid the canyon of hippies who had encamped there and proceeded to trash the place.

Like that episode two decades previous, something had to be done. By

The cover of Sonny's 1991 book.

the late 1980s the need was there to rid the town of its unsavory visitors, to nullify the "dying" image of Palm Springs, and to once again attract the upscale tourists. Help came from several fronts, and one of the more interesting ones was the election of entertainer Sonny Bono as mayor.

Why Sonny ran

Up until this time Bono was known as the "other" half of the singing team Sonny and Cher. Divorced from Cher for years and remarried, he and his wife Mary had moved to Palm Springs where they ran an Italian restaurant on North Indian Canyon. Bono encountered problems with the city over a proposed sign for the restaurant as well as permit and inspection problems with his home in the Mesa area of Palm Springs.

In his 1991 autobiography *And The Beat Goes On* the entertainer revealed, "I began to see City Hall as a tired complex of unfair contradictions...The town was a sleeper...Palm Springs relied on tourism, yet, as far as I could tell, the stodgy old guard had driven the once glittery desert oasis straight into economic torpor."

After fighting and complaining, Sonny finally made the decision to run for mayor. With the election set for April 12, 1988, Sonny went on the attack stating, "All the city's growth had gone 'down valley,' into neighboring resort communities like Rancho Mirage and Palm Desert; the city was suffering from a 2.8 million dollar deficit, resulting in cuts for city services, including the police and fire departments."

On Election Day eve, Sonny, apprehensive over the next day's voting, watched television to see his ex-wife Cher win the Academy Award for "Moonstruck." The momentum of the famous team was on the upswing.

And Sonny's election? Surprising many who thought it was just a joke, a confident and upbeat Sonny Bono won by the biggest landslide in the city's history. To continue his natural high, a few days after the election Mary delivered their first child, a boy they named Chesare.

Sonny as Mayor

Mayor Bono's objective was to make Palm Springs a family-friendly destination. With the help and support of the merchants, Palm Springs effectively closed off Palm Canyon Drive for Spring Break. The Palm Springs police got strict about enforcing drinking laws, and one of Mayor Bono's decrees that brought him perhaps unwanted national attention was his ban on thong bikinis in public places.

Even though he initially received a lot of criticism—called Mayor Bonehead and worse—Mayor Bono did much of what he set out to do.

Instead of the cowboy culture of previous decades, Bono envisioned Palm Springs as a motion picture industry showplace. Even though he and former cowboy Mayor Frank Bogert were publicly friendly, the two differed greatly. That 1988 changing of the guard between Bogert and Bono signified a dramatic change in direction and created a source of friction. Outspoken Bogert has called Bono a "pissant," and still denounces him.

To a historian, it appears that they were each the right man for the times in which they served.

Sonny Bono, while small in stature, had a large presence. His tremendous energy and enthusiasm set out to rekindle attitudes in a town that had not changed much over the past two decades.

He brought a major film festival to town, the Nortel Networks Film Festival. Now called the Palm Springs International Film Festival, the mega-January event is in its 15th year and a showcase for many eventual Academy Award winners. The increasing list of Hollywood stars in attendance helps underscore its importance.

The success of that prestigious event has brought other festivals to town, a Festival of Festivals, which made its debut in 2001, and the Palm Springs International Festival of Short Films held each September.

Buoyed by enthusiasm, the city began to respond and soon there was a marathon, a vintage-car race, a Grand Prix Bicycle Race, and much more.

Now there are so many events and parades in downtown Palm Springs throughout the year you never know what you'll encounter as new ones are added all the time.

As an example, during a recent three month period from September to November 2003, traffic on Palm Canyon was rerouted for the following events: Rocktoberfest—selected by the American Bus Association as one of the top 100 events in North America, American Heat Motorcycle and Hot Rod Weekend, a Palm Springs High School Homecoming parade, the popular Gay Pride Parade, a Veterans Day Parade, and an Antique Car Show.

Today there are numerous art shows and other gatherings at Frances Stevens Park (North Palm

Sign on Palm Canyon Drive in the village of Palm Springs.

Canyon Drive and Alejo Road), including the annual Palm Springs Old World Renaissance Festival.

Lots of things were going on during Mayor Bono's tenure from 1988 to 1992. The Plaza Theatre downtown was vacant, and in 1990 Riff Markowitz put together The Fabulous Palm Springs Follies, which has been bring-

Villagefest draws big crowds.

ing in more adult tourists ever since. *The Desert Sun* newspaper said, "The Palm Springs Fabulous Follies helped the city discover its glitzy roots."

Then there is the popular Villagefest. Begun in 1991 the Villagefest is now a Thursday night tradition all year long except for Thanksgiving. Every Thursday evening Palm Canyon Drive downtown is closed to traffic and up to 160 venders set up booths selling produce, handicrafts, art, jewelry, and food. There are entertainers and a kiddy zone. It has been so successful most of the stores stay open late for the strollers and browsers.

Congressman Bono

Buoyed by his run as mayor, and fired up with a renewed confidence, Sonny Bono ran for and was elected to the U.S. House of Representatives representing California's 44th District. He was reelected in 1996. As a conservative who opposed big government and overall spending, he did however support legislation that benefited the local Indian tribes. He also supported extending tax credits for producing energy from the wind.

From one whose political career began with people thinking he was a joke, Bono became a respected congressman. He was killed in a skiing accident in January 1998 and the world watched the touching services held at St. Theresa's Catholic Church in Palm Springs.

Mary Bono, widowed with two children, ran for his congressional seat, won, and has since been reelected, serving with distinction in her own right.

Sonny Bono left a legacy on Palm Springs, and he is remembered. The terminal at Palm Springs Airport was named in his honor. The Salton Sea wildlife sanctuary, which he supported, has been renamed the Sonny Bono

Salton Sea National Wildlife Refuge. Interstate 10 through the Coachella Valley is now called the Sonny Bono Memorial Highway, and a life-size bronze sculpture of Mayor Bono has been placed at 155 South Palm Canyon Drive at the entrance to the Plaza Mercado.

Location and Timing

In real estate the adage about the three most important things goes "Location, Location, Location." Palm Springs has always had the location, nestled up against Mt. San Jacinto; it just needed a reminder.

By the late eighties and early nineties there were numerous forces, including the energy of entertainer-turned-politician Sonny Bono, that helped put Palm Springs back in the forefront. The renaissance of the late nineties is still going strong with real estate prices soaring, new businesses opening, older ones expanding, and a renewed enthusiasm in town.

Under the later leadership of Mayor Will Kleindienst (1992-2003), there was considerable revitalization downtown, including the Mercado Plaza, The Plaza, the Desert Fashion Plaza upgrade, the Arenas Road upgrade, the Spa Resort and Casino, and more. Mayor Kleindienst also noted that the Palm Springs International Airport was expanded and now offers increased service and flights.

One of Mayor Kleindienst' most visible achievements is the Festival of Lights parade, a December dazzler that he started in 1991. Growing every year, now over 100 floats, marching bands and other groups entertain about 150,000 spectators on Palm Canyon Drive between Ramon Road and Tamarisk Drive.

Uptown Palm Springs—North Palm Canyon Drive—has established an identity. Now called the Uptown Heritage Galleries and Antique District, approximately 20-30 shops line both sides of the street between Alejo Road and Tachevah Road. There is new Uptown lighting and "First Friday" was introduced there. That's when the Palm Canyon merchants and antique dealers stay open late on the first Friday of each month and provide refreshments and entertainment.

Mayor Ron Oden, a former city councilman who took office in November 2003, pledged to continue his pro-business voting and improve the city's relationship with local merchants and businesses. His spirited 2005 State of the City address ended on this upbeat note, "We *are* Palm Springs, a magical place, and this is our time—now!"

To quote *Vanity Fair* magazine in its June 1999 issue, "Palm Springs is hot, hot, hot."

CHAPTER 38

Showcasing Movies
PALM SPRINGS INTERNATIONAL FILM FESTIVAL

Palm Springs has long been the setting for movie making, and more importantly, it has been a resort hideaway for the moviemakers, producers, directors, writers, and actors. Now it is also an important venue where some of the world's most significant movies are screened. The Palm Springs International Film Festival, originated by former entertainer Sonny Bono during his tenure as mayor, has evolved into the world's largest festival of foreign films.

Now in its 17th season, the Palm Springs International Film Festival (PSIFF) is held every January and gets bigger and more prestigious every year. The two-week festival now draws over 200 movies from 65 countries as well as a handful of American independent movies and documentaries.

During 2004, the festival attracted 53 out of a possible 56 of the year's official foreign language submissions seeking an Oscar from the Academy of Motion Picture Arts and Sciences. This, in turn, brought producers, directors, and actors from around the world to Palm Springs to tout their movies.

Foreign movie makers mingled with top Hollywood producers and stars at the many gala parties and events. At a 2004 black-tie awards presentation held at the Palm Springs Convention Center, several Americans garnered awards, including producer Richard D. Zanuck, actor/director Kevin Costner, actress Naomi Watts, and composer Danny Elfman.

The January 6-17, 2005 event was emceed by *Entertainment Tonight* co-host Mary Hart, who has a home in the desert. The largest glittering array of stars ever was in attendance, including Nicole Kidman, Kirk Douglas, Kevin Spacey, Samuel L. Jackson and Liam Neeson.

There was an overlap in January 2004 as the established Sundance Film Festival in Utah started five days before the PSIFF finished. However, the Sundance festival specializes in independent films, while the PSIFF focuses on international movies.

Even with the overlap, there were 86,000 attendees at the movies showcased in Palm Springs. Over 100,000 attendees made the 2005 event the largest ever. Ten local theaters are used to show the movies, the main venue being the seven-screen Signature Theater.

While movie people from around the world are in town to see movies and be seen, the local community is a big factor in the festival's success. Retirees, snowbirds, and other residents make up a good percentage of film buffs drawn to the screenings. Film fans of all ages flock to Palm Springs from the Los Angeles area for the festival. More and more celebrity entertainers attend each year fulfilling the original dream of Sonny Bono.

Palm Springs International Film Festival Executive Director Darryl Macdonald paid tribute to the founder in his opening message for the 2004 festival:

> *During those early years, Sonny Bono was the driving force behind the event, and though there were skeptics who in the beginning doubted the Festival's purpose and staying power, no one could doubt now that the vision that drove Sonny to launch the Festival and throw the city's weight behind the event was anything less than prescient. Sonny always felt that Palm Springs had an identity and a destiny that was tied to its romantic past as an artists' colony and its history as a premiere resort getaway for people who worked in the movies. If he were alive today, I know he'd be proud of the wonder he created and nurtured through those ambitious early years.*
>
> *What began fifteen years ago as an ambitious, 55 film showcase celebrating the art of film has evolved into one of America's premiere festivals, encompassing some 200 films annually, hosting hundreds of filmmakers, national and international press and film industry executives, and tens of thousands of filmgoers. What draws them here initially is the strong reputation that this Festival has built for itself in the course of those fifteen years; what keeps them coming back for more is the amazing natural beauty of the area and warmth and welcoming embrace of its people.*

The city of Palm Springs considers the PSIFF its flagship event and contributes $350,000 a year to ensure its success.

In addition to the Palm Springs International Film Festival, other film festivals have found a home in Palm Springs. The Palm Springs Festival of Festivals was established by former PSIFF Executive Director Craig Prater and in 2001 featured 116 films from 25 countries.

The fourth annual Coachella Valley International Hispanic Film Festival moved from Palm Springs to nearby Palm Desert in October 2004 to be near the greater Hispanic population of the east valley.

The popular Palm Springs International Short Film Festival is now in its 11th season. A step-child of the PSIFF, it is held every September and features 40 to 50 themed programs of from four to seven short movies each. The individual movies generally run from about eight to 15 minutes each.

Now that Palm Springs is firmly established as a major film festival site, it appears that the village that has always been entertainment and celebrity friendly has come full circle in its long history with moviemaking.

CHAPTER 39

As Young As You Feel
THE FABULOUS PALM SPRINGS FOLLIES

A variety show featuring seasoned performers at least 55 years of age works well in a nostalgic town like Palm Springs. The Fabulous Palm Springs Follies still packs 'em in and has served as a major catalyst for the resurgence of Palm Springs as a resort destination.

Palm Springs today is a place where vintage tunes, not from the sixties and seventies but from the thirties, forties, and fifties, bleat out over the radio waves all day. The sentimental music is a part of daily life, enough to cause some visitors to comment on the apparent "time warp."

These days celebrity bus tours drive past homes of movie stars who have passed away so long ago that most people, all those under 50, say, "Who was that celebrity again?"

But for a town whose population swells each winter with retirees from around the country and Canada, and is only a two-hour bus ride from millions of others, nostalgia plays quite well.

The first time I attended the Fabulous Palm Springs Follies at the historic Plaza Theatre on Palm Canyon I was 59 years old. Looking at the white-haired crowd, I felt like one of the youngest people in the place. That's something today's Palm Springs in winter can do for you.

The show's producer, director, and master of ceremonies Riff Markowitz, in his biting role as M.C., plays well the age of the patrons. During each show he works the crowd, singling out those over 90 and 100 for recognition. Don't forget, most of his audience appear to be in their 70s and 80s. Move over, Branson.

Long-legged lovelies

Most are not disappointed in the show; in fact over 98 percent vow to return. Age vanishes once the curtain opens. You know those long-legged lovelies on the stage are from 56-87 years old—but it's hard to believe. Flashing as much leg and torso as is prudent, they dance, sing, even do the splits, and appear in elaborate costumes and headdresses that can weigh 15 pounds or more.

One, 87-year-old trouper Beverly Allen, has been listed as "The World's Oldest Still Performing Showgirl" according to the *Guinness Book of Records*. Like most of the seasoned Follies showgirls, her credits are dazzling, going back to dancing with Eddie Duchin and Tommy Dorsey and entertaining troops for the USO in Europe during WW II.

Today the Follies is in its 15th season, constantly playing to sell-out crowds filling the restored theatre of 760 seats. Over 2,500 performances have delighted crowds since opening in 1990, and well over 2½ million people have seen the show.

Follies dancer Angela Paige. *Photo courtesy Ned Redway, Palm Springs Follies.*

The season runs from November through March, mostly Wednesday through Sunday, two daunting three-hour-plus shows four days, and one show on Sunday, about 115-120 days a year, for about 200 plus shows each season. The shows are long too, with two intermissions.

Timing was perfect

The timing of need and opportunity was perfect for such an enterprise as the Fabulous Follies. The city wanted a tenant for the Plaza Theatre abandoned in 1989 by the Metropolitan Theater Company. And former Hollywood producer Riff Markowitz was bored with his retirement to La Quinta, having spent 30 years of his life producing, writing, and directing award-winning television series and variety specials for a host of famous talents. He also co-created and produced the dramatic series *The Hitchhiker* for HBO and *Tales From The Darkside*.

Upon his first visit, he realized the theater's charm and sense of history would be perfect for his dream. Markowitz recalls, "Well this was just the ultimate sandbox for someone whose dream had always been to perform upon an authentic vaudeville stage.

But first he had to convince the city, which he finally did with a 3-2 vote.

Then in addition to assuaging the concerns of neighboring businesses, he had to sink about $900,000 into renovating the old place.

The show opened with slow sales the first week. Then word of mouth took over, and Markowitz has never looked back. The show's 165 employees have commanded a large payroll, but more important to the community are the approximately 170,000 attendees each year.

Local businesses rave

Over 40 percent of visitors come to Palm Springs just for the show. While only about 20 percent spend the night, over 75 percent grab a bite to eat and 50 percent buy something locally. So the concerns of the neighboring businesses have turned to raves.

In fact, group organizers bus them in all season long. Locals can set their watches by the busses dropping off their charges around the corner on Tahquitz Canyon Way.

Not only were the townspeople won over, but so was the media. *The Washington Post* said, "The regular standing ovations suggest that this is the right stuff in the right place at the right time." *The Today Show* reported, "Great legs, great stamina, great sense of humor! Dazzling." Doing them one better was ABC's *Day One* with Diane Sawyer and Forrest Sawyer which gushed, "The sexiest, most stunning showgirls in the business."

A first-rate show

Everything about the show is first rate, and the costumes are no small matter. Markowitz acquired designer Paul McAvene whose movie credits include *King Kong* and *The Jungle Book* while for the stage his costumes for *Les Miserables* and *Cats* helped ensure their success. Each of the showgirls' costumes is designed for the individual body.

Along with the popular song and dance numbers each show features various variety acts and a headliner. The most endearing variety acts have been pure vaudeville. With straw hats and banjos, the Mercer Brothers, Jim and Bud, 85 and 88 years old, sang, tap-danced, and just plain had fun as they have since the show's second season. Bud, unfortunately, passed away in 2004.

Early on, one big name was hired for the entire season, but sometimes illness forced Markowitz to scramble to find replacements. The late Donald

O'Conner, who sang, but admitted he could no longer do the soft shoe work for which he had become known, was the guest headliner for my first visit. O'Conner got ill shortly after that show, and replacements filled the remainder of the season.

Today, Markowitz signs up four headliners to cover the entire season, each doing about 50 shows. In my second visit my friends and I were impressed by Carol Lawrence who did a great job involving several members of the audience. Howard Keel, Frankie Laine, Anna Marie Alberghetti, The Modernaires, Peter Marshall, The Four Aces, and Barbara McNair, Buddy Greco, and Kaye Ballard have also been headliners at the Fabulous Follies.

Audience involvement

Markowitz loves interacting with the audience. During the show he recognizes various groups who have come to town for the show. As each is introduced, that section applauds itself. If one group is way in the back, he might make a comment like, "Boy, I hope you didn't pay your leader for the expensive seats."

As a special treat after each show, the cast adjourns to the lobby to greet visitors departing the historic theater. In 2003 we got a photo of my friend posing with lovely dance manager Leila Burgess who could pass for 20 years younger than her admitted 69 years. The active show business lifestyle obviously agrees with her.

The show is more of a "Fountain of Youth" for the cast than it is for the audience. Former Radio City Rockette and runway model Glenda Guilfoyle, 71, who is also a mother of seven and grandmother of eight, said it succinctly what most know and feel, "The Follies keeps me young."

Dorothy Kloss, 81, in her 9th Follies season, simply added, "I no longer think about getting old."

It's a show that makes you feel good about the inevitable aging process. In one fun afternoon, you're transported back in time and honored, because whether it was your time or not, age became timeless. After all, you're as young as you feel!

CHAPTER 40

Reliving the Big One – WW II
PALM SPRINGS AIR MUSEUM

It was the greatest conflict the world had ever seen in terms of cost, of lives lost, and worldwide significance. World War II spanned the globe from capital cities of Europe to small dots of islands in the Pacific Ocean.

Ultimately, it was air power that helped turn the tide of the war toward the Allied Forces, just as air dominance has been a major factor in every war since. Recognizing that, in the mid-1990s the Palm Springs Air Museum, a non-profit educational institution, opened to showcase those aircraft that changed the course of the world.

Just a few weeks after America went to war again, I paid another visit to the museum. While on that day modern aircraft were methodically bombarding Afghanistan and its Taliban regime, I walked among the well-maintained planes from World War II. Their proud histories were displayed, leaving the visitor to imagine the havoc they wrought upon the enemy.

Palm Springs Air Museum.

Was the spike in attendance that day because it was a weekend at the beginning of the "desert season" or was it a continuing patriotic display of support caused by the attack on the World Trade Center? These were new times and the military had taken on a renewed significance and importance.

Among the white-haired veteran visitors you'd expect to see at such a tribute were numerous families, young couples, and teen-agers, all soaking up the history of World War II. Scores of volunteer docents, mostly in their 70s and 80s, mingled, many offering anecdotes about their involvement in the big war.

A visit to a museum became a day of memories, of pride, of patriotism. The old veterans through the decades have seen the public treat them in every fashion possible, from abhorrence and disgust, to mild interest and avoidance, to unflinching reverence and appreciation.

The museum, located on Gene Autry Trail on the east side of the Palm Springs Airport, contains one of the world's largest collection of flyable World War II military aircraft, many owned by Mr. Robert Pond, who became chairman of the board of directors of the museum. There are also aircraft on loan from other private owners, the U.S. Navy and the National Air and Space Museum, rendering a total of about 26 on daily display.

Included are everything from Grumman Wildcats, Hellcats, Tigercats, and Bearcats to a Boeing B-17 Flying Fortress.

From conception in late 1993 until the public grand opening that attracted approximately 5,000 visitors on Veteran's Day, November 11, 1996, there was a lot of cooperation and work.

Bob Pond made it happen

It started when two residents, Charlie Mayer and Bill Byrne, got the idea after seeing a P-51 flying low overhead. They got their friend Pete Madison, a former P-38 pilot, who in turn approached his friend Bob Pond, a former naval aviator who had been collecting and rebuilding old planes and cars.

They incorporated early in 1994, leased a 10-acre parcel of land on the Palm Springs Airport property, and set about getting funding, as no public funds were used. During 1995, a 50,000 square foot facility was constructed while the following year planes were acquired and the interior was prepared. Due to later additions, the environmentally controlled interior display space is now approximately 70,000 square feet.

The mission of the museum is to exhibit, educate, and eternalize the role of the World War II combat aircraft and the role of the pilots and the American citizens in achieving this great victory. In addition to the warplanes, it houses rare and original combat photography, original artwork, artifacts,

Palm Springs Air Museum.

memorabilia and uniforms, graphics and continuous video documentaries.

There are two large hangars, the European and the Pacific hangars, and a smaller hangar, the Thomas L. Phillips Hangar, which houses the B-17G "Miss Angela" as well as a P-47 Thunderbolt.

The European Hangar features the flyable aircraft, classic cars and motorcycles, murals, many exhibits from the war in Europe, timelines and clippings from the war, uniforms, ribbons, and more.

A tribute to Bob Hope

The Pacific Hangar has outstanding displays, timelines and murals of the Pacific Theatre of Operations. In addition to the aircraft are miniature models of the ships on Warship Row in Pearl Harbor, surrender documents, battlefield weapons, and a display providing tribute to Bob Hope and the USO tours.

The Buddy Rogers Theater hosts regular events, programs, and three or four movies each day. Scheduled the week I was there was a Navajo Code Talker Program, hosting Thomas H. Begay USMC-WW II Navajo Code Talker.

A delightful surprise was the upstairs library called the James C. Ray Educational Resource Center. I'd never seen a grander collection of aviation books from World War II. The state of the art education center offers flight simulators for a modest fee.

Acquisitions and donations have been nothing short of phenomenal with the Donor's Wall recognizing many prominent valley residents including Jane Wyman, Gene Autry, Baron Hilton, and Buddy Rogers.

Planes have gone to Hollywood

Hollywood has come to the planes and the planes have gone to Hollywood. Most recently, the 2001 movie *Pearl Harbor* featured several planes from the museum, the Spitfire, P-40 and P-25 in photographic action sequences.

The energetic museum trustees offer group tours, school and youth-oriented tours, corporate events, and catered events and site rentals. They also offer six levels of membership.

The pride of the Palm Springs Air Museum goes way beyond the fine aircraft and professional exhibits. What really helps this museum and makes it special are the hundreds of docents, many who served and survived air combat during WW II. When they take the time to explain an exhibit, you pay attention, because that oldster was likely actually there, fighting for America in a war that changed the course of history.

CHAPTER 41

An Army of Giants
THE PALM SPRINGS WINDMILLS

"It's an army of giants," proclaimed Don Quixote, and despite the urgent warnings of his companion Sancho Panza, the erstwhile Spanish gentleman charged the "giants," only to have his lance jam into the sail of a windmill. He and his horse both fell to the ground but the hero of the Cervantes novel was not as hurt as his pride when he realized that instead of giants, he had attacked a field of windmills.

If Don Quixote felt that small field of windmills on the plains of long-ago Spain deserved a singular attack, he would have called in air strikes against the massive fields of windmills blanketing the desert floor near Palm Springs today.

One of the country's largest "wind farms," the one in the windy San Gorgonio Pass at the entrance to Palm Springs contains more than 4,000 separate windmills and provides enough electricity to power not only Palm Springs, but the entire Coachella Valley. According to the U.S. Weather Service, the San Gorgonio Pass is the "Finest natural wind tunnel in the world."

One of the oldest forms of energy, farmers have been harnessing wind for millennia to pump water or turn large stones to grind wheat or corn.

With the political instability of oil supplies and escalating oil prices, using wind to create non-polluting power has become an excellent alternative source of energy in recent decades.

Wind creates electricity by spinning the blades on a wind turbine. The turbine has a brake so if the wind blows too hard, the brake can stop the blade from becoming damaged. As wind has to blow at speeds of 12 to 14 miles an hour to turn the turbines fast enough to create electricity, turbines are placed in wind farms in perennially windy passes.

California has three such locations—one near Tehachapi, one in the Altamont Pass in northern California, and the local one. Those three wind farms alone provide 30 percent of the world's wind-generated power. Together, the three can illuminate a city the size of San Francisco.

The turbines each produce from about 50 to 300 kilowatts of electricity per hour. Most of the local windmills are 80 feet high, but many newer ones stand 150 feet tall with blades half the distance of a football field. With the blade in the top position, some of the windmills soar to 300 feet above the desert floor. The compartments at the top of the tower contain the generator, hub, and gearbox and weigh between 30,000 and 45,000 pounds.

A wind turbine producing the typical monthly needs of a household—300 kilowatt hours—can cost up to $300,000. Federal and state subsidies help offset the initial costs.

The larger, two-bladed 250 Kw wind turbine is an advanced technology developed by the New World Power Technology Company and uses aircraft-style aileron controls designed especially for high winds.

To learn more about the windmills and mingle among this amazing "army of giants," four regular 90-minute tours are offered daily, Wednesday through Saturday. Group tours can also be scheduled for other times.

The guided tours, operated by Windmill Tours, Wind Farms of Palm Springs, www.windmilltours.com or (760) 251-1997, take guests on electric vehicles amid the towering turbines. The giant blades "whooshing" overhead create an experience not soon to be forgotten as you can actually "feel" the cleaner and more environmentally friendly electricity being created.

Huell Howser, popular television producer and host, said this about the windmill tour, "This has been an absolutely wonderful experience... Standing here in front of these things is amazing, because this is the future right here."

The Palm Springs tour, the only tour of a working wind farm in the world, also offers photo taking opportunities, introduction to desert flora and fauna, and a gift shop.

The 4,000 windmills that make such a dramatic presence in the pass on the northern limits of Palm Springs may not

The Palm Springs windmills look like an army of giants.

be the "army of giants" as perceived by the hapless Don Quixote, or are they? They're extremely large, they're lined up military fashion, and they're capable of effecting incredible change as they harness nature's force, the wind, to create a new/old type of clean and efficient energy.

CHAPTER 42

Indian Casinos Big Desert Draw
AGUA CALIENTE BAND SETS PACE

Palm Springs had already started on its economic recovery with new attractions and a renewed vigor. Then California Indians won gambling rights in a 1987 U.S. Supreme Court decision and were the country's first to cash in by offering gaming. Indian casinos began springing up in all sorts of places throughout California.

In 1998 Californians further supported Indian gambling with a two-thirds majority passing Proposition 5. Not effective immediately, the state of California and the Indian tribes then struck a deal that allowed the tribes to offer house-banked card games and Las Vegas-style slot machines. The tribes were off and running.

Guidelines and restrictions were established including limiting a tribe to two casinos and 2,000 slot machines. With proposition 1A in March 2000 also passing and supporting the deal, the Indian casinos began further expansions. They are bigger, offer more in games and amenities, and are growing with more than 20 casinos in southern California alone. Today they seriously compete with Las Vegas.

The one location benefiting the most is the Coachella Valley, those low-desert destination resort communities only about 100-120 miles away from most of Los Angeles and Orange Counties.

By year 2000, four Indian casinos had already graced the valley from the San Gorgonio Pass to Coachella, then a fifth opened in 2001, and another in 2002. Today most are undergoing expansions and creating full-service destination resorts. The casinos have undergone such rapid growth this chapter became out-of-date after each draft was written.

The Casino Morongo is right off Interstate-10 in Cabazon at the entrance to the valley. At the other end of the valley in Indio/Coachella are the Fantasy Springs Casino and the Spotlight 29 Casino. In downtown Palm Springs is the Spa Hotel and Casino. The Spa's sister casino, the Agua Caliente, opened next to Interstate 10 in Rancho Mirage in spring 2001. In Coachella the Augustine Casino opened in 2002.

In 2003 the valley's six casinos formed the Palm Springs Casino Association with a goal to publicize that the Palm Springs area is truly the Gaming Capital of California.

The Casino Morongo

The Casino Morongo enjoys a great freeway location between metropolitan southern California and the desert communities. It is run by the Morongo Band of Mission Indians, most of whom are descendents of the area's earlier Cahuilla band.

Originally opened as a bingo hall in 1983, it was poised for expansion once legislative issues were resolved. The first expansion was in 1995. Another expansion created a large casino of 100,000 square feet with a 60,000 square-foot gaming area that offered 46 table games and 2,000 slot machines, the maximum allotment per tribe. The Casino Morongo for a while also operated a 53,000 square-foot 7,000 seat entertainment venue in a huge white tent in the parking lot next to the casino.

Not content with the Interstate 10 traffic stopping off, the Casino Morongo has completed construction on a true destination resort. In late 2004 a huge 23-story, 272 room, 600,000 square-foot resort hotel and casino opened to the public. Costing $250 million, Casino Morongo was designed by the same people who built the Bellagio and Treasure Island in Las Vegas. The 309-foot tall complex, the tallest structure in California east of Los Angeles, now dominates the pass, making those dinosaur structures at the next Cabazon turnoff look like toys.

Spa Hotel and Casino

The original Spa Hotel and Casino was located right in downtown Palm Springs on the nine-acre site of the original springs from which the town evolved. The Agua Caliente Band of Cahuilla Indians, the original settlers, had leased the spa area since the 1880s and purchased it back in 1992.

They renovated the hotel and added a casino which they continually expanded, earning enough profits to have been giving close to $1 million of their gambling windfall back to the city of Palm Springs each year.

The current 120,000 square-foot Spa Resort Casino opened November 6, 2003 on 6.8 acres just a block northeast of the original casino. It cost $90 million and is a "shot in the arm" in the revitalization of downtown Palm Springs. Even the older casino was a major draw and a bus tour destination. Referring to the new casino, Jeff Hocker of the Palm Springs Bureau of Tourism said, "It'll be huge—a very big draw."

In addition to the existing hotel, the Spa Resort Casino features three restaurants, including a 300-seat buffet, a 150-seat lounge, and a central bar on the casino floor. There are about 1,000 slot machines, some with progressive jackpots, and 40 table games. The Spa Hotel and Casino, which is open

24 hours a day, seven days a week, offers valet parking and free shuttle to the tribe's other casino, the Agua Caliente in Rancho Mirage.

Today the entire Palm Springs Spa Resort offers 230 hotel rooms, a renovated men's and women's spa, restaurants, meeting rooms and the casino. The original Spa casino employed 860 people and the new casino added about 250 more jobs.

The cream-colored stucco building with a distinctive roof complete with turrets and bright blue awnings is not only a new draw for the city of Palm Springs, it reminds all how far the Agua Caliente Band of Cahuilla have come since the days of the old bath house next to the springs that bubbled hot water.

The Spa Casino is owned by the Agua Caliente Band of Cahuilla Indians..

Agua Caliente Casino

The Agua Caliente Casino is the sister casino to the Spa Resort and makes the Agua Caliente Band the only Indian band with two casinos as of the end of 2004. This Las Vegas style casino features 35,000 square feet of gaming area, 1,100 slot and video poker machines, 33 table games, a 10-table poker room, and six restaurants, including a popular 24-hour all-you-can-eat buffet.

Big name entertainment has been attracted to the 1,000-seat Cahuilla Showroom at the Agua Caliente from the start.

The upscale Agua Caliente casino also features the latest in slot machine technology, offering ticket machines along with coin-based payouts. Executives from Las Vegas casinos have actually come to the Coachella Valley to research the new machines.

The Agua Caliente casino is right off the I-10 freeway at Ramon Road and Bob Hope Drive in Rancho Mirage and is more central to the valley's entire population.

Already plans are being made for expansion. The tribe wants to add a 14-story, 400-room hotel next to the casino, a 65,000 square-foot expansion of the casino, and a 90,000 square-foot showroom and meeting area. They also want to add a 350,000 square-foot retail complex on the west side of Bob Hope Drive, connected to the casino by a pedestrian bridge. Appropriate environmental reports and approvals are expected to be completed by late 2005.

Fantasy Springs Casino

Fantasy Springs Casino has been voted by valley residents as the "Best Overall Casino" in the area for the past nine years. It is run by the Cabazon Band of Mission Indians, descended from the Desert Cahuilla Indians and named for the great Cahuilla Chief Cabezon. The "Mission Indians" title is a bit misleading as the Cabazon Band was never part of the Spanish mission system.

Fantasy Springs began as a card room in 1980, later adding bingo. It now incorporates a 265,000 square foot gaming and entertainment area offering poker, blackjack, slots, live entertainment and a 24-lane bowling alley. Fantasy Springs now attracts over one million visitors a year.

Ongoing shows are the popular Joey and Maria's Comedy Italian Wedding and Kenny Kerr's impersonator cabaret show "Boylieve It Or Not" which has wowed 'em in Las Vegas for years.

Fantasy Springs has completed a $200 million expansion program that includes a hotel, an event center and a golf course. The 12-story, 250-room hotel opened in December 2004 and features a top-floor bar, a spa, restaurants and stores. A 100,000 square-foot convention and entertainment hall, with seating for 4,500 people, opened in February 2005. Along with a new parking structure, casino expansion and other improvements, it is reported that the new improvements created an additional 1,000 jobs.

The Cabazon Band of Mission Indians has made Fantasy Springs a true destination resort.

The Spotlight 29 Casino

The Spotlight 29 Casino in Coachella regained its former name after a couple of years of being called the Trump 29 Casino, reflecting a partnership between the Twentynine Palms Band of Mission Indians and entrepreneur

Donald Trump. Following a planned buyout, Tribal Chairman Dean Mike said, "We enjoyed a very beneficial relationship with the Trump organization, and now we are excited to put the Spotlight on our guests."

The Twentynine Palms Band of Mission Indians are descendents of the Chemehuevi Indians who settled at the Oasis of Mara in 29 Palms. The renegade Indian Willie Boy was a Chemehuevi who joined many of his tribe working at a ranch in Banning.

The casino, which originally opened in January 1996, is growing at a rapid rate. Already offering "Vegas-style" slot machines including progressive jackpots, blackjack, poker, mini baccarat, Caribbean stud poker, and Pai Gow, more is planned.

Phase 1 of a $60 million expansion opened and features 100,000 square feet of gaming area in a casino twice that size. The completed casino now boasts 2,000 slots, 35 gaming tables, a seven table poker room, banquet rooms, six restaurants, a private lounge, and an ultra-hip nightclub. The former casino has been revamped to accommodate boxing and other entertainment. Featured entertainers have included The Commodores, Don Rickles, Howie Mandell, Rita Coolidge, and LeAnn Rimes.

The Rattlesnake restaurant in the casino is one of the valley's finest. A five star dining experience, it has already won several culinary awards.

Expansion is currently underway for a 400-room hotel and spa, and a larger 200,000 square-foot casino and conference/entertainment center.

Augustine Casino

The Augustine Casino opened in July 2002 in Coachella. Owned by the Augustine Band of Cahuilla Mission Indians, it features 359 slot machines and 10 table games. At only 32,000 square feet, it is the smallest casino in the Coachella Valley, has two restaurants, and caters more to locals with lower priced gambling, including nickel and penny slot machines. It also offers $1 minimum blackjack during the early morning and graveyard shifts.

The Augustine Reservation, created by executive order in 1891, is only one square mile in size, and the band presently has only one adult member, Chairman Maryann Martin. The casino is operated by Paragon Venture, a Las Vegas company.

More in the future

During his final days in office, former Governor Gray Davis signed numerous bills favorable to Indian gaming allowing about a dozen other tribes to also open their casinos. In 2004 there were 22 Indian casinos in southern California. Several others are near completion.

The Torres-Martinez Band of Cahuilla Indians plans to open a large casino with 1,650 slots on their reservation not far from the Fantasy Springs and Trump 29 casinos. They also plan to put 350 slot machines at a truck stop near the Salton Sea.

In early 2004 new Governor Arnold Schwarzenegger called on California's gaming tribes to contribute more of their gambling revenue to the state and he set out to renegotiate compacts with them.

Meanwhile a coalition of race tracks and card clubs got an initiative on the ballot (Proposition 68) which would require tribes to pay 25 percent of their net slot revenues to the state or forfeit their monopoly. The Indians countered with their initiative (Proposition 70). Led by the Agua Caliente Band of Cahuilla Indians, Proposition 70 would require gaming tribes to pay 8.84%/year in taxes on their gambling revenue, equal to the state's corporate tax rate, and would remove all limits in scope and size in their casinos.

Governor Schwarzenegger opposed both measures, instead opting for his new compacts. The measures were both soundly defeated in November 2004 and the new compacts appear to be a win-win for both the Indians and the state.

The compacts preserve the tribes' monopoly on casino-style gambling but require them to make an initial $1 billion payment to the state, and thereafter annual payments estimated to range between $150 and $375 million. Tribes may exceed the 2,000 slot machine limit, but pay increasingly more to do so. Additionally, tribes must abide by binding arbitration in disputes, and submit to various environmental, labor relations and building safety constraints.

On the national scene, the U.S. Supreme Court, on October 4, 2004, refused to rule on an appeal against the states allowing Indian tribes to operate casinos, creating another victory for the Indians.

It appears demand, rather than regulations, will most likely determine the saturation point for Indian gambling in the Coachella Valley. All six casinos are doing whatever they can to draw customers, and big-name entertainment has stepped up a notch.

Pat Benatar has performed to a sold-out outside amphitheater at the old Spa; Gladys Knight sold 3,200 seats there over two nights, and Tom Jones also has performed. At the Agua Caliente, the 15,000 square feet Cahuilla Showroom has attracted Wynona Ryder, Burt Reynolds and David Brenner. Fantasy Springs has the Stars Amphitheater featuring outside concerts by Wayne Newton, Bill Cosby, Carrot Top, and the Doobie Brothers.

For decades Las Vegas was North America's undisputed gaming capital, replete with dazzling entertainment, nightlife and thousands of enticing slot machines. A lot of Los Angeles and Orange County people are already passing on Las Vegas and Laughlin in favor of the closer Palm Springs area, which is roughly a third the distance of Las Vegas. Popular are bus packages that offer casino chips and coupons.

With each casino employing between about 600-800 people, it has been a boon to the local economy. According to David J. Valley and Diana Lindsay, authors of *Jackpot Trail: Indian Gaming in Southern California*, non-Indians fill 95% of those jobs. They add that for every 1,000 employees, about $25 million in payroll is generated. Even more is spent by the casinos on local goods and services, creating more local jobs outside. The authors conclude that for every casino job, there are approximately an additional 1.5 jobs created.

On top of the tourist dollars brought to town, a booming economy has been developed. To Palm Springs it has been another factor in its revitalization. To the local Indians, it has been a wealth-generating windfall.

CHAPTER 43

The Naked Bridge
UPBEAT TOWN WELCOMES DIVERSITY

The gala opening of the first pedestrian bridge in Palm Springs made national news and was the talk of late night shows. What made the newscasters snicker at this widely-covered February 2003 media event was the fact that this bridge was built for the exclusive use of nudists.

The 13-year-old naturist Desert Shadows Inn Resort and Villas had expanded. A pedestrian bridge was needed to link the main nudist resort with newly built member condos across Indian Canyon Drive, a major north-south thoroughfare. Desert Shadows already took up the entire block from Indian Canyon east to Chaparral Road and built the new condos once they received city approval for the bridge.

The condos and 140-foot-long walled bridge are the newest additions to the growing Desert Shadows, by many accounts the country's number one naturist resort. In April 1992 Ray and Sue Lovato and Steve and Linda Payne opened an 11-room bed and breakfast for naturists. That has grown to now be a full-service resort with hotel, full spa, salon and steam room, a three meal restaurant with menus, three swimming pools, Jacuzzis, lighted tennis court, fountains with streams and waterfalls, 59 private villas and the new condos. Every time there is an improvement or addition at Desert Shadows, the envelope is pushed a little farther for nude recreation.

Coincidentally, the Desert Shadows is on the site of an old clothing optional hotel originally called the Casa del Sol. It was built in 1943 and owned by that Hollywood sheik himself, Errol Flynn. The old hotel at 1550 North Indian Canyon Drive lay abandoned for years and finally burned in 1990.

The Palm Springs Chamber of Commerce honored the Desert Shadows with the "Entrepreneur Development Award" in 1998. In 2001 the Palm Springs Resorts Authority voted them the "Best Managed Resort" award for under 200 rooms. Even *USA Today* called the Desert Shadows "the jewel in the crown of nude resorts."

The American Association of Nude Recreation (AANR) has held several board meetings at the Desert Shadows, and city officials have made appearances to welcome them to Palm Springs. Mayor pro-tem Ron Oden even stressed to them the importance of AANR becoming part of their respective communities.

The famous "Naked Bridge" crosses Indian Canyon Drive..

At the bridge opening, in recognizing the role nude recreation plays in Palm Springs, then Mayor Will Kleindienst, in attendance with three council members, said, "The bridge represents opportunity. We see it as an image, a landmark, an icon, a portal into Palm Springs."

Nudism in Palm Springs

Indeed, the Desert Shadows is not the only nude or clothing-optional resort in Palm Springs. There are approximately 30 nudist hotels in Palm Springs but only a handful are for straights, with most catering exclusively to gays or lesbians.

For straight couples there are two notable longstanding naturist destinations. One is the Terra Cotta Inn, run by Tom and Mary Clare Mulhall, a 17-room hideaway on Racquet Club Road that was designed by Albert Frey in 1960 and originally called the Monkey Tree. Tom has served as president of the Palm Springs Chamber of Commerce, and he and Mary Clare even coordinate "Nude Hikes Along the San Andreas Fault."

There's also the 12-room Morningside Inn on Indian Canyon Drive, run by former bankers Vern and Jill Sorensen. After spending numerous weekends at Palm Springs resorts from their Santa Clarita home, the Sorensens purchased the already clothing-optional hotel in 1999. The cozy B&B offers Continental breakfast poolside every morning and wine and snacks in the afternoon.

The newest clothing optional resort hotel opened in Palm Springs in early 2005. Called the Desert Fountain Inn, it is located on North Palm Canyon Drive.

The Hermit of Palm Canyon

In addition to the resorts, skinny-dipping behind one's own confines has been going on since the days of the original hot springs.

The first acknowledged nudist in Palm Springs perhaps was a hermit named William Pester. Born in Germany in 1886, he showed up in Palm Springs one day and lived in a shack he made of palm fronds near Palm Canyon.

During the 1920s and 1930s, Pester would often come into town at night and charge people 10 cents to look at the moon through his telescope. But during the days he lolled around the canyon *au naturel* and only put on clothes when he had visitors or when he went to town. According to former Mayor Frank Bogert, "He was a hippie long before anyone heard of the word."

William Pester, the Palm Springs hermit. *Photo courtesy Palm Springs Historical Society.*

Tolerance rules

A live-and-let-live attitude has prevailed in Palm Springs since the early days, creating a city so diverse that currently, Indians are the largest landowners, the mayor is a black man who is openly gay, and the president of the chamber of commerce operates a nude resort.

There's also a blending of numerous nationalities which can be reflected by the eclectic mix of restaurants in downtown Palm Springs alone: American, Brazilian, British, Chinese, Continental, Country, French, Greek, Indian, Irish, Italian, Japanese, Jewish, Mediterranean, Mexican, Mid-eastern, Persian, Southern BBQ, Southwest, Thai, and Vegetarian.

But it's not the mix of nationalities that makes Palm Springs so unique. More, it's the tolerant, even purveying, attitude of the town toward all types of cultural, social and unorthodox lifestyles and beliefs. Unlike so much of middle America, in Palm Springs people rarely care about what their neighbors are doing.

Even middle-class neighborhoods in Palm Springs have homes and pools well hidden behind walls or large ficus hedges. Many people have never met next door neighbors, let alone those a few doors away. Privacy is respected, and so is individual style and taste. Custom homes predominate, and CC&Rs do not cut it in Palm Springs.

Other desert communities, where tract homes surrounding a golf course are more dominant, seem to lack the blatant and coveted individualism of Palm Springs. Those developments may offer a private gate at the tract's entrance, but regardless of how exclusive it is, there is often a tight-knit community that amuses itself with dances and other social events. Middle America has been transplanted to the desert. But not to Palm Springs.

A Mecca for Gays & Lesbians

The guidebook *Best Places: Palm Springs and the Desert Communities*, in reference to Palm Springs, noted, "The area is also home to a thriving, highly visible gay crowd, many of whom stay at hotels and resorts catering exclusively to gay men and women."

In fact, at this writing, there were approximately 32 hotels and B&Bs for gay men and lesbian women in Palm Springs. There are an additional three or four in neighboring Cathedral City.

Out & About magazine noted that Palm Springs led the list in the country's exclusively gay male accommodations. Top honors went to: Cobalt, Desert Paradise, East Canyon Hotel and Spa, Hacienda, Inn Exile, INNdulge, La Posada de las Palmas, Santiago, Terrazo, and the Triangle Inn.

According to the city of Palm Springs census, gay men and women make up 25-30 percent of the resident population. Sometimes it seems like much more when there are gay-oriented events in town. Two of the largest of these are Easter week's big White Party, billed as the world's largest gay bash, and the Greater Palm Springs Gay Pride Festival and Parade that draws thousands to Palm Canyon Drive each November.

Palm Springs hosts the Gay and Lesbian Pride parade every November.

In addition, each March is the Dinah Shore Golf Classic in Rancho Mirage, during which time the Palm Springs area becomes the unofficial lesbian capital of the world. An estimated 15,000 lesbian tourists make their way to Palm Springs that weekend.

Gay Mayor and City Council

To further illustrate the entrenchment of the gay community in Palm Springs, in November 2003 councilman Ron Oden won the mayoral election, defeating incumbent Will Kleindienst, who was accused of being unfriendly toward gays. While his record tended to discount that perception, he couldn't convince the gay community and lost.

Thus, Ron Oden became the nation's first openly gay, black mayor. Also elected as city council members in that November election were two other openly gay politicians, Steve Pougnet and Ginny Foat, giving gays/lesbians a majority on the Palm Springs City Council. November's top council vote-getter was actually Mike McCulloch who joined incumbent Chris Mills as the two straight council members, the pair later finding themselves often out-voted by the gay majority.

With over a dozen gay bars and restaurants and many more gay friendly places, there are activities for the crowd all year long. It is so common to see two men together shopping, or two women dining, that residents hardly notice.

Real estate in Palm Springs is booming largely because of the gay influence.

Many brokers and agents are gay and so are their clientele. Several brokers advertise in San Francisco offering Palm Springs properties to baby boomer same-sex couples who want to retire to the sunshine in a gay-tolerant atmosphere.

They come and they buy. Most of the homes sold in the established and upscale old Las Palmas area over the past few years have been purchased by gay men, who often totally remodel them. The influence of the homosexual community upon Palm Springs has been enormous. The economy has been revitalized because of their presence and spending.

It's not uncommon to see more same-sex couples than straights at some restaurants. People not accustomed to living among a gay population and who may have formed negative expectations might be surprised. The reality is: except for those couple of events where unattached men come to town, the gay population is almost always in couples doing the same things straight couples do. And the unattached men congregate at places where they know they're welcome.

An example of the growth of gay enterprises would be the Adobe Restaurant on the site of an old cosmetic company's "beauty farm." A couple of years ago, the venerable old resort was refurbished and reopened with the name changed to The Villa—Palm Springs and features two quality dining areas, the Adobe Restaurant and Dates Café. The restored property and entire venture now caters to gay, lesbian and straight guests.

Reflecting on the emergent population in town, a new restaurant called Bloody Marys—part of a small gay chain that originated in San Francisco, recently opened on North Palm Canyon Drive. There are several gay-oriented publications printed in town, and the Revivals Thrift Shops are gay-operated with profits going into AIDS research.

Snowbirds visit their winter nests

There are some Palm Springs residents who have no problem with nudists or gays in their midst, but go absolutely bananas over the "snowbirds." "It's their driving," one local said. "They go so slow, never know where they're going, and can barely see over the steering wheel."

Others lament the longer lines at the post office, the waiting for tables at restaurants, the lack of abundant parking, the rising prices on everything with the increased population, the preponderance of "blue hairs" that makes you sometimes feel you live in a retirement home, and the uneasy feeling that someone is invading your own personal space.

The easy-going and carefree days of summer, when traffic is sparse and lines nonexistent, come to an abrupt halt about the first of November each year when snowbirds start returning to their winter nests. The Palm Springs species of this migratory fowl comes primarily from Oregon, Washington, Idaho, Montana, and the western provinces of Canada, although they hail from every state in the union and beyond.

Sometimes it seems like half of the cars in the Costco parking lot in winter are either from Oregon or Washington, according to their vehicle license plates.

Most snowbirds stay from five to six months and make their trek back northward in April leaving the dog days of summer to the locals.

They come and stay in accommodations based on their budget, from small trailers to huge motor homes, to condos, to beautiful estates which are only occupied during "the season."

Even though it makes the desert more crowded, the snowbirds are an integral and vital part of the Coachella Valley economy. The population rises by about one third, adding about 125,000 people to the valley's 318,000 (2000 census).

The Palm Springs population is 43,715, of whom 82 percent are permanent residents. Other communities are even more greatly impacted. Palm Desert, for example, sees an increase of 28,225 people on top of their 37,634 permanent residents.

The impact of this influx is enormous as snowbirds contribute over a half-billion dollars in sales tax revenue alone each year. Most are retired and have a greater spending ability, and they often spend freely. Needless to say, the arrival of these seasonal visitors is anticipated and welcomed by merchants and restaurateurs.

In addition to their spending, many of these visitors occupy their time in service and commitment to their winter communities. Many serve as volunteers or docents at local hospitals, museums, libraries, and other cultural affairs. Along with their physical and hands-on help, the snowbirds are significant contributors to charities and non-profit organizations throughout the valley.

Cognizant of the value to the area and the enmeshed and complex nature of the snowbird with the community, locals have learned to appreciate their presence. The arrival of the snow-white headed snowbird signifies not only that cooler days are ahead but the advent of a special time in Palm Springs, "the season" when activities and events are so numerous one can't attend them all.

In the summertime

In summer, when temperatures soar over 110-115 degrees many days and over 100 degrees daily for about four months, life slows down in Palm

Springs. Many restaurants and businesses close down for several weeks yet tourists still stroll Palm Canyon Drive.

Summers these days have brought a new species of migratory fowl. Europeans, especially the Germans and French, have discovered the entire American west and delight in flocking to the desert in summer. In fact, Death Valley National Park, which used to close down in summer, stays open all year now to a crowd that one ranger said, "In summer it's 99 percent Europeans here. That's why we stay open."

Europeans state they enjoy the wide open spaces that they see in movies and on television, yet are non-existent in densely-packed Europe. They also seem to not only tolerate, but are challenged by the record heat. Plus, Europeans like the bargain prices that traveling to desert locations in summer offer.

There's something for everyone in the city of Palm Springs. There are 28 churches of all denominations and four synagogues. There are 141 hotels with 6,333 rooms, and families from around the world come, enjoy the sunshine, play in the pools, golf or play tennis, stroll the Thursday night Villagefest, go hiking or shopping, sample the numerous restaurants, and usually never care about nor notice the town's diverse demographic statistics.

SECTION 7

❋

A Sense of History

With the short life expectancy of so many businesses, even those that have come and gone after brief runs along Palm Canyon Drive, special tribute goes to those long-time enterprises of Palm Springs that have endured the uncertain swings of the economic pendulum for decades.

Many of these long-time businesses, along with the preservation efforts of the museums and the lore and physical legacy of the Agua Caliente Band of Cahuilla Indians, are truly links to the past and are integral parts of the area's colorful heritage.

CHAPTER 44

Preserving The Past
PALM SPRINGS ART MUSEUM/INDIAN MUSEUMS

Palm Springs Art Museum

Established in January 1938, the 65-year-old Palm Springs Art Museum (formerly the Desert Museum) is a community effort and a real treasure. For its 50th anniversary, then-President Ronald Reagan wrote, "Nancy joins me in offering congratulations and warmest regards. We are confident that the Palm Springs Desert Museum will continue its role as a leading cultural force during its second 50 years."

From inauspicious beginnings in January 1938 when naturalist, author, and educator Don Admiral opened a small museum for desert study in La Plaza downtown, what is now the Palm Springs Art Museum has evolved into wonderful permanent collections, periodic cultural exhibits, showings of noted artists, as well as an entertainment venue.

Admiral did what a couple of earlier naturalists in the area had hoped to. Back in 1916, educator Edmund Jaeger formed a "nature club" through which he led hikes in the area. In 1932 resident naturalist Theodore Zschokke, and a friend of Don Admiral, also lectured on desert nature and led field trips.

Months after the opening in 1938, the museum incorporated. Admiral was elected as the first director while local merchant Carl Lykken became the museum's first president. Through most of the 1940s, Lloyd Mason Smith directed the fledgling museum; he initiated the concept of permanent and rotating exhibits.

The museum was relocated to a wing of the Welwood Murray Memorial Library, but by the late 1940s both entities needed to expand. On land donated by village pioneer Cornelia White, the museum built its first permanent home, a 10,000 square foot structure at the corner of Tahquitz Canyon Drive and Indian Canyon Drive. It was dedicated on December 5, 1958.

Steady growth forced a later board to seek a new and larger site. The current museum at 101 Museum Drive, between the Desert Fashion Plaza and the mountain, opened on January 24, 1976. The beautiful building was a result of hard work by the fundraising Women's Committee, and donations from numerous benefactors.

Palm Springs Art Museum.

Ambassador and Mrs. Walter Annenberg donated the Annenberg Art Wing and the 450-seat Annenberg Theater. The McCallum Natural Science Wing came from a foundation established in the will of pioneer developer Pearl McCallum McManus. The Sinatra Sculpture Court was donated by Frank Sinatra, and Walt Disney's widow provided for one of the art galleries.

Especially interesting are the permanent exhibits, the Oriental art donated by William Holden, the art and sculptures by George Montgomery, and the originals by the famous western artists Frederic S. Remington (*You Can Hear The Hoofbeats*), Charlie Russell, and Thomas Moran. They also have a Diego Rivera painting and an Auguste Rodin statue. Reflecting on the area's roots, there's also a room featuring Cahuilla baskets with the intricate work of Dolores Patencio, Dolores Lubo, and others.

The museum decided to change focus as it kicked off its 2004-05 season, switching from a multi-disciplinary museum to a world-class art museum, and is now called the Palm Springs Art Museum. They plan innovative art programs and the museum's theater program is expected to continue with increased vitality and celebrity headliners.

In a letter to members, Bob Armstrong, president of the museum's board of trustees, wrote, "We will seek avenues to share the natural science assets which we hold in public trust with regional organizations."

While the past was preserved at the former Palm Springs Desert Museum, it appears much of the collection of artifacts will soon be located in other venues.

Village Green Heritage Center

Smack dab in the center of downtown Palm Springs is the Village Green (200 block of South Palm Canyon Drive). It's a restful little square enhanced by some of the most historical buildings in Palm Springs—the McCallum Adobe and Miss Cornelia White's house—and the Agua Caliente Cultural Museum.

The McCallum Adobe, the oldest remaining building in Palm Springs, was built by John McCallum, the first permanent white settler in 1884. Today it serves as headquarters of the Palm Springs Historical Society and is a small museum, housing old photographs, books, tools, paintings, memorabilia, and much more from the early days of Palm Springs.

The "Little House" of Miss Cornelia White was originally built from railroad ties by Welwood Murray in 1893. Murray was the owner of the village's first hotel. It has been restored and furnished with donated antiques reminiscent of the era. A small donation to the Palm Springs Historical Society covers admission to both houses.

The Cornelia White House was originally built by Welwood Murray from railroad ties from the defunct Palmdale railroad.

The Agua Caliente Cultural Museum

"The Spirit Lives! Through you, my ancient people, I am." According to its Mission Statement, the Agua Caliente Cultural Museum was established "…to leave our prints, as our ancestors did for us, so that our children will have a sense of knowing that they are important."

Established by the Agua Caliente Band of Cahuilla Indians, the museum opened in 1991 at the Village Green Heritage Center at 219 South Palm Canyon Drive. A new 100,000 square foot museum is under construction on 52 acres at the base of Andreas Canyon south of Palm Springs. Once publicly owned, the land was purchased by the county and tribe in recent years.

The current museum offers a retail shop and educational programs, the Flora Patencio Basketry Exhibit, the ACCM Library, and a newsletter called *The Spirit*. "Preserving the Spirit" classes in Cahuilla pottery and walking sticks are held along with children's programs, including mask making.

The Agua Caliente Cultural Museum also sponsors a Native American Film Festival and Cultural Weekend in March.

The museum of the future, a large new $40 million facility, is expected to bring the message of the Cahuilla to the public. Plans include permanent and changing exhibits, a 150-seat multi-purpose theater, classrooms, a library, a re-creation of a Cahuilla village, a botanical garden, a café, museum store, and picnic facilities. There will also be hiking trails emanating from the museum.

According to a museum flyer, "The Cahuilla people do not think of themselves as holding a unique place in the world. They have always considered themselves an integral part of nature and accept the responsibility of protection of other life and the environment."

Their new museum, planned to open in December 2005, will help re-enforce the relationship between the Cahuilla and nature for future generations. With the purpose of preservation and a link to the past, it is solemnly and resolutely "leaving prints."

The Malki Museum

On the Morongo Reservation behind the outlet centers in Cabazon, about a mile up Fields Road toward the mountains, is a simple building with a complex mission. It is the non-profit Malki Museum, the first public museum established on an Indian reservation in southern California.

While its primarily function is to collect, preserve and display historical artifacts and materials of the Indians of the San Gorgonio Pass and all the Cahuilla-speaking peoples, it also serves as a research center for scholars seeking material on all the southern California Indians.

Open to the public Thursday through Sunday, the Malki Museum was co-founded in 1964 by Cahuilla women Jane K. Penn and Katherine Siva Sauvel. The Malki's first president and driving force for 40 years has been Sauvel, still active as president, a Cahuilla elder, and spokesperson. The museum is financed by contributions from patrons, visitor donations and dues from members of the Malki Museum Association.

The Malki Museum Press also prints books, booklets and brochures about Indian life in southern California. Early publications were informative booklets on the various southern California tribes, including *The Cahuilla Indians of Southern California* by Lowell John Bean and Harry Lawton.

Researcher and author Dr. Bean is a member of the Malki Museum Board and the Malki Press Editorial Board. As one who lived for years on the reservation, his books *Mukat's People, The Cahuilla Indians of Southern California and Temalpakh*, which he co-authored among others, makes him highly respected not only among scholars, but more importantly, among the Indians themselves.

CHAPTER 45

Still Going After All Those Years
LEGENDARY PLACES IN PALM SPRINGS

Many of the legendary places of Palm Springs are still around today. Numerous hotels, resorts, restaurants, and other businesses have survived for decades in some form or another and have become part of the heritage that is Palm Springs. Their history is intertwined with, and inseparable from that of the city.

Listed here are many of those businesses still extant that go back decades. A rigid establishment date was not used to determine inclusion; instead this book chooses to recognize older businesses that made a difference or quickly became part of the lore of Palm Springs.

Angel View

High on the mountain coming into Palm Springs on Highway 111 is a rock cluster that is much lighter than the surrounding terrain. With "wings" on either side, the formation very much resembles an angel.

Using the protective analogy an angel represents, Angel View Crippled Children's Foundation is a non-profit business that has served the community for over 50 years. Beginning with one rehabilitation facility in Desert Hot Springs in 1954, Angel View has expanded to 17 specially equipped 6-bed transitional houses throughout the valley and a summer camp on 17 acres in Joshua Tree.

In addition, Angel View operates 11 Thrift Shops and Prestige Boutiques in Palm Springs and surrounding areas. The community has long embraced the work performed by Angel View where 96 percent of every dollar donated goes directly to those in need. Several benefits involving some of the city's key business people and philanthropists, including Mel Haber of Ingleside Inn, and Jackie Houston, owner of the CBS affiliate television station, are held each year.

Dr. Robert Bingham began what emerged into the foundation by donating Desert Hot Springs land with a "view to the angel" hoping the hot mineral

Angel View: The light rock formation creates an "angel" on the mountain.

waters there would help polio patients. It turns out the therapeutic waters of the natural hot springs did wonders for the children.

Angel View went on to become home to thousands of children over the past half century, including 39-year-old Dan Philbin, son of TV personality Regis Philbin, who was born with missing vertebrae and leg muscles. He entered Angel View at age three and eventually had to have both legs amputated. The younger Philbin went on to Palm Springs High School, and eventually got two college degrees. He was the featured speaker at the Angel View Foundation's 50th Anniversary celebration in February 2004.

One key person who helped create national attention for Angel View was writer and journalist Glory Hartley. When her son Danny Munday became statistically one of the last children afflicted with polio, Hartley brought him to the original Angel View center in the 1950s.

She was so impressed with Angel View and the curative work being done she brought Mamie Eisenhower out to see the distinctive rock formation for which the organization is named. Later even President Eisenhower made a visit to Angel View.

While Danny Munday unfortunately died at age 15, Hartley has continued to support Angel View and personally make an impact on Palm Springs. She and Sally Presley Rippingale co-founded the Palm Springs Women's Press Club in 1980, which now has over 75 members. Hartley writes for several publications and also publishes the *Desert Insider*, an historical guide magazine.

Builders Supply

The oldest continuously operated business in Palm Springs is Builders Supply, a hardware store founded in 1926 by Alvah Hicks. (see "A Legacy of Commitment—Alvah Hicks"). It was sold by the Hicks family in 1960 to Frank De Benedetti, of De Benedetti Enterprises and was owned by his daughter and son-in-law, Joy and Frank Purcell, for nearly 40 years until January 2000.

Richard Barnes, John Thompson, and Kyle Kincaid bought De Benedetti Enterprises and continue to run the business. A second store was established in Desert Hot Springs in the early 1970s.

Now called Ace Hardware, the place is always crawling with contractors who still refer to it as Builders Supply.

Postcard recognizing the 75th birthday of Builders Supply Company in Palm Springs. *Photo courtesy Builders Supply Company.*

Caliente Tropics Motor Lodge

The Caliente Tropics Motor Lodge (now the Caliente Tropics Resort), at 411 East Palm Canyon Drive is considered by the Palm Springs Historical Site Board to be the best remaining example of a Polynesian-themed motel in southern California. Extremely popular during the '50s and '60s, the tropical island theme had pretty much vanished two decades later.

Designed by Ken Kines in 1964, the Tropics, as it was originally called, features a dominant peaked A-frame entrance and the typical tropical landscaping replete with the obligatory Tiki god statues.

The old motor hotel underwent an extensive $2.2 million renovation building upon and enhancing its Polynesian theme. Now the upscale Caliente Tropics Resort features custom-furnished and boutique-styled guestrooms, complimentary breakfast, newspaper, beverages, and more.

Interestingly, a local statute prohibited the use of the word "motel," which is what this place is. In Palm Springs, they have to be called either inn, or lodge, or resort, or motor hotel, or something—just don't call it a motel.

Casa Cody

Tucked away in the old Palm Springs Tennis Club area is the Casa Cody, one of the oldest continually operated inns in Palm Springs. Built in the 1920s by Harriet Cody (see "Making a Difference—Harriet Cody"), its 17 charming rooms still attract celebrities and those wishing a restful respite.

Del Marcos Hotel

A good example of Mid-century Modern architecture is the Del Marcos Hotel at the corner of Baristo Road and Belardo Road. (225 West Baristo Road.) in downtown Palm Springs. Designed in 1947 by the famed architect William F. Cody (see "Design Palm Springs Style"), it has 16 guestrooms ranging from private patios or balconies to suites with full kitchens.

At one time it was called the San Marino, but it has since reverted to its original name. The spacious rooms have been refurbished to reflect Cody's original design. And in keeping with the Mid-century Modern theme, music from the '40s and '50s is heard poolside.

Ingleside Inn

The Ingleside Inn, an original estate built in the 1920s for Carrie Birge and turned into a first class hotel in 1935 by Ruth Hardy, (see "Prominent Palm Springs Women—Ruth Hardy"), is still going strong.

Melvyn Haber bought the inn in 1975, added the upscale Melvyn's restaurant, and the venerable old hideaway at Belardo Road and Ramon Road (200 West Ramon Road) still attracts the celebrities and is now an historical site.

Brooklyn-born Haber was a New York businessman who admittedly fell in "love at first sight" with the Ingleside in a visit to Palm Springs and has run it with loving care ever since. Haber's book *Bedtime Stories of the Legendary Ingleside Inn in Palm Springs* features a special dedication from no less a personage than actor-turned-governor Arnold Schwarzenegger.

It's a place where Frank and Barbara Sinatra held their engagement party, Debbie Reynolds celebrated her 50th birthday, Rita Hayworth recuperated following a hospital stay, and Kurt Russell and Goldie Hawn flew in just for lunch.

Live music in the Casablanca Lounge provides a romantic scene for dancing, and in October 2003, Haber completed a $400,000 renovation which included updating Melvyn's restaurant with new décor.

Mel Haber himself is a very active volunteer chairing and supporting various Angel View Crippled Children's Foundation activities. The Ingleside Inn is a Palm Springs legend that has not only survived but mellowed to a rich piece of Palm Springs history.

Le Parker Meridien (Givenchy Spa)

It's still going strong, but has changed hands and names so often it is hard to figure out that this storied place is the same one that has been owned by a couple of famous names.

Thus the Holiday Inn/Melody Ranch/Gene Autry Hotel/Givenchy Spa/Merv Griffin's Resort Hotel and Givenchy Spa at 4200 East Palm Canyon Drive is now Le Parker Meridien, also called the Parker Palm Springs.

California's first Holiday Inn, initially a small cinderblock and concrete building, was built in 1959 on the site, then at the far edge of Palm Springs. Cowboy singer Gene Autry, who had just acquired the California Angels baseball team, bought the hotel in 1961 partially to house the team for spring training. The team was training in Palm Springs at the newly named Angel Stadium, originally called the Polo Grounds when built in 1949.

Autry changed the name of the Holiday Inn to Melody Ranch and increased the number of rooms, added tennis courts, a second swimming pool, first class suites, bars and restaurants. The name that stuck over the next 30 years, however, was The Autry Hotel. Before the Cowboy sold the hotel he went on to make a big impression upon Palm Springs.

Along with major league baseball and its attendant glamour and economic clout, Autry and his wife Jackie gave back much to the community. For example, in 1984 they donated $5 million for an expansion at the Eisenhower Medical Center, now called the Autry Tower. Gene Autry Trail is a major north-south artery running adjacent to the Palm Springs Airport and named for the popular singing cowboy.

Autry sold the hotel to Rose Narva, his hotel general manager, in 1992. Narva worked out an arrangement with French designer Hubert de Givenchy, who lent the resort its name.

In 1998 television personality and businessman Merv Griffin bought the Givenchy and renamed it Merv Griffin's Resort Hotel and Givenchy Spa. By this time the Givenchy Spa sat on 14 beautifully manicured gardens and orchards, boasted 107 rooms and villas and had become a favorite respite for Hollywood celebrities. The Versailles-inspired white colonnaded resort featured a top restaurant called GiGi's, a full-service spa, six tennis courts, 10,500 square feet of indoor meeting space, and outdoor event space as well.

The world-class spa was ranked No. 4 by readers of Conde Nast Traveler magazine.

Griffin sold it in late 2002 to Epix Hotels and Resorts, who only owned it a short time. It closed for a while and was purchased in 2003 by the parent company of Le Parker Meridien. The Parker group made significant renovations and it reopened in 2004, immediately becoming the desert's first and only five star resort.

Now there are 144 luxurious rooms, suites, and villas, the famous spa now called the Palm Springs Yacht Club, and two restaurants—Norma's, a five star diner, and Mr. Parkers, a five star family-style gourmet dining experience. A highly trained staff helps insure that all possible amenities are offered and delivered with flair.

Le Vallauris

While there may be older restaurants, this one has survived three decades in one of the town's oldest buildings and is widely considered as the finest dining in Palm Springs. Le Vallauris restaurant was established in January 1974 by Paul Bruggemans and Camille Bardet, owners of the noted Le St. Germain restaurant in Los Angeles.

The building at 385 West Tahquitz Canyon Way was for 50 years the former home of the son of village pioneer Nellie Coffman, George and Alta Roberson and their family. The Mediterranean/Spanish Revival building was designed by Charles Tanner and built in 1924. It is a Palm Springs Historical Landmark.

In 30 years the restaurant has become a landmark in its own right. It was named after a small village in the south of France where Picasso made his ceramics, and the French cuisine is from the same area. The valley's top rated and award winning restaurant has welcomed many famous personages, including President and Mrs. Gerald Ford, the Bob Hopes, the Frank Sinatras, the Gregory Pecks, Ambassador Walter Annenberg, Leonard Firestone, Lee Iacoca, and royal princes and princesses.

Moorten Botanical Garden

Moorten Botanical Garden has been a Palm Springs landmark since its 1957 founding (see "Prominent Palm Springs Women—Patricia Moorten").

Oasis Hotel

Built in 1924 by village pioneers Pearl and Austin McManus at the corner of Belardo Road and Tahquitz Canyon Way and still in operation (see "Reclaiming a Heritage").

O'Donnell Golf Club

The Coachella Valley's first golf course built in 1926 is still in operation (see "The Desert's Premier Golf Course").

Palm Springs Spa Resort

The social heart of Palm Springs for hundreds of years has been the hot mineral water spa in what is now the center of town at 100 North Indian Canyon Road at corner of Tahquitz Canyon Way. It was the gathering place of the Agua Caliente Band of Cahuilla Indians.

While the Palm Springs Spa Resort on the site today is a far cry from its two forerunner enterprises, the Spa could be considered the oldest business still going. From as early as 1870 when a primitive, rough-planked shack was erected on the site, the local Indians have been known to charge admission to their Anglo visitors.

They later replaced that structure with a bathhouse that had some primitive bathing cubicles. For years the main financial sustenance of the Agua Caliente Band were fees from those health seekers who came from far and wide for the curative properties the mineral water provided.

The Spa Hotel that incorporates those hot mineral springs was the first long-term (99 years) lease enacted by the tribe after passage of an amendment to Public Law 86-326 in 1959. The ownership was later returned to the Agua Caliente Indians and now is a full-scale resort with a brand new casino. The sleek Mid-century Modern structure itself was designed by noted architect William F. Cody and is a Palm Springs Historic Site.

Plaza Theatre

The long-legged lovelies of the world famous Fabulous Palm Springs Follies have been performing out of the historic Plaza Theatre, built by Earle

Strebe in 1936, for the past 13 years. The storied theater is a perfect venue for this popular variety show (see "As Young As You Feel" and "Theaters Come To Town").

Racquet Club

The venerable Racquet Club, established by Charlie Farrell and Ralph Bellamy in 1934 is one of the most famous of the classic Palm Springs institutions (see "Racquet Club Becomes Hollywood Haven").

Riviera Hotel

The successful owner of the famous "Chi Chi" nightclub, Irwin Schuman, always thought big. Back in 1954 he and his brother Mark acquired 40 acres at the northeast corner of Indian Canyon Drive and Vista Chino from the Indians with plans to build the biggest hotel in Palm Springs as well as its first convention hall. (See "The Legendary Chi Chi").

Considered risky at the time because the town still closed down in summer, and the location was "too far north," the Schumans' Riviera Hotel opened in the mid-1950s and has never closed its doors since.

In 1975, Irwin Schuman spent $3 million to upgrade the Riviera Hotel. He even took two statues that had flanked the stage of the Starlite Room in his "Chi Chi" and moved them to the Riviera to be part of a fountain.

The Riviera Hotel and Resort. The large resort is readily spotted from the top of the tram.

Today the Riviera Hotel and Convention Center, 1600 North Indian Canyon Drive is a full service resort on 24 acres of land. Its 476 guestrooms are in eight two- and three-story buildings fanning out from two swimming pools, one of which is the largest in Palm Springs. There are banquet and convention facilities, nine tennis courts and a tennis stadium, an 18-hole putting green, a fitness center, volleyball and basketball courts.

The Riviera caters to big groups and is large and sprawling. One conference attendee, in a later web site review, said, "…the place is huge. Several times I got lost going from point to point."

Smoke Tree Ranch

On the remains of a failed 1887 enterprise called Palmdale (see "The Little Train That Couldn't") rose a ranch that would one day be one of the most exclusive in the Coachella Valley.

The Smoke Tree Ranch on the Palmdale site was purchased in 1936 by Fred and Maziebelle Markham who transformed it into a colony of homes where Western-style living prevailed. Once it was successful, in 1945 the Markhams sold the property to the 85 homeowners, or "colonists" as they are called. The Markhams continued on, serving on the board of directors which administers the affairs of the ranch.

Smoke Tree Ranch encompasses approximately 400 acres just south of East Palm Canyon Drive between Sunrise Way and Farrell Road. Three hundred acres are reserved for the 85 colonists and their homes, and the guest ranch occupies 20 acres. Part of the remaining acreage is leased for stables, and part is the Smoke Tree Village Shopping Center, which acts as a buffer zone between the colony and East Palm Canyon Drive.

There are 57 guest cottages on the guest ranch, horses, swimming pool, a bowling green, and tennis courts.

Smoke Tree regulars and members included President Eisenhower, Cary Grant, and Walt Disney, and today numerous corporate leaders spend winters in the private enclave where desert authenticity is preserved.

Walt Disney and his wife Lily bought into the Smoke Tree lifestyle in 1948 but sold the house in 1954 when trying to raise money to open Disneyland. He loved Smoke Tree so much he bought his second home there in 1957 after the rousing success of the Magic Kingdom was assured. Disney liked lawn bowling and was influential in getting the bowling green at Smoke Tree. He also lent the expertise of his studio and designed some of the Smoke Tree Ranch guest cottages.

Palm Springs Tennis Club

Built by Pearl McManus in 1937 (see "Reclaiming a Heritage"), the Palm Springs Tennis Club (PSTC) had the world's two finest tennis courts and a round swimming pool flanked by v-shaped palm trees. Nestled against the rocks, the pool became the most photographed and copied swimming pool in the west.

The clubhouse, which opened in February 1938, was designed by Los Angeles architect Paul Williams, the first black member of the American Institute of Architects. It was inspired by a monastery in Amalfi, Italy.

Early tennis club members included Ronald Coleman and Gilbert Roland, both major movie stars at the time. Along with numerous celebrities, some tennis greats also played there.

In 1939 "Auntie Pearl" hired Tony Burke to manage the PSTC and with his promotional flair he got a lot of things done. He even inaugurated trout fishing by bringing in trout from the Whitewater hatchery and dumping them into the stream which ran from Tahquitz Canyon through the property to The Desert Inn.

The tennis club became a timeshare property in 1980 and rentals are open to the public. Today there is a 63-unit hotel, plus 63 private bungalows with up to two bedrooms. There are now 11 tennis courts, three swimming pools (including the original), five spas, a fitness center and more. The stylish Spencer's restaurant features Continental cuisine and patio dining. It is owned by Harold Matzner.

The Palm Springs Tennis Club, at the extreme west end of Baristo Road, is a Palm Springs Historical Site.

The Desert Sun

In many respects the 75-year-old *The Desert Sun* is the pulse of the valley. It was begun by Carl Barkow and Harvey Johnson in August 1927 as a free weekly publication.

Prophetically, in that first issue, the publishers wrote, "...that this remarkable winter resort is in line for still greater development and extensive progress is not to be denied."

As the Coachella Valley grew so did *The Desert Sun*. Barkow, who was one of the visionaries of the Palm Springs Aerial Tramway, sold the paper to Oliver Jaynes in 1946. It was expanded in 1955 to Monday through Friday. In 1988 The Desert Sun Publishing Company was formed and in 1991 a Sunday edition was added.

Today, Robert J. Dickey is the publisher and president of *The Desert*

Sun. In a 75th anniversary article of the paper in 2002, he wrote, "Seventy five years of technology has brought *The Desert Sun* from typewriters and letterpresses to cell phone-equipped laptop computers, full-color offset printing presses and a Web site, www.thedesertsun.com, that brings you news as it happens."

Today *The Desert Sun* employs over 350 people, including long-time newspaperman Steve Silberman who joined the paper in 2001 as executive editor. Silberman instituted numerous changes both in content and appearance. He increased local news, added more color to the pages, and announced a teamwork venture with local television station CBS2.

The Desert Sun now publishes three magazines for Coachella Valley communities: *Desert Post Weekly, Desert Magazine*, and the *Hispanic Viva Monthly*.

As part of its 75th anniversary celebration in 2002, *The Desert Sun* published a book featuring milestones stories and photos covered over the decades. In the introduction to *Desert Memories: Historic Images of the Coachella Valley*, Congresswoman Mary Bono wrote, "*The Desert Sun* cried with us, cheered with us, celebrated with us, and mourned with us. They praised accomplishments and criticized excesses. Our success as a community is tied to the success of *The Desert Sun*."

The Willows

Set against the hillside where Tahquitz Canyon Way runs into the mountain is The Willows, a charming eight-room inn lovingly restored as an Italian villa.

Built in 1927, it was the home of New York lawyer Samuel Untermyer who lived there until his 1940 death. He had many notable friends and acquaintances, including Albert Einstein, who was a guest in his Palm Springs home on numerous occasions.

There were several owners until Paul Marut and his wife Tracy Conrad bought it in 1997 and began a meticulous restoration that included handmade Moorish tiles and mahogany French doors. The eight guestrooms are unique and feature antiques, Italian burled walnut furniture, luxurious private baths, fireplaces and more.

The Willows Historic Inn.

One, called the Rock Room, is named for a boulder from the cliff that protrudes into the bathroom.

The Library Room was said to have been the honeymoon quarters of Clark Gable and Carole Lombard. And the Marion Davies Room was named for its former tenant.

The Willows management also restored the O'Donnell House (see "The Desert's Premier Golf Course") just a little farther up the hill which can be reserved for weddings or special occasions. In 2002, The Willows received the Conde Nast Johansen's "Most Outstanding Inn Award." It is a Palm Springs Historical Site.

Other Historic Inns of Palm Springs

In addition to those businesses covered, there are several charming historic hotels and inns, primarily in the Palm Springs Tennis Club district, that have been catering to guests for years. Most of these hotels date from the '40s and '50s, and are small (4 to 18 rooms). Many of them have changed names over the years. These hotels include:

- **"A Place In The Sun" Garden Hotel**, built in 1948 and housed the crew of the classic movie *A Place In The Sun* with Elizabeth Taylor and Montgomery Clift.

- **Arenas Gardens West**, five Spanish revival style units, part of property originally owned by village pioneer Pearl McCallum McManus.

- **Ballentines Hotel**, on Indian Canyon Drive. Built in 1952, 13 rooms have been redone in classic Mid-century style.

- **The Chase Hotel**, 200 West Arenas Road, originally called The Holiday House when built in the late 1940s, was a Doris Day favorite. Classic Mid-century Modern architecture is a fitting setting for its 26 guestrooms.

- **Desert Hills Apartment Hotel**, another Mid-century Modern design, built in 1956, has 14 studios and suites.

- **Desert House Inn**. Over 50 years old, its six rooms are done in Southwest ranch style.

- **The Indianola, INNdulge** and **Triangle Inn** are three gay resorts with long histories. The Indianola Tiki Guest Resort, with 11 rooms, is Polynesian style. Rooms feature original '50s furniture, including bamboo lamps.

INNdulge, built in 1958 as Golden Palm Villas became a gay resort in 1995. The late '50s Mid-century Modern Triangle Inn was originally called the Impala Lodge.

- **La Bella Villas** offers six Southwest-style villas refurbished from a small 1939 inn.

- **The Ocotillo Lodge** on East Palm Canyon Drive is not so small, and features all-suite bungalows and villas. Ownership has changed over the years, but at one time Gene Autry was part owner before it was purchased by Lakers owner Jerry Buss. It is now owned by the Doric Company which owns hotels in Santa Barbara, Santa Monica and Miami Beach.

- **The Orbit Inn** on West Arenas Road offers 18 rooms in Mid-century Modern style. Travel & Leisure magazine referred to it as "a desert oasis where the 1950s never went out of style."

- **The Orchid Tree**, originally built in 1934, offers 45 rooms with differing architectural styles, from Spanish to Modern.

- **The Viceroy Palm Springs** is a new name for the Estrella Resort and Spa on South Belardo Road. The 74-room newly revamped hotel was originally built in 1933.

- **The Villa Royale** on South Indian Trail, is a Palm Springs classic. Built in 1947 as a Mediterranean-inspired hideaway for Hollywood celebrities, the Villa Royale offers 31 exclusive villas, each adorned with antiques and fine furnishings, and lush, landscaped grounds. The accompanying upscale Europa restaurant, which features Mediterranean fare, was once the innkeeper's home.

CHAPTER 46

Do You Remember?
GONE BUT NOT FORGOTTEN

While much of the Palm Springs heritage is still in evidence today, many businesses that helped put the resort city on the map are no longer around. The original Palm Springs Hotel, The Desert Inn, and the Del Tahquitz Hotel have long been razed in the city's progress.

Gone too are those legendary places that catered to legions of party-goers, like the famous Chi Chi, the Dunes Club, or the Doll House.

The rich history of some of these establishments of earlier eras helped define the Palm Springs of today.

The Desert Inn

The "original" Palm Springs desert resort, The Desert Inn, was established by village pioneers Dr. Harry Coffman and Nellie Coffman in 1909 and run by Nellie and her sons for decades (see "Mother Coffman's Boardinghouse"). It was sold by the family in 1955 and later razed to be part of the Desert Fashion Shopping Plaza.

El Mirador

After a gala opening on New Year's Eve 1927, the El Mirador Hotel was the "in" spot in Palm Springs for decades and is now a medical center (see "El Mirador Draws the Celebrities")

Hotel Del Tahquitz

The Hotel Del Tahquitz was one of the big attractions in town during the 1930s and 1940s. At the southeast corner of South Palm Canyon Drive and

Baristo Road in downtown Palm Springs, the Del Tahquitz was completed by 1930. It was erected by a motion picture actress who soon thereafter sold her investment to Tom and Billie "Mom" Lipps in 1931.

The popular Del Tahquitz was a two-story pueblo-style building featuring broad balconies with thatched roofs and stucco walls. The Western motif included saddles for seats in the Saddle Bar Cocktail Lounge as well as an outdoor dining grill. The Del Tahquitz offered a tennis court, badminton, ping-pong, and a swimming pool.

Excellent cuisine was featured in the Azure Room. There was even an ice rink

Del Tahquitz Hotel. *Photo courtesy Palm Springs Historical Society.*

floorshow in the dining room which was a Palm Springs first. In the 1940s, there were big shows in the '49er Room, featuring vaudeville, comedy acts, impersonations and much more.

During World War II, Tom and Billie Lipps kept the Del Tahquitz Hotel open during the summer, at a loss to themselves, for the Ferry Command pilots stationed in town. That "pleasant gray-haired lady" Billie became "Mom" to scores of servicemen. Word got out that the guys were always welcome and Mom would even allow them to sleep four or six to a room, keeping their expenses down.

They had enormous respect for her and she always took care of "her boys" as she called them. Many of them corresponded with her for years, even up to her death in 1991 at age 96.

Billie "Mom" Lipps was another Palm Springs woman who made things happen. She became the first woman president of the California Hotel Association.

She sold the hotel in 1946 to M.A. Charleston who continued to run it. It closed in 1958 and original plans called for a bowling alley on the site, which didn't materialize. It was then bought by Santa Fe Federal Savings and Loan Association who demolished it in 1960 to build their new headquarters. The building now houses the offices of John Wessman, developer of several real estate projects in Palm Springs.

Howard Manor

While the Howard Manor is still in operation these days as The Palms at Palm Springs, an upscale fitness retreat, the Howard Manor days are but a wistful memory. Actually the hotel at 572 North Indian Canyon Drive goes back before the Howard Manor tenure to 1935 when the hotel was constructed.

Originally called the Colonial House, it was built by former Las Vegas casino owner Al Wertheimer who also owned the Dunes Club, one of Cathedral City's nightspots. It was originally a more-or-less private hotel housing the owner and his gambling bud-dies. It is said that the Colonial House had a large illegal gambling room downstairs which was entered through a secret stair-well concealed behind a locked pantry cupboard.

The long run as a popular resort hotel began in the late 1940s when Robert S. and Andrea Leeds Howard bought the property. Robert was the son of Charles Howard, successful car dealer and owner of the famous racehorse *Seabiscuit*. Andrea Leeds was an actress who had achieved fame in the 1937 movie *Stage Door* with Katharine Hepburn.

For three decades the Howard Manor on North Indian Canyon Drive gave the other larger resorts a run for their money and was also visited by celebrity guests, including Jack Dempsey, David Janssen, and others.

The old Howard Manor is now a spa called The Palms.

The Howards sold the hotel in 1979 to fitness pioneer Sheila Cuff and her husband Don who established one of the first spas in the desert. Sheila was a former figure skater and physical education teacher and soon had her charges doing aerobics and other fitness routines.

The Cuffs made major renovations and The Palms, a 45-room health resort with a fascinating history has been placed on the market for $3.5 million. Meanwhile The Palms is not only one of the oldest spas in Palm Springs, but one of its most popular.

Palm Springs Biltmore Hotel

Another "in place" during the golden age of Palm Springs was the Palm Springs Biltmore Hotel. It opened in February 1948 and was popular with celebrities and wealthy tourists during the 1950s and 1960s, saw decline begin in the 1970s, and finally closed its doors in 1988.

It was advertised as "The Last Word in Informal Elegance" when it was opened in 1948 by Samuel H. Levin and his two sons, Richard and Robert Levin. The senior Levin was in the motion picture publicity business in San Francisco, moved to Palm Springs in 1945, and bought 50 acres on East Palm Canyon, building the Biltmore on 11.5 of those acres.

The Biltmore opened with 50 rooms and was the first large hotel to stay open all summer. From an opening-day full house, the Biltmore attracted wealthy easterners and Midwesterners who would stay for weeks at a time.

At 1000 East Palm Canyon Drive, the Biltmore was among the most popular in Palm Springs during the 1950s and 1960s, also welcoming many celebrities as guests, including Jack Benny, Fernando Lamas, Mary Martin, and Spencer Tracy.

There was a championship size tennis court and a nine-hole golf course. The hotel was later expanded to 72 rooms with numerous single-story bungalows, some with rock fireplaces. The restaurant and lounge, which featured entertainment, were also big draws.

Early on, Samuel turned the hotel over to the family: Robert, who managed it since the opening; Richard, and another brother and sister in San Francisco.

With the incredible growth of the condominium concept in the 1970s, and shorter visits in general by clients, Palm Springs had turned into a weekend town. The Biltmore was among those venerable old hotels that had begun to decline.

Then in 1983, a man who said the food at the Biltmore made him ill was awarded $75,000.

Lacking group facilities and walk-in traffic, the Biltmore finally closed in 1988. It languished for years. By this time Samuel was long gone, son Richard later passed away

The last remnants of the former Biltmore Hotel.

in 1993, and Robert and the others wanted to sell. It was originally listed in 1994 at $6 million, then dropped to $3.9 million, and a sale was finally consummated in 1999.

The buyer, Linda Grant from Los Angeles, had plans to refurbish the property into an art-deco 1950s style hotel, including the addition of high-end 1950s specialty shops. Unfortunately, her plans never got off the ground, and the property continued to deteriorate.

Becoming an eyesore, the city of Palm Springs cited that the 11.5 acre property was in poor condition, had many code violations, and the owner was given 30 days to bring it to code or raze it. It continued to languish and was finally demolished in Fall 2003, ending an era of one of the hot spots of Palm Springs.

Robert Levin, now 85, who lives nearby and witnessed the demolition, expressed sadness at seeing his family's old Biltmore reduced to rubble.

New owner Nexus Residential Communities, Inc. is building 19 single family homes and 133 condos on the site, and plans to link with the past by calling the new development—the Biltmore Colony.

The Doll House

It was only a 14 year run, but what a run it was! It was one of only three nightspots in Palm Springs (El Mirador and the Chi Chi were the others) during the golden years of 1945-1959. The Doll House, at 1032 North Palm Canyon Drive was one of the most popular restaurants and watering holes in town.

Opened by Ethel and George L. Strebe (the brother of theater owner Earle Strebe), after George's release from the service in 1945, The Doll House became an immediate favorite among locals, tourists, and the movie crowd.

Many visitors to town stopped at The Doll House for dinner and cocktails before checking into their hotels. It became a second home for many celebrities and regulars included Marlene Dietrich, Doris Day, Eddie Fisher, Ava Gardner, Dick Haynes, Ida Lupino, Howard Hughes, Rosalind Russell, Frank Sinatra, Elizabeth Taylor, Jack Warner, and Darryl Zanuck. Peggy Lee was a singer there who credits The Doll House for her "discovery."

One Doll House waitress who resembled actress Joan Crawford, asked for the star's autograph when she stopped by. The visiting star had fun trading places with the waitress and taking orders, to which some customers said, "You know, you look just like Joan Crawford."

Before the war, George and Ethel bought the Zanzibar, which later became the Sportsman, from Irwin Schuman, but they sold it after George went in the navy.

The Strebes also bought The Doll House in the Balboa area of Newport Beach in 1950, which they ran during the summer months.

George and Ethel went their separate ways in 1959, and The Doll House's fabulous days were over. Ethel married John Harutun and they established Ethel's Hideaway on the Deep Well Guest Ranch, which they ran for four years. Then in 1962 they opened That John's on the former location of the Latin Quarter.

George helped his brother with the movies, was one of the founders of the Desert Circus, an annual fundraising event, was past president of both the local Shrine Club and the Los Compadres Riding Club. He died in September 1989.

Ethel Strebe Harutun is in her 80s, is vice president of Classic Homes Realty, and has been living in her Palm Springs Las Palmas area home for 34 years. She received a star on the Palm Springs Walk of Fame in 2002.

The Doll House became Sorrentino's Restaurant in 1966, an Italian favorite for many years and a regular haunt of Frank Sinatra's. You could order Steak Sinatra, a meal named after him, and maybe bump into Kirk Douglas, who also dined there. But no more, as Sorrentino's closed its doors in 2002.

Deep Well Guest Ranch

The Deep Well Guest Ranch was "horses in the desert" with all the western trappings. It was operated by Frank and Melba Bennett for 16 years. (see "Prominent Palm Springs Women: Melba Berry Bennett"). It is now a private housing enclave off of East Palm Canyon Drive.

The Deep Well Ranch was originally a dude ranch.

Dunes Club

Today with all the Indian casinos, gambling is ubiquitous in the desert communities, but it was taboo back in the 1930s and 1940s. However, that didn't stop the popular pastime from surfacing.

In the years just before Palm Springs became a city, the town leaders, including the indominitable Nellie Coffman, effectively squelched attempts to opening gambling clubs.

One easterner who had relocated to Palm Springs via Las Vegas, Al Wertheimer, was denied opening a club. Undaunted, he crossed the border into Cathedral City and opened the Dunes Club in 1934. At the time the Spanish style building was out in the middle of the desert on a newly bulldozed street now called Date Palm Drive.

It is said that Wertheimer had sufficiently bribed the local constable who, in turn, notified the Dunes when a "raid" might take place. The accommodation worked well, and for years the Dunes Club was the place you might end up throwing the crap dice with a celebrity. Errol Flynn, Clark Gable, Carole Lombard, and Daryl Zanuck were all visitors.

The Dunes was first class, with elegant chandeliers, gilt-edged china, cut crystal, and French cuisine. There was even a dress code for the patrons requiring formal evening gowns and suits. The finery seemed at odds a bit to the green felt tables and heavily armed guards. It was alleged that the games could be rigged for the house.

The success of the Dunes prompted others to get into the game in Cathedral City. The 139 Club was opened by Earl Sausser and featured free

The Dunes Club attracted gamblers to the desert in nearby Cathedral City. *Photo courtesy Palm Springs Historical Society.*

chili, sawdust on the floor and became the most popular by appealing to a broader audience with numerous slot machines. Sausser died in 1942 and his lawyer Walter Melrose ran it until it closed in 1947. The building became a thrift shop and was finally torn down in 1985.

An associate of Wertheimer's, Frank Portnoy, along with parking lot mogul Jake Katelman, opened The Cove, an upscale gambling club in Cathedral City. Constantly hassled by the authorities, they closed it down and moved to Las Vegas.

The original Dunes Club burned to the ground in a suspicious fire in 1943.

Irwin Rubenstein then opened a Dunes Club in Palm Springs, later changing its name to Ruby's Dunes. It underwent numerous ownerships and name changes ever since.

Wertheimer himself tried to operate an illegal gambling operation out of his own home and intimate hotel called the Colonial House (see "Howard Manor" above). He was busted and given a 60-day sentence. The man who originally brought gambling to the desert died in 1953.

The Legendary Chi Chi

If there was ever an establishment that catered to the Hollywood crowd that found Palm Springs a relaxing haven, it was the long-standing Chi Chi downtown.

The list of those luminaries tableside matched those who performed live at the Chi Chi. The fabled performers included such personalities as Louis Armstrong, Desi Arnaz, Pearl Bailey, Milton Berle, Ray Bolger, Nat King Cole, Vic Damone, Sammy Davis Jr., Duke Ellington, Lena Horne, Eartha Kitt, Gypsy Rose Lee, Peggy Lee, Liberace, Jerry Lewis, Tony Martin, Mills Brothers, Patti Page, Louie Prima & Keely Smith, Lili St. Cyr, Sophie Tucker, and Mae West.

The venue started in 1931 when Irwin S. Schuman converted his little Waffle Shop into the Desert Grill, the first dinner house in the village outside the three hotels—The Desert Inn, El Mirador and Oasis. It was on property leased from Zaddie Bunker just north of The Desert Inn on Palm Canyon Drive (where the Desert Shopping Plaza is now). The hotels closed down from shortly after Easter until October, but Schuman's Desert Grill stayed open in the summer.

Schuman transformed the Desert Grill in 1935 into the legendary Chi Chi, a bar replete with bamboo and russet leather décor, a fine restaurant, and the "Blue Room" for entertainment.

Schuman, along with Jack Freeman, owned and operated the popular Silk Hat nightclub next door to the Chi Chi. Originally run by Lee Humbard, the old Silk Hat had become famous and was known from Hollywood to New York. But it was the Chi Chi that would survive, as in 1938 Schuman tore the wall down between the two nightclubs, doubling the floor space of the Chi Chi and adding dressing rooms.

During World War II, the Chi Chi was also a favorite haunt for GIs stationed at the Torney General Hospital, the converted El Mirador Hotel, and the temporary Camp Young out past Indio.

But it was the Hollywood crowd who regularly showed up to party that built the Chi Chi reputation. It became the "in" place of the "in" resort destination.

Responding to demand of bigger shows and bigger entertainment, Schuman opened the Chi Chi's famous "Starlite Room" in 1950. With a raised dance floor, the Starlite Room was terraced and seated 750 people. The adjacent dining room seated an additional 250 people. The opening was a major social event for Palm Springs. On hand were Mayor Charlie Farrell and his wife actress Virginia Valli, leading actor William Powell and his wife Mousie, along with most of the city officials and many of its illustrious citizens.

Desi Arnaz headlined opening

Headlining the Starlite Room opening was Desi Arnaz, unknown to television viewers at the time, and introduced as a well-known Cuban bandleader in the accompanying flyer. It was where he first performed "Babaloo"

Interior of the world-famed Chi Chi, where stars entertained and were entertained. *Photo courtesy Palm Springs Historical Society.*

on the bongos. It was reported that he "set the pace for the big-timers that followed: Carl Ravazza, The Vagabonds, Carl Brisson, and Rudy Vallee."

It was common to see celebrities tableside at the Chi Chi's Starlite Room. Limousines often dropped off recognizable entertainers like Bing Crosby, Bob Hope, or Frank Sinatra.

Schuman hired the Bill Alexander Band for dancing and accompanying the vast variety of entertainers. They stayed at the Chi Chi for 13 years. A 1959 flyer boasted "Louis Armstrong and All Star Band with Bill Alexander's Orchestra."

In 1961, Schuman gave up managing the Chi Chi and accompanying Starlite Room so he could devote his energies on his new enterprise, the Riviera Hotel. The Chi Chi went through a series of managers, and in 1964, Schulman resumed operating it. Then in 1965, he put it up for sale, and the Chi Chi was closed for most of the 1965-66 season.

A nude extravaganza

New entrepreneurs George Arnold, Philip Richards and Helen Stoddard acquired the Chi Chi from Schuman in a $500,000 lease-purchase deal. They remodeled the place and on February 3, 1966, reopened it for a month's run of a nude extravaganza called "Follies de Pigalle" featuring expensive sets and a glamorous cast of 40 showgirls.

After that run, they started with big name entertainment and French singer Denise Darcel started a new show. However, less than a week later it was closed by the marshal after a $10,111 contracting bill for the remodel was attached against the property. Arnold later declared bankruptcy.

The doors of the famed Chi Chi were closed. While an era had passed, the Chi Chi was down, but not out. In September 1968 owner Zaddie Bunker signed a 15-year, $1 million lease with Seymour (Sy) Weiss, a former professional baseball player, who had owned three International House of Pancake franchises and the Westward Ho restaurant in Pasadena.

For a short while the club flourished. The "velvet fog" crooner Hoagy Carmichael gave a 2-day appearance in 1969, but the Chi Chi's new life was short-lived. After extensive redecorating and a large overhead, the devastating floods of 1969 kept people away, and two charity events were considered flops. Finally, in March 1969, Weiss threw in the towel, lamenting, "I tried. I tried every way I know. I've had it."

In 1970, Zaddie Bunker's son-in-law and manager of her estate Earle Strebe tried to make a go of it himself. He reopened the Chi Chi as a cabaret serving cocktails and dinner. The city council approved a dance license for him if he made improvements in the parking lot behind the club. Nevertheless, after one season awash in red ink, he discontinued the operation.

Then in 1971, Don Cone leased the Chi Chi from Earle Strebe in hopes of sub-letting the place to theater groups and to film television musicals upon the stage. All that amounted to was during two nights in February 1971, the Palm Springs Playhouse presented "The Unsinkable Molly Brown" in the Starlite Room.

Another revival attempt, a discotheque, interestingly called "Jilly's-in-the-Bush," lasted but a short time in early 1972.

Then it was outsiders, a group from Denver called the EMT Corporation, in February 1973, who used the center third of the large Chi Chi nightclub for an Italian "singing restaurant" called Mario's, patterned after the ones in Denver and San Diego. The President of EMT was Mario Lalli.

The other two thirds of the illustrious Chi Chi? Well, on the south side of Mario's was the Original House of Pies, and on the north—The Wonderful World of Wax Museum.

The knockout punch

While the Chi Chi was down for over a dozen years, the knockout punch came in 1977 when the entire site was transformed to house three retail shops. The renowned basket weave brickwork on the building's face that signified the desert's most popular nightclub came down, and with it, an institution.

The story of the Chi Chi, unfortunately, did not end there. A decade later in 1987, John DeBoard opened a "New" Chi Chi, a lounge in an "also-new" Desert Inn Hotel and Resort which opened at 155 South Belardo. While he may have had fun restoring the name, it too was short-lived.

Famous Chi Chi logo on medallion. *Photo courtesy Palm Springs Historical Society.*

The original Chi Chi nightclub is more than a memory, it represents an era, one that is gone, but it helped put Palm Springs on the map.

CHAPTER 47

The Legacy of the Indian Canyons
CAHUILLA THROUGH THE YEARS

The Agua Caliente Band of Cahuilla Indians never left Palm Springs, and there was very little assimilation into the population at large. Today, the tribe's legacy is evident everywhere, from the Indian Canyons, to numerous places and streets named for early Agua Caliente family members.

The Agua Caliente Reservation, originally established in 1876, comprises 31,128 acres of which 2,961 have been allotted to individuals. About 6,700 of these acres are located in the heart of Palm Springs, surrounding the hot water spa from where the band gets its name.

The most visible legacy of the Agua Caliente is obvious today in a spectacular way. In the beginning tourists came for the therapeutic value of the hot springs; in contrast, today many visitors come seeking a different type of therapy and pay homage to the local Indians through the games of chance and entertainment provided in the flourishing casinos.

The local canyons

It is the local, scenic Indian Canyons, however, that will be around for millennia, long after the last casino will board shut its doors. The canyons are what makes Palm Springs special, and to enter their beckoning palm-shaded chambers gives you the same sensation of awe one experiences after passing through the ponderous doors of a great cathedral.

Along Mt. San Jacinto's eastern escarpment six major canyons tumble into the resort city of Palm Springs: Chino Canyon, Tachevah Canyon, Tahquitz Canyon, Andreas Canyon, Murray Canyon and Palm Canyon.

Chino Canyon is northernmost. Named for Pedro Chino, the Agua Caliente Indian who lived there, the canyon is best known as housing the Palm Springs Aerial Tramway.

Farther south just opposite the Las Palmas area is Tachevah Canyon. Its highlight is what the locals call Dry Falls, a permanent stain on a large sheer rock that divides the canyon into upper and lower reaches. "Ta che va" means "plain view" in Cahuillan, and the falls, which actually do get wet in the rainy months, are definitely in plain view. There was plenty of water tumbling down the rocky face during the heavy rains of early 2005. The North Lykken Trail can take you to the base of the Tachevah Canyon.

Tahquitz Canyon

The sharp rocky crag creating the huge gash in the mountain casts a large shadow across Tahquitz Canyon. The shadow's outline resembles a profile of an unmistakable "Witch," visible from most of town in the morning hours. The evil spirit Tahquitz, according to local legend, has haunted the canyon and to this day, some tribal members refuse to enter it.

According to Eric Meeks in his book *The Witch of Tahquitz*, mysteries still inhabit the area. He cautions, "But beware of the shadow. For as long as her shadow is in the canyon there is a Witch of Tahquitz."

For years the canyon attracted hikers and skinny-dippers who enjoyed the picturesque falls and respected the serene scene, but some vandals had dumped garbage on the canyon floor and spray-painted graffiti on the boulders. Hippies, hermits, and homeless people had taken up residence in the canyon's caves. Then in 1969, a rowdy crowd left a rock concert and went up into Tahquitz Canyon for days of partying. That was the last straw. The Agua

The "Witch of Tahquitz Canyon" is visible in the early mornings from much of Palm Springs.

Caliente Band of Cahuilla Indians shortly thereafter closed the canyon to the public. For years "No Trespassing" signs blocked ingress to this, one of the most beautiful of Palm Springs canyons, and site of the oldest known Cahuilla village.

In the late 1990s, the Indians built a visitor center with educational and cultural exhibits and, after a three-year cleanup, reopened the canyon in 2001 by offering guided hikes only along the 1.8-mile trail. Because of the water and shade there are no palm trees, but plenty of sycamores and other foliage.

The canyon has a year-round stream, several pools, and the beautiful 60-foot Tahquitz Falls. The canyon is full of native plants, many used by the Cahuilla for food and medicine. The knowledgeable rangers point out interesting sites and flora and fauna. It's an invigorating and refreshing hike that is a must-do for visitors and worth the fee to see such beauty protected.

The hike into Tahquitz Canyon ends at restful Tahquitz Falls.

The Indian Canyons

Favorite places to take visitors are the Indian Canyons to the south of town. Of the six canyons, these southern three are commonly referred to as the Indian Canyons, and a fee is charged for their use. From north to south they are Andreas, Murray, and Palm Canyons. All three, along with Tahquitz Canyon, are listed in the National Register of Historic Places. Palm Canyon has the largest concentration of palm trees in the world, and Andreas Canyon is second; Murray Canyon is fourth.

Immediately past the Agua Caliente entrance booth where a day-use fee is collected, the macadam road to the right takes you to Andreas Canyon, where Andreas Creek forms beautiful pools at the base of large, towering cliffs. The one-mile mostly shady trail up one side of the creek and down the other passes hundreds of native stately palms and impressive large rock formations, some of which contain Cahuilla rock art. The tranquil setting has long been a favorite of visitors to Palm Springs.

Murray Canyon to the south is a little harder to reach as you must take a trail from the Andreas Canyon parking lot around the point to enter the canyon. On one visit, I found I was the only hiker and enjoyed the tranquil setting, the only sounds being water over rocks. The endangered Least Bells Vireo is known to nest in Murray Canyon.

At the south end of the paved road is the great Palm Canyon, 15 miles long and one of the most naturally beautiful spots in the west. Photos of it are everywhere. From the small Trading Post in the parking lot, a trail meanders up into the canyon which is the solemn setting for over 3,000 native Washingtonia filifera palm trees.

Trails to nearby locations can be accessed from the main Palm Canyon Trail, but it's hard to understand why hikers would want to head off across the barren hills when there is so much exploring in the beautiful canyon itself. It's easy to appreciate the Indian Canyons, the natural legacy of the Cahuilla.

Street names recognize Agua Caliente members

A fitting tribute was paid to the members of the Agua Caliente Band of Cahuilla Indians in 1930 when the supervisors granted the petitions of many Palm Springs villagers and changed the street names in town, many to recognize members of the Agua Caliente. Fittingly, only Indian Avenue, which bisected the village along the reservation line, remained similar, however it is now Indian Canyon Drive.

The original street names had reflected what was in the beginning an agricultural community with Lime, Lemon, Orange and Vine streets. In 1930 Main Street became Palm Canyon Drive, Orange Street became Cahuilla Road, and North, South and West streets were renamed Alejo Road, Ramon Road, and Patencio Road, respectfully.

Palm Springs streets and roads honoring Agua Caliente members include those named: Andreas, Arenas, Belardo, Chino, Lugo, Marcus, Patencio, Segundo, and Saturnino.

A position of power

Of all the Cahuilla, the Agua Caliente Band has been the most fortunate from an economic point of view. Seeing the Agua Caliente Tribal Council is like watching a board meeting of successful business people, which they have become. Current Tribal Chairman Richard M. Milanovich was elected to that office in 1984.

The Agua Caliente Band of Cahuilla Indians is the largest landowner within the city limits of Palm Springs with nearly 6,700 acres. Along with real estate, the band now owns the Spa Casino Resort, the Agua Caliente Casino, the Agua Caliente Cultural Museum, Canyon National Bank, Canyon Country Club (land only), and the Tahquitz Canyon Visitor's Center.

Contrary to an early white stereotype that Indian women were no more than domesticated beasts of burden, women have always played a large role in the tribal council. In fact, there have been occasions where the entire council was made up of women. Much like the white female contribution to the history of the area, Indian women played a dominant role in the development of Palm Springs.

In fact, in the mid-1950s it was an all-woman Agua Caliente Tribal Council, the first Indian

The Agua Caliente Visitors Center at the entrance to Tahquitz Canyon.

all-female tribal council in the United States, that lobbied Congress for progressive legislation, including land lease rights to promote economic development.

Today the economic impact of the Agua Caliente Band of Cahuilla Indians is significant. In April 2003, the tribe donated $1.1 million to 64 charities and civic organizations throughout the Coachella Valley. It included a gift of $60,000 to the Palm Springs Fire Department and $10,000 to the Palm Springs Desert Museum. Even to a casual observer, it appears that there has been a reversal of fortunes.

The legacy and legends of the Agua Caliente are the real history of Palm Springs. The farmers, respiratory patients, artists, movie stars, celebrities, politicians, tourists, snowbirds, hikers, equestrians, and golfers have all found solace in Palm Springs. For many, their time has come and gone. But the Agua Caliente remain. And remain they will.

According to Chief Francisco Patencio in *The Stories and Legends of the Palm Springs Indians*, there is a leaning rock in Chino Canyon. He says, "In coming to Palm Springs, or leaving it, there is to be noticed a great Leaning Rock on the hillside entering Chino Canyon...the Leaning Rock is to cure as well as to love. It is the 'Calling Rock.' It says, 'Come, come back' Always it is calling, and all people that leave Palm Springs, they all come back."

Bibliography

Admiral, Don. *Palm Springs Desert Area*. Palm Springs: The Desert Sun, 1932

Ainsworth, Katherine. *The McCallum Saga: The Story of the Founding of Palm Springs*. Palm Springs: Palm Springs Desert Museum, 1973

Ainsworth, Ed. *Golden Checkerboard*. Palm Desert: Desert Southwest Inc. 1965

Bean, Lowell John. *Mukat's People: The Cahuilla Indians of Southern California*. Berkeley: University of California Press, 1972

——————and Lisa Bourgeault. *The Cahuilla*. New York: Chelsea House Publishers. 1989

——————and Lawton, Harry. *The Cahuilla Indians of Southern California*. Banning, CA: Malki Museum Press, 1965

Bogert, Mayor Frank M. *Palm Springs: First Hundred Years*. Palm Springs: Palm Springs Heritage Associates, 1987/Palm Springs Public Library, 2003

Bono, Sonny. *And The Beat Goes On*. New York: Simon & Schuster Inc. 1991

Bright, Marjorie Belle. *Nellie's Boardinghouse: A Dual Biography of Nellie Coffman and Palm Springs*. Palm Springs: ETC Publications, 1981

Brumgardt, John R. and Larry L. Bowles. *People of Magic Waters: The Cahuilla Indians of Palm Springs*. Palm Springs: ETC Publications, 1981

Burke, Tony. *Palm Springs: Why I Love You*. Palm Desert: Palmesa Inc. 1978

Chase, J. Smeaton. *Our Araby: Palm Springs*. Pasadena: Star News Publishing, 1920

Churchwell, Mary Jo. *Palm Springs: The Landscape, The History, The Lore*. Palm Springs: Ironwood Editions, 2001

Deller, John J., M.D. *The Palm Springs Formula*. Rancho Mirage: LesStrang Publishing, 1995

Durham, David L. *Place-Names of California's Desert Counties*. Clovis, CA: Word Dancer Press, 2001

Ferranti, Philip. *100 great Hikes In and Near Palm Springs*. Englewood, CO: Westcliffe Publications, 2000

Findley, Rowe. *Great American Deserts*. Washington: National Geographic Society, 1972

Fleming, John A. *Coachella Valley Hiking Guide*. Palm Springs: Nature Trails Press, 1996

Frenzel, Gerhard G. *Portrait of the Stars*. Palm Springs: The Palm Springs Walk of Stars. 1999

Furbush, Patty A. *On Foot In Joshua Tree National Park*. Lebanon, Maine: M.I. Adventure Publications, 1995

Gudde, Erwin G. *1,000 California Place Names*. Berkeley, Los Angeles and London: University of California Press, 1959 (3rd Edition)

Haber, Mel. *Bedtime Stories of the Legendary Ingleside Inn in Palm Springs*. Palm Springs: Ingleside Press, 1995

Hartley, Glory. *The Desert Insider*. Rancho Mirage: Glory Hartley, 2001

Hicks, John D. *History of the Desert Riders*. Palm Springs Desert Riders, 1980

Hillinger, Charles. *Hillinger's California*. Santa Barbara: Capra Press, 1997

Hudson, Roy F. *Forgotten Desert Artist*. Palm Springs: Desert Museum, 1979

Jackson, Helen Hunt. *Ramona, A Story*. Boston: Roberts Brothers, 1884

Jaeger, Edmund C. *The California Deserts*. Stanford: Stanford University Press, 1933

James, George Wharton. *California: Beautiful & Romantic*. Boston: The Page Company Publishers, 1914

————— *Traveler's Handbook to Southern California*. Pasadena: George Wharton James, 1904

James, Harry C. *The Cahuilla Indians*. Morongo Indian Reservation, Cabazon: Malki Museum Press, 1960

Johns, Howard. *Palm Springs Confidential*. Fort Lee, N.J.: Barricade Books, 2004

Kelley, Kitty. *His Way: The Unauthorized Biography of Frank Sinatra*. New York: Bantam Books, 1986

Kleven, Robin. *Best Places Palm Springs*. Seattle: Sasquatch Books, 2001

Kotzen, Alice. *Malki Museum's Native Food Tasting Experiences*. Morongo Indian Reservation, Cabazon: Malki Museum Press, 1994

Lawton, Harry. *Willie Boy: A Desert Manhunt*. Balboa Island, CA: Paisano Press, 1960

Lindsay, Lowell and Diana Lindsay. *The Anza-Borrego Desert Region*. Berkeley: Wilderness Press, 1978

McKenney, J. Wilson. *Desert Editor: The Story of Randall Henderson and Palm Desert*. Georgetown, CA 1972

McKinney, John. *Walking California's Desert Parks*. San Francisco: Harper Collins, 1996

Meeks, Eric. *The Witch of Tahquitz*. Palm Springs: Celebrity Books, 2003

Miller, Ronald Dean and Peggy Jeanne Miller. *The Chemehuevi Indians of Southern California*. Morongo Indian Reservation, Cabazon: Malki Museum Press, 1967

Moore, Terry. *The Passions of Howard Hughes*. Los Angeles: General Publishing Group, 1996

Mungo, Ray. *Palm Springs Babylon*. New York: St. Martin's Press. 1993

Nordland, Ole J. *Coachella Valley's Golden Years*. Coachella: Coachella Valley County Water District, 1978

Palm Springs Desert Museum Women's Committee. *Palm Springs Desert Museum 1938-1988*. Palm Springs: PSDM, 1988

Palm Springs Historical Site Preservation Board. *Palm Springs: Brief History and Architectural Guide*. Palm Springs: City of Palm Springs, 2001

Patencio, Chief Francisco (As told to Margaret Boynton). *Stories and Legends of the Palm Springs Indians*. Los Angeles: Times Mirror, 1943

Pepper, Choral. *Desert Lore of Southern California*. San Diego: Sunbelt Publications, 1999 (2nd Edition)

Pittman, Ruth. *Roadside History of California*. Missoula, MT: Mountain Press Publishing Co. 1995

Pomeroy, Elizabeth. *John Muir: A Naturalist in Southern California*. Pasadena: Many Moons Press, 2001

Powell, Lawrence Clark. *California Classics*. Los Angeles: The Ward Ritchie Press, 1971

Presley, Sally. *The Village of Palm Springs*. Palm Springs: Celebrity Publishers, 2001

Pryor, Alton. *Little Known Tales in California History*. Roseville: Stagecoach Publishing. 1997

Pyle, Linda McMillin. *Peaks, Palms & Picnics*. Philadelphia: Xlibris, 1999/San Diego: Sunbelt Publications, 2002

Ramona Pageant Association. *Ramona Program*. Hemet: Ramona Pageant, 1956

Richards, Elizabeth W. *A Look Into Palm Springs' Past*. Palm Springs: Santa Fe Federal Savings and Loan Association, 1962

Rippingale, Sally Presley. *The History of the Racquet Club of Palm Springs*. Yucaipa, CA: U.S. Business Specialties, 1985

Sandos, James A. and Larry E. Burgess. *The Hunt For Willie Boy*. Norman and Landon, OK: University of Oklahoma Press, 1994

Saroyan, Aram. *Rancho Mirage*. New York: Barricade Books, 1993

Shoumatoff, Alex. *Legends of the American Desert*. New York: Harper Perennial, 1997

Silberman, Steve (Editor). *Desert Memories*. Palm Springs: The Desert Sun, 2002

Sullivan, Noelle. *It Happened in Southern California*. Helena, MT: Twodot Books, 1996

Titus, Jack. *Palm Springs Close Up*. Palm Desert: Prickley Pear Publishing, 2000 (5th Edition).

Valley, David J., with Diana Lindsay. *Jackpot Trail: Indian Gaming in Southern California*. San Diego: Sunbelt Publications, 2003

Women's Committee. *Palm Springs Desert Museum 1938-1988*. Palm Springs: Desert Museum, 1988

Young, Patricia Mastick. *Desert Dream Fulfilled*. Palm Springs: Palm Springs Desert Museum, 1983

Young, Stanley. *Beautiful Spas and Hot Springs of California*. San Francisco: Chronicle Books, 1998

Periodicals/Magazines

Coachella Valley Family News. Coachella Valley Historical Society

Desert Entertainer. Palm Desert: Hi Desert Publishing

Desert Guide. Palm Springs: Desert Publications, Milton Jones, publisher

Desert Key Magazine. Palm Desert: Cactus Publications, Corp.

Desert Magazine. Palm Springs: The Desert Sun

Desert Post Weekly. Cathedral City: Desert Community Newspaper Group

Desert Weeky. Palm Springs

Desert Woman. Sally Benson article "Frances S. Stevens," January 1998

Palm Springs Life. Palm Springs: Desert Publications, Milton Jones, publisher

The Limelight. Palm Springs (1938)

The "D" Different Desert Daily. Riverside: The Press Enterprise publication

The Desert Sun. Palm Springs

The Press Enterprise. Riverside

Whispering Palms. Palm Springs Historical Society

Index

M

Sunbelt's Southern California Bookshelf

Incorporated in 1988, with roots in publishing since 1973, **Sunbelt Publications** produces and distributes natural science and outdoor guidebooks, regional histories, multi-language pictorials, and stories that celebrate the land and its people.

Sunbelt books help to discover and conserve the natural, historical, and cultural heritage of unique regions on the frontiers of adventure and learning. Our books guide readers into distinctive communities and special places, both natural and man-made.

We carry hundreds of books on southern California!
Visit us online at:

www.sunbeltbooks.com